MENDING
GOD'S CREATURES

TRUE STORIES OF A SMALL-TOWN VETERINARIAN

MENDING
GOD'S CREATURES

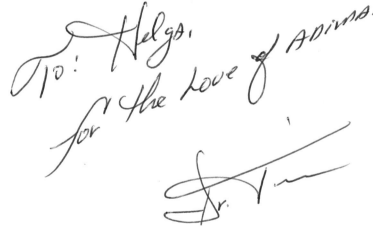

To: Helga,
for the Love of Animals.

Dr. [signature]

JIM ROLOFF DVM

TATE PUBLISHING
AND ENTERPRISES, LLC

Published by Tate Publishing & Enterprises, LLC
127 E. Trade Center Terrace | Mustang, Oklahoma 73064 USA
1.888.361.9473 | www.tatepublishing.com

Tate Publishing is committed to excellence in the publishing industry. The company reflects the philosophy established by the founders, based on Psalm 68:11,
"The Lord gave the word and great was the company of those who published it."

Published in the United States of America

ISBN: 978-1-62854-929-4
1. Medical / Veterinary Medicine / General
2. Nature / Animals / General
14.02.07

DEDICATION

This book is dedicated to my lovely wife, Sandy. It was her faithful support, encouragement, willing sacrifices, and sincere compassion for animals that inspired and sustained me through the years. Together we achieved our hopes and dreams.

ACKNOWLEDGMENT

A special thank-you goes to all the receptionists, veterinary assistants, veterinary technicians, and veterinarians for their conscientious efforts and professionalism throughout the years. I couldn't have done it without you, and I'm eternally grateful for your devoted service.

VETERINARY TECHNICIANS, VETERINARY ASSISTANTS, AND RECEPTIONISTS:

Angela, Barb, Chandra, Christine, Darlene, Donna S., Donna Sl., Heather S., Heather W., Heidi, Hillary, Ivy, Janice, Jennifer, Kathleen, Megan, Melanie, Melody, Merle, Rachel M., Rachel Mc., Robbie, Sarah, Sharon, Tami, Taryn, Tauni, Vashon, Vickie, Whitney, and Candace, our special friend and consultant.

ASSOCIATE VETERINARIANS:

Dr. Al, Dr. Bill ("Wild Bill"), Dr. Dee, Dr. Kate, Dr. Paul,

TABLE OF CONTENTS

OUT ON MY OWN

PREFACE

What defines a true friend? To many of us, our animal companions are true friends because they often demonstrate that supreme measure of devotion—unconditional love. They can give us joy, provide us with peace and comfort, and teach us how to be more forgiving. In many cases, they inspire us to be better individuals. Many years ago, Chief Seattle of the Suquamesh Indian Tribe said it perfectly:

> What is man without the beasts?
> If all the beasts were gone, men would die from
> great loneliness of spirit.
> For whatever happens to the beasts will soon
> happen to man.
> All things are connected.

Growing up on a farm provided me an opportunity to interact with all kinds of animals. It wasn't long before I sensed a definite connection with them. They were my friends, and witnessing them battle pain, sickness, and disease inspired me to find a way to relieve the discomfort and provide healing, hence the calling to become a veterinarian.

THE LETTER

"Time stands still for no man." I forget who actually said that, but it is certainly true. That burning desire, down deep inside, to become a veterinarian was never quenched. I was twenty-six years old, married to a beautiful young lady, had a young son, and had recently graduated from Eastern Washington University, having completed a four-year premed curriculum with a major in Biology. I'd applied to the Washington State University College of Veterinary Medicine, gone through the admissions interviews, and was at the mercy of the selection board. It was a well known fact that many students weren't accepted on their first application, but I was still hopeful, although somewhat apprehensive.

This whole thing of striving for that goal of becoming a veterinarian had been a major sacrifice for all of us—Sandy, Eric, and myself. We had been through four years of doing without a lot of things, and now, if I got accepted into vet school, we'd have four more lean years to endure. We were willing. We were a team. Even though we were poor financially and drove a clunker, we were rich in hope and faith. Now, all we had to do was wait patiently for *that* letter. It was difficult going to the mailbox daily and finding it empty. Would I be one of the lucky ones to get accepted on my first application, or would I have to find a farm job and reapply the following year? Could I ask Sandy and Eric to hang on for another year while many other guys my age were now gainfully employed? Those were very sobering questions that kept running through my mind.

Then one beautiful day, as I opened the mailbox, there it was! The letter from Washington State University College of Veterinary Medicine, and it was addressed to me. As I held that letter in my hands, all my hopes, dreams, and sacrifices of the past, just to get to this point, flashed before my eyes. The first words I read when I opened the letter were, "Congratulations, you've been selected into the College of Veterinary Medicine." I didn't have to read any further. Tears of joy and relief welled up in my eyes as I showed the letter to Sandy. We made it! Thank you, Lord! As reality sank in, I knew that being accepted into vet school was a major turning point in our lives, and the beginning of a new adventure.

THE COLLEGE DAYS

VETERINARY SCHOOL

The four years of vet school were far from being a cakewalk. The introduction speech given by one of the vet school profs to our incoming class of sixty students was short, sweet, and definitely to the point. Doctor Brachen leaned over the podium, paused, and sternly warned, "Do not fall behind! If you do, you'll never catch up!" Believe me, truer words were never spoken. The courses of study were intense; the professors, demanding; and the competition, fierce. There was no letup for the four years of study. The very high stress level had an adverse effect on some of my classmates, and it unfortunately resulted in them withdrawing from school. The great majority of us, however, endured with determined and committed resolve. The driving forces that kept me going were my love and respect for animals, a good sense of humor, the support and encouragement of my family, and most importantly, my strong faith.

"RED"

It was in the anesthesiology laboratory class during my second year of vet school when I first ventured outside the box, and it wouldn't be the last time either! The students were paired up and assigned a dog for the hands-on lab sessions. We were to observe and record the patient's physiological responses to various forms of anesthesia, and at the end of the course, the dogs were to be humanely euthanized. We were emphatically told that these laboratory dogs were property of the state of Washington, and they didn't belong to us. I had been assigned a young, happy, very energetic Irish Setter, who I later named Red. He was a real kick in the pants! He loved the attention and was always excited about going to the laboratory. He'd pull hard on the leash, seemingly looking forward to his next hit of anesthesia. I guess you could say that Red had become an anesthesia junkie. I really liked that goofy guy. He was a very good patient, and we sort of connected.

The last day of the course had arrived, and it was now time to relinquish the dogs to their unfortunate fate. As I held Red's head in my hands and looked into his big brown eyes, I paused momentarily, then told him, "Red, let's get you out of here!" So I quickly grabbed a leash and jetted out the door with Red gleefully prancing in tow. He was his usual happy-go-lucky self, looking up at me as if saying, "Oh boy! Where're we goin'?" We made it out of the building, undetected, and by some act of providence, standing right next to the exit door was a fellow student taking a smoke break. I handed him the leash and said, "Here, take this dog for a short walk for me, okay? Take him somewhere, right now, where I can't see him. I'll catch up with you later and get the dog, but just get him out of here!" The other student could tell something was up, but thankfully he didn't ask any questions. He just took off with Red, who was happily pulling on the leash. I then went back to the lab to pick up my books and suddenly encountered the instructor, who was standing by the door.

"Roloff, where's your dog? You're aware that these dogs are State property, aren't you? If you've taken that dog, that would be considered stealing from the state of Washington, and you'd be breaking the law."

I swallowed hard, looked the instructor straight in the eyes, and replied, "I got rid of him, and I don't know where he is." That was the truth! I didn't know *exactly* where he was at that *exact* moment. So in my mind, I wasn't lying. Instead, I considered it to be a matter of semantics. The instructor just stood there, looking me eyeball to eyeball. The stare-down probably lasted only a few seconds, but it seemed like an eternity to me. I kept telling myself, *Don't sweat! Don't blink!*

Finally the instructor looked away, shook his head, and I heard him mutter under his breath as he turned to walk away, "Don't get caught." I didn't, and eventually we found Red a nice home in the country where he could run free and live a carefree life. I'd helped save a friend's life. I felt good about that, and still do.

A GOOD LAUGH

I'll never forget one particularly humorous incident that occurred during my third year of veterinary school. Jake Burns and I were classmates and were scheduled to work together on large animal reception one Saturday morning in late September. Our duties were to get the medical histories of the patients and perform the initial examinations. If any treatments were necessary, we'd do those under the direct supervision of an instructor. Jake and I were hoping for a light caseload that morning because there was a football game scheduled at Martin Stadium at 2:00 p.m., and both of us were planning to go see it. Everything had been going along smoothly up until 11:00 a.m. Then it happened! An old cattle truck pulled up to the unloading dock, and the stench of rotting afterbirth permeated the air. The cow was unloaded and placed in the treatment stanchion. The smell was so foul that we had to place menthol rub up our noses to keep from gagging. Naturally, the instructor turned to Jake and me and said, "Boys, now's the time to see what you're made of." Jake gave me a quick glance and rolled his eyes. We both knew what was coming.

The cow's rectal temperature was understandably elevated since she'd become septic from the retained putrefying afterbirth tissue. It had to be manually removed, and believe me, that was one messy, stinky job! Jake and I both worked at it, and finally we got all that rotten stuff out of there. The cow was good to go, but we weren't! We stunk to high heaven, even though we wore coveralls and shoulder-length obstetric gloves. We didn't notice it at the time, but our coveralls had shrunk somewhat from repeated washings, and now these "high water" overalls left the bottoms of our jeans totally exposed to anything and everything.

We finished up a little late but still had time to make a quick run home, clean up, and get to the game on time. I got to the game and noticed Jake sitting with a group of people in the end zone section. He seemed to be enjoying himself, but as time passed, most of the people around Jake had left. He looked pretty lonely over there, sitting all by himself, so I ventured over to sit with him. When sitting down next to Jake, I got a whiff of that rotten afterbirth stench. So I asked him, "Jake, did you go back to your dorm and clean up? Because you smell just like that dang cow." Jake told me he'd cleaned up, but as I looked down at the cuffs of his jeans, there it was, a piece of rotten afterbirth stuck on his pant leg. No wonder the people around him took off! They couldn't stand the smell. Jake told me that his sense of smell had never been very good—no kidding! He tore out a page from his game program, wiped off his pants, and we had a good laugh. There we were, watching the rest of the game all by ourselves, undisturbed in our own little section, just like two guys in church, sitting in our own pew.

"RUFUS," THE ELEVATOR CAT

It was the summer between my sophomore and junior years of vet school that I found myself in dire need of earning some extra income. Working while attending vet school was discouraged, so

Sandy was our main source of income. She worked as a nurse for a local physician and had a definite gift of compassion for the patients. I was so proud of her. I applied for summer employment at the Whitman County Grain Growers, hoping that my experiences on a wheat and cattle ranch would help me get hired. It did!

The early part of the summer job consisted of getting the elevators prepared for the upcoming harvest season. There were bins to be cleaned, augers repaired, conveyor belts replaced, and holdover grain needed to be loaded into rail cars and shipped out. The hours were long, and the labor was intense. My immediate foreman was about eight years younger than myself, had completed only high school, and seemed to delight in calling me "college boy." Hey, I didn't mind. I respected his position, and I worked hard for him. The company manager noticed my work ethic and placed me in charge of the Fallon elevator during the harvest season. Once again, hard work was noticed and would be rewarded.

On one routine day at the elevator, while sitting in the shade having lunch, I noticed some fast, staccato-type movement out of the corner of my eye. My first thought was, *Rat!* I grabbed a nearby shovel, ready for action. Unexpectedly, the head of a young cat peered around the corner. With ears up, eyes opened wide, he bounded toward me from behind his cover and unabashedly invited himself to share my lunch. So now I had company for dining. We ate and talked—I did most of the talking, of course. This little gray shorthair tabby, about four months old, ended up eating most of my food, but I enjoyed our time together. After devouring as much as possible, he delightedly excused himself and left. The next day, at about the same time, he magically reappeared for more lunch, pets, and conversation. That scenario continued throughout the duration of the harvest season.

When the wheat and pea harvest had come to a close, it was time to shut down the elevator, lock up, and go home. As I was getting into my car and about to leave the elevator for the last time, that little lunch buddy suddenly appeared and sauntered toward the car. I'd grown fond of that little moocher, so I held the car door open and asked him, "You comin' or stayin'?" He jumped right in without a moment's hesitation, plopped himself down on the seat right next to me as if he'd done it a hundred times before, and home we went. We named him Rufus, and we were the best of friends for many years. Rufus was more of a purr-son than he was a cat, and together we forged wonderful enduring memories.

THE GENTLE GIANT

Clinical rotations were a part of the veterinary curriculum wherein the third- and fourth-year veterinary students assisted in the examinations, diagnosis, and treatments of the hospitalized cases. The large animal rotation segment dealt primarily with horses, pigs, cattle, sheep, and goats. One of my most memorable large animal rotation cases was "Mike", a big and powerful four-year-old Clydesdale stallion. He was truly a gentle giant. Mike was pitch black in color, with a white stripe down his forehead, and he had those long tufts of white hair, called feathers, above each hoof. He was a very handsome horse, and he knew it too.

Mike was at the veterinary school hospital because of a medical problem that involved his left front hoof, and the treatment consisted of cleaning, medicating, and bandaging that enormous hoof twice daily. I was assigned to Mike's care during my two-week rotation stint, and we became pretty good buddies over that extended period of time. Mike was a smart one, and had more than his share of that proverbial horse sense.

He seemed to instinctively know when it was treatment time. He'd stand there with his big head draped over the paddock wall, eagerly eyeballing me as I approached. Mike was a good patient, surprisingly easy to handle and lead. He was very cooperative, and liked all the attention. I was extremely thankful too, because Mike stood over eighteen hands (about six feet) tall at the withers, weighed over two thousand pounds, and had hooves the size of dinner plates. I got him cross-tied in the treatment stanchion and struggled to position that huge, heavy hoof between my knees so it could be cleaned and treated. Believe me, I was in a vulnerable position, and Mike knew it. He didn't struggled or object—thank goodness—but he was a trickster, and he couldn't resist nibbling on my ear, sensing that I was in a compromised stance where I couldn't defend myself. As I was intently working on his hoof, I'd occasionally feel this delicate tickling sensation on my ear. It was from the small hairs on his muzzle. It's hard to believe that this huge, powerful horse with a muzzle the size of an overinflated football could be so gentle. I'd reach up with one hand, tap him on the muzzle, and tell him in no uncertain terms, "Knock it off, Mike." That only slowed him down for a minute or two, and then he was back at it again.

He had that look in his eyes not unlike that of some mischievous little kid just annoying someone for the fun of it. I swear, there were times that it sounded like he was actually snickering. The treatment sessions took quite a while to complete because it went something like this: clean, swat, clean, tap—"Knock it off, Mike"—clean, swat, etc. His hoof eventually healed, and when he went back home, I honestly missed that big dude. One thing for sure, I thoroughly enjoyed working with Mike. He was my gentle giant buddy.

THE SIMPLOT ROTATION

Another of the clinical rotations, especially for those individuals who would be treating large animals in the future, was the two-week block at the Simplot cattle ranch located in southern Idaho. The Simplot Company was involved in various business ventures, including potato production, feedlots, and cow-calf operations, just to name a few. We were to go to the cow-calf center, where about one thousand young cows and first-calf heifers would be calving. Most of the cows were brought in directly from the range lands to the holding pens without having much prior exposure to humans. That made for a very interesting situation. The Simplot managers gave full permission to the third-year veterinary students to perform any medical procedure necessary, including caesareans. It was a win-win deal—Simplot got extra veterinary help, and we, as eager students, had an opportunity to gain invaluable hands-on experience.

Some of Simplot's hired hands included hardcore cowboys, who looked and acted as if they'd just stepped out of the 1800s, and some Basques who provided care for the sheep primarily, but they also pitched in with the cattle. The chow hall was extremely clean, but Spartan, —- no frills! The menu was carefully planned to meet the high caloric requirements of a hardworking crew, and the food was very tasty and plentiful. There were strict time schedules for meals—you better not be late—and there wasn't much time to sit and shoot the bull. It was strictly regimented—eat quickly, refuel, and get back to work. We were essentially on call 24-7 and slept only when time permitted, but it was a great experience, one which I'm grateful to have had.

Our duties were to assist with the calving. Some calves were coming backward (i.e. posterior presentation), and there were hip lock cases, breaches, uterine inertias (wherein the muscles of the uterus fatigued and there were hardly any contractions), and we also surgically performed caesarean sections. The hours were long, but the experience was priceless! Many of the cowboys called us "Doc," and that sounded good for a change. Even better was earning the trust and confidence of the regular crew.

On one particular occasion, there was a very wild Charolais-cross cow standing out in the center of the large corral, with a calf dangling out of her with its hips locked tight in her pelvis. From a distance, the calf appeared alive, but we couldn't tell for sure because the cow wouldn't let anyone get close. Whenever someone attempted to direct her into one of the calving stalls, she'd snort, paw at the ground, bellow, and swing her head wildly in the air, getting ready to charge. All the while, the calf was swinging back and forth under her tail. The calf's position hadn't changed, and something needed to be done for that calf and done quickly or else it would surely die. The smaller calving stalls were located on both sides of a long runway that was connected to the large open corral. Getting that wild cow down the runway and into one of those stalls would be pretty tricky. None of the guys had any solutions, so I chimed, "I've got an idea!" You see, I'd grown up around cattle. I'd learned, by experience, how to read their body language and how to react and respond to their moves. I'd been to the "school of hard knocks" literally. Over the years I'd been charged, butted, kicked, run over, and horn-whipped. I'd learned how to watch their eyes, how to time their charges, and I felt confident that I could get this wild cow into one of those holding stalls and come away clean! I wasn't intimidated or afraid of that cow, but I had a healthy respect for her and the damage she could potentially inflict. It was always an exhilarating adrenaline rush to go one-on-one against a big charging animal! Believe me, my heart would really get a-pounding! It was exciting! I loved it!

I told the guys, "I'll go out there and approach her. She'll charge me, and when she does, I'll run down the alley way, with her right on my tail. I'll swing into one of the calving stalls and get out by climbing over the rear wall." Everybody thought I was nuts, but it seemed like a good plan to me. "Everybody ready?" I shouted. Then into the large holding corral I went. When the cow spotted me, she immediately swung her head high in the air, blew snot, pawed the ground with her hooves, bellowed, then lowered her head, and—"Here she comes!"—*run*! I thought that I was doing pretty good until some of the guys yelled, "Faster! She's gaining on ya!" I ran down the alley, made a quick turn into a stall, and got my hands on the top board of the stall to make my great escape. At that precise moment, the cow whipped her head and caught me square in the seat of my pants! She launched me into the air—up, out, and over the wall. It all happened in the blink of an eye. Then that deranged cow attempted to jump over the almost six-foot tall enclosure, and in so doing, got temporarily hung up on the top board. The pressure on her abdomen and her frantic struggling caused the *live* calf's hips to free up, and the calf fell unceremoniously to the ground. That maniacal cow eventually maneuvered herself over the wall—high-tailed it out of there—and never looked back. Gone!

Hey, that was a wild experience and a lot of fun too! I'd managed to escape with only a few bruises, and on the positive side, we'd found a new and novel method to free up a hip-locked calf!

THE NEXT STEP

Those first three years of vet school had gone by in a flash. Here I was, in my final year, and almost ready to go out into the real world as a full-fledged veterinarian. It was almost unbelievable. The past three years had been intense, stressful, and also humbling. Many sacrifices had been made to get to this point in our lives, yet we would have gladly done it all over again. We didn't have much money during those college years, so we were forced to live very frugally. Our dining out consisted of going to the local drive-in once a month for the five burgers for $1.00 special. We also splurged on a small side of fries and one milkshake. I had two of the cardboard burgers, while Sandy and our four-year-old son, Eric, shared the remaining three. The greasy fries were a real treat, and Eric thoroughly enjoyed the runny shake. Hey, we were happy and didn't realize how poor we really were. Our entertainment was simple and, most importantly, affordable. We didn't have a TV, so we listened to the radio, went for walks, sang songs, took short trips to nearby Kamiak Butte for day hikes, and went to the pig barns to watch the little piglets scurry all over the place. They were really funny! Believe me, those times of simple pleasures and cheap entertainment provided us with many fond memories.

Then the time came to carefully think about finding employment after graduation. That was a new and exciting thought, considering the fact that I'd been a student for the last eight years. All the senior vet students would make their daily pilgrimage to the jobs board to peruse the latest postings of employment opportunities. There were positions available in all kinds of practices from all over the country. You could actually choose where you wanted to live and work. It was such a different concept to realize that I was about to enter a medical profession that was in demand and that my days of looking for part-time summer work were over.

There was one particular posting that seemed to appeal to me more than the others. It was a veterinary practice located in a small town near Mount Rainier. It was a mixed practice—meaning, veterinary services were provided for both large and small animals—and there were many dairy operations in the area as well. I wrote down the telephone number of the veterinary clinic from the posting and was anxious to contact the practice and find out if the position was still available. When I got home from school that day, I said to Sandy, "How would you like to live near Mount Rainier?" She quickly replied, "How close?" I told her that I didn't know, but I'd find out.

This was starting to get exciting! I proceeded to make the call, talked to the veterinarian, and we set up a time for an interview. The name of the town was Enumclaw, population about five thousand, located near Crystal Mountain Ski Resort, and surrounded by several smaller communities. It sounded like a great place to live and work. Looking at the map, we saw that Enumclaw was located at the base of Chinook Pass, not far from the larger neighboring city of Auburn. So far, so good.

The interview with Dr. Wagner went very well. He was enthusiastic, congenial, easy to talk to, and I felt comfortable with the relationship. Dr. Wagner must have had the same impression because he offered me the position of associate veterinarian at the Enumclaw Veterinary Clinic. I accepted, sight unseen. Sandy was extremely excited too, and we decided to make a weekend trip over the mountains to actually see this community that would become our future home. The weather was absolutely stunning on the day of our trip. The clear blue sky and gentle warm breezes made the drive over to Western Washington very enjoyable. We took an exit from I-90, headed south on Highway 18, then turned left on Highway 169. The forest of tall dark-green cedar trees stood as silent sentinels, hugging and dwarfing the road leading to Enumclaw. Suddenly, as we rounded a bend in the road, there it stood in all its glory, *the* mountain, Mount Rainier. There wasn't a cloud in the sky, and that majestic snow-capped mountain stood directly in the center of the road, framed by the towering cedars. That sight was absolutely breathtaking. It made a person so very thankful just to be alive and to be able to experience such beauty.

As we drove by the numerous dairy farms and smaller ranches with horses and dogs running about, it became quite evident that veterinary services were really needed here. When finally arriving in Enumclaw, I told Sandy, "I think we made the right decision. I *know* we made the right decision."

INTO THE FRAY

HEY, DOC

Rumbling down the road with all our belongings packed into the back of my dad's cattle truck made us strangely resemble the *Beverly Hillbillies*. What can I say, it worked, and the price was right. We lucked out that day because the weather was good— no rain. There we were, on our way to a new town, and I was starting my career as a veterinarian. The whole experience seemed almost unreal. A dream, along with a lot of effort and willing sacrifice, had finally come true. We were filled with excitement and anticipation of what the future had in store for us. There were plenty of butterflies in our stomachs as well, especially mine as I tried to grasp all the major changes that were rapidly impacting our lives.

My first day as a practicing veterinarian was unlike anything that I'd expected. Instead of jumping directly into the fray, I was given a short introduction to the countryside and the overall thrust of the practice. I was to observe the way things were done. The practice was extremely busy, phones ringing incessantly and staff scurrying about frantically in preparation for the day's schedule of activity. I quickly learned that they were shorthanded. The previous associate veterinarian had moved on, and Dr. Wagner, the owner, had been the sole veterinarian for quite sometime now and was in dire need of some relief. It appeared to me that the workload of the practice could easily keep three veterinarians busy. Nothing like jumping right into the fire! I accompanied Dr. Wagner on his rounds that first day, taking notes on all the different roads, medications and treatments used, and how to charge for services rendered. Believe me, it was like mental overload big time! Dr. Wagner told me, "Don't worry. You'll get the hang of it."

Over the next couple of weeks, I became familiar with the area, the people, and the practice. One day, I noticed an old beat-up portable medical case called a "Pandora" sitting next to the garbage can at the rear of the clinic. The medical case was all scuffed up, had hinges missing, and some of the compartments were damaged and displaced. It looked pretty sad. I knew that those boxes were quite expensive, and I'd always wanted to purchase one but couldn't afford paying the price. I asked Dr. Wagner why the medical case was sitting by the garbage can.

Dr. Wagner answered, "It's junk! It's seen its better days. It's been dropped, stepped on and into, crapped on, and the goats have even tried to eat it. It's going into file 13."

"Can I have it?" I asked.

"Sure, if you want it, it's yours," came the reply.

It has been said that beauty is in the eye of the beholder, and my previous eight years of poverty had taught me how to make a silk purse out of a sow's ear. As I feasted my eyes on that old dilapidated medical case, I could see that it had definite possibilities. So down to the hardware store I went. I bought hinges, tape, and black shoe polish, hoping to resurrect my newly acquired prized possession. It's truly amazing what a little sweat equity and some ingenuity can accomplish. Dr. Wagner just laughed and shook his head when he saw how good that ole beat-up box looked after I'd performed my magic on it. That restored "Pandora" medical case served me well for over ten years.

I arrived at the clinic a little early the next morning, partly because of excitement, but I also needed to prepare myself for the coming events of the day. Roberta, the receptionist-assistant, was already there, but Dr. Wagner hadn't yet arrived.

"What time does Dr. Wagner get in?" I asked.

"Oh, he's not coming in today because he really needs some time off. He's been going at it pretty hard since the other vet left, and now he deserves a break. Roberta retorted. "You're it."

Momentary panic and an overwhelming sense of responsibility hit me all at the same time. "You need to be here, then there, by 10:00 a.m., so get the surgeries done quickly, and be ready for emergencies," she added.

I told myself, *Focus, just stay focused! Don't make any mistakes. Eat on the run. Don't get lost on the farm calls. Get through the cases, even if it takes all day and most of the night.* So this is what it was *really* like being a veterinarian in a busy practice. It was fun, challenging, and at times, physically and mentally exhausting. But through it all, being addressed as "Doc", made it all worthwhile.

A VALUABLE LESSON

Walking into the clinic each morning was not unlike being announced as the blue light special. I was greeted with "Get ready, Doc, it's going to be a wild and bumpy one today." One quick glance at the handwritten schedule of booked and double-booked appointments verified Roberta's prophetic statement. Strangely missing was "lunch." Was that just an accidental omission, or was she really serious? The way things were to turn out that day, she was serious.

The first surgical case of the day was an ovariohysterectomy (spay) on an eight-month-old white cat named Pinkie. She was a good little girl, purred constantly, and seemed overly affectionate. She rubbed her head against everything and everybody. These not-so-subtle amorous marking cues suggested that Pinkie was very possibly in heat. If she were, then the uterine tissues would be much more delicate and fragile, requiring extra care and caution during surgery. Pinkie was anesthetized, prepped, and readied for surgery. The initial abdominal incision was made, and the uterus, along with the ovaries, was quickly isolated. The uterus was slightly enlarged, there were follicles plainly visible on the ovaries, and the adjacent blood vessels appeared enlarged . The verdict—this little lady was in roaring heat, and I'd need some additional assistance to retract the delicate uterus while placing the ligatures. So I called out to Roberta for some help, "Roberta, could you please come and retract for me?" No response. I called out again, only this time with more volume and urgency. Finally, a disgruntled Roberta appeared.

"Why can't you do this yourself? Dr. Wagner doesn't ever need help."

"Roberta," I said, "Dr. Wagner has about fifteen more years of experience than me, and after a few more of these, I won't need any help either, but for now, I need an extra hand, okay?" I explained the delicate tissue concern and the extra care needed, but it obviously went in one ear and out the other, because when I gently handed Roberta the forceps, which were attached to the uterus, she impatiently and forcefully jerked up on them. The fragile tissue instantly snapped, causing the body of the uterus and the adjacent vessels to plunge back down into the recesses of the abdominal cavity. There was immediate panic! Roberta's face turned pale, and she was speechless—for a change. I could feel my chest tighten and my heart rate increase, sensing the gravity of what had just happened. Pinkie could possibly bleed internally if I couldn't quickly find the uterine stump and vessels and tie them off. I enlarged the incision for better exposure, and to my amazement, there was no bleeding. The quick jerk on the fragile tissue had caused the vessels to constrict and stopped any potential hemorrhaging. I did find the vessels and tied them off, just to avoid any further complications. Pinkie recovered very nicely and went home the next day happy and none the worse for wear.

The whole incident was an extremely valuable lesson for both Roberta and myself. She never again questioned my request for assistance. She also became a more gentle, proficient, and compassionate assistant, and I'd learned how to effectively respond in high-stress, life-threatening situations. That experience was a real adrenaline rush, but more importantly, the patient survived and was doing well.

NEW MEDICINE

As I walked into the clinic that morning, our receptionist, Roberta, greeted me with, "Hey, Doc, you've got to go out to Van Leeuwen's place today. He's got a cow that he thinks has mastitis, and he says her bag is hot and pretty big and hard too. Don't try to get him to use penicillin on any of his cows because he doesn't believe in the stuff. Oh yeah, and don't even try to get him to come into the clinic, for anything, because Dr. Wagner has tried that for years, and Sam has never come in, ever."

This ole Dutch dairyman, Sam Van Leeuwen, sounded like a real character and a challenge. I was actually looking forward to going on this farm call and meet Sam. You see, I grew up in an ethnically German community, heard farmers and ranchers converse a lot in German, and I'd experienced the stubbornness of some of those people and how they could be firmly set in their ways. Believe me, I'd seen firsthand how change was hard for many of them to accept. Heck, dealing with ole Sam would be like "old home week." It sounded like fun!

Driving through the countryside on the way to Sam's place was great. The scenery was a real feast for the eyes, especially on that nice day with the sun shining down on all the cattle and horses grazing contentedly on the pastures. Once in a while, I'd get a perfect view of snow-capped Mount Rainier towering majestically in the distance. It was a sight to behold. I definitely understood why people had chosen to live and work in this part of the country.

My sightseeing venture ended as I pulled up to the Van Leeuwen dairy farm. It wasn't a large operation, but dairies didn't have to be big to be good. Suddenly a skinny little man dressed in overalls, wearing black barn boots, and sporting an old misshapen baseball cap came marching out from one of the white barns. He waved an arm in the air with a welcoming gesture and approached my vehicle.

"*Wie gehts*, Sam," I said, hoping he could understand my German greeting.

Sam replied with a wry smile, "*Gute.*"

Well, that was a good ice breaker. So far, so good.

"*You da nu Dokk?*" he asked.

"*Ja, Ich bin der tierarzt.*" (Yes, I am the animal doctor, veterinarian.) "I understand that you've got a cow with udder problems. Is that right?

"*Ja*, her bag is hot, and dere's some blud in da mielk too."

Sam led the way to the barn, and I followed close behind with my stainless steel bucket in one hand and the medical bag in the other. I examined the cow, and Sam was right on the money with his diagnosis. The cow's rectal temperature was elevated, her udder was swollen, discolored, very warm to the touch, and when I stripped milk from one of the teats, it was bloody, thick, and stringy. I told Sam that his cow did indeed have a bad case of mastitis, and I had a "new," very special mastitis medicine with me that I wanted to use on his cow. I had taken a brand-new bottle of penicillin, added 2 cc of azosulfamide solution, which was deep red in color, mixed the contents, and—voila!—the "new medicine." I reached into my medicine bag, grabbed the unlabeled pink concoction, showed it to Sam, and told him, "I'll give the cow an injection of this new medicine now, and if it appears to work, then you'll have to come to the clinic and pick up another syringe of the stuff, okay?"

Sam nodded his head in agreement. As I was about to leave, I told him that I was pretty confident that this new mastitis treatment would help. Deep down inside, I knew it would. Now the big question, could I get Sam to show up at the clinic— something he'd never done before? Time would tell.

Three days later, Roberta came rushing back into the clinic treatment area, and with a shocked expression on her face, she said, "You'll never believe who just walked into the clinic. Sam Van Leeuwen, and he wants to see...you! How'd you do that?"

Looking nonchalantly at Roberta, I said, "A trade secret." Oh yeah, the treatment on Sam's cow was a success, and in time, his confidence in the healing powers of penicillin was restored.

THAT WAS FAST!

Holstein cows tend to be very large animals, and when they have problems, those problems can be rather big too. Such was the case with Lawrence Purdy's cow. The drive to Mr. Purdy's dairy that morning was enjoyable. As I passed by the numerous wild blackberry patches alongside the road, the sun began to peek out between the clouds that had brought rain earlier that morning. The sky was blue, the air was clean and clear, and the sun was shining. *This should be a wonderful day,* I said to myself as I entered Mr. Purdy's driveway.

This dairy was one of the largest in the area. The outbuildings and barns appeared well maintained, suggesting that the owner was very conscientious and took pride in his work. I pulled into the farmyard and stopped my truck at the exact moment that Mr. Purdy emerged from one of the barns. He walked up to the truck, saw me, and said, "He didn't send me another newbie again, did he?" Mr. Purdy appeared and sounded disgusted.

I stretched forth my hand and introduced myself, "I'm Dr. Roloff, Dr. Wagner's new associate." Mr. Purdy ignored my handshake, looked to the side and said, "Yeah, that's what I thought. He always sends me somebody who's green. Well, you're all I got…so. It's this way to the cow. She prolapsed her uterus."

I knew, right then and there, that this was going to be a tough case, and there'd be a lot of equipment and medications to carry to the barn. I asked Mr. Purdy, "Could you help me carry some of this stuff?" He opened the gate and just kept walking, not looking back. I wasn't sure if he heard me, or if he was just being rude and simply ignored my request. Anyway, there I was, buckets and ropes in one hand, and portable medical case in the other, shutting the gates with my shoulders and feet. I sure could have used some help, but I didn't get any. As I entered the barn, there she stood! This huge, behemoth of a cow with her uterus totally prolapsed. Gads! It's not unusual to find a mature Holstein cow that tips the scales at between 1,500 and 2,000 pounds, stands over five feet tall at the shoulders, and is close to three feet across the hips. These gals are big, and so are their parts, both inside and out. Reducing (replacing) this uterus would be a long and difficult task—that was for sure. As I proceeded to clean the bloody, swollen, edematous, straw-covered mass of tissue, I heard Mr. Purdy comment, "I suppose we'll be here almost all day because it takes Doc Wagner quite a while to do these, and he's good." Boy, that was sure a confidence builder! I didn't respond to his put-down; instead, I just kept on doing my job. I then gave the cow an epidural anesthetic injection to decrease the cow's straining and to make the whole replacement procedure easier on both of us. That pendulous uterus weighed almost seventy pounds, was about two feet wide, and hung down over half way to her hocks. Attempting to push something that big back into a 1,500-pound cow through a small opening, while she was still straining in resistance, was definitely not a walk in the park. All the while, Mr. Purdy was standing silently to the side with an "I knew it" smirk on his face.

As I grunted to get the weighty uterus into position, suddenly I felt the tissue beginning to involute (turn in on itself), and that

48

was the key. The use of steady even force allowed the uterus to magically fold in on itself, and in the blink of an eye, the mass tumbled completely back into its normal position. Quite honestly, I was shocked. It was a minor miracle! I wanted that thing to stay put, so I placed a few temporary restraining sutures (stitches), gave her several antibiotic injections, and I was done! It took less than ten minutes! I nonchalantly looked over at Mr. Purdy with a Cheshire cat smile on my face. His mouth was hanging wide open, and he looked as if he'd just seen a ghost.

"How'd you do that so fast?" he asked.

Very calmly and without smiling, I said, "If you know what you're doing, it should always work like that."

Mr. Purdy was speechless! I grabbed my buckets and equipment, handed them to Mr. Purdy, and said, "Now, here, help me carry my stuff to the truck."

Without a moment's hesitation, the stunned Mr. Purdy grabbed the buckets and even managed to open the gates for me as we returned to the truck. His demeanor had suddenly become much more civil. He actually seemed appreciative and somewhat humbled, but more likely, he was in a state of shock and disbelief at what he'd just witnessed. I couldn't stop smiling on the drive back to the vet clinic because replacing a prolapsed uterus on a cow that big, that fast, was almost unbelievable. I'd definitely been graced out. Thank you, Lord. Hey, the day really did turn out to be beautiful, in more ways than one.

THE GRAY STALLION

Being a veterinarian in a mixed practice was never boring or mundane. It was exciting going to work each day, anticipating what interesting cases lay ahead. Most days were, as Forrest Gump put it, "like a box of chocolates. You didn't know what you were going to get." Truer words were never spoken.

"Doc, you got to get out to Milton Stables. They've got a horse that hurt his mouth."

"Is that it? They didn't tell you any more?" I asked. Roberta curtly replied, "Nope."

I grabbed what I thought I'd need to handle just about anything. Heck, the horse could have an abscessed tooth, or maybe he had bitten himself, or his teeth might need to be floated—all kinds of things could be going on here. I'd just have to wait and see. Milton Stables was a first-class equine breeding operation. White wooden fences flanked the long entry lane that led up to the headquarters atop a grassy knoll.

There were numerous white and green barns surrounded by various-sized separation pens. White fences were everywhere, and it all appeared perfectly manicured. Well-groomed horses were all about, whinnying in delight as they ran and jumped around in their corrals. It looked like something you'd expect to see in an oil painting. The foreman approached. I introduced myself and asked to see the horse with a mouth problem. He led me over to a small corral where this big, muscular, gray Quarter Horse stallion was busily eating grass hay. I thought to myself, *He's eating, so this shouldn't be too bad.* That's what I thought until the foreman turned the horse's head toward me.

"Holy cow." I said. "His jaw is broken."

"Yup," the foreman responded. "I shouldn't have put those two stallions so close together. They're always fighting over the mares and trying to bite each other through the fence. Something must've happened.

No kidding, I thought to myself. The horse didn't seem to be in much pain or discomfort, and that in itself was amazing. His lower jaw was totally split in half, and the now separated jaw bones moved freely and independently.. "This horse needs surgery, and pronto!" I told the foreman.

Thank goodness the weather was cooperating. The day was warm, sunny, and best of all, no rain. I placed the horse under general anesthetic upon the lawn atop the grassy knoll. As I opened the horse's mouth, the lower jaw separated approximately four inches. What a mess! The symphysis, the union point of the right and left sides of the lower jaw, was completely split. Pieces of grass and plant seeds were stuck into the exposed porous openings of the bone marrow. All the debris had to be painstakingly removed to prevent a severe bone infection from occurring. Once the cleaning of the tissues had been completed, I wired the horse's jaw back into place with some very stout stainless steel surgical wire and reconstructed the soft tissue. Upon completion, it looked really good, almost as if nothing had happened.

The stainless steel wires would stay for eight to ten weeks. Antibiotics were to be given, and my final instruction: *keep those stallions apart*! He did, and the big, gray stallion did just fine.

SHE'S SO SMALL

Why do emergencies always seem to happen at the most inopportune times? The unspoken code in the medical profession is "You must attend," but what does that really mean? It essentially means that you drop whatever you're presently doing and immediately address the problem at hand. Such was the case on one particular Saturday evening.

The caseload had been pretty hectic the last few weeks, and I was seriously in need of a break. That Saturday morning's appointments were basically routine cases, fairly easy stuff, no major problems to deal with. I was looking forward to getting off at noon but was scheduled to be on call that evening. Saturday evenings were usually rather quiet, so Sandy and I thought we'd treat ourselves by going out to dinner at one of the local restaurants. We definitely needed and deserved some quiet, relaxed time together.

It was 7:30 p.m., and just as we were about to leave on our dinner date, the phone rang. "I hope it isn't what I think it is," Sandy said as she picked up the receiver. She stood there, listening for a minute or so, then said, "Here's Doc," and handed me the phone.

I listened to the concerned owner, told him that I'd be right out, and hung up the phone. I turned to Sandy and dejectedly said, "The guy on the phone has a first-calf heifer that's been straining hard for several hours, trying to deliver a calf, but nothing's happened. I'm so sorry, dear, but I've got to go. I'm on call, and small first-calf heifers usually have more trouble calving, and those difficult births can be life-threatening to the cow, the calf, or both of them. It sounds like a bona fide emergency, and I might end up doing a C-section tonight. I guess we'll have to take a rain check on that dinner date."

Sandy, bless her heart, said, "That's all right. Would you mind if I came along?"

I told her, "That would be great."

Sandy had never seen a caesarian section performed on a cow, so this would be a first. She was a nurse by profession, and she was willing to pitch in and help if I needed assistance. We quickly changed clothes because now we were headed out on a "dystocia (difficult birthing) date," instead of a dinner date.

The small farm was located on the edge of town, so it didn't take long to get there. The hobby farmer and his wife were standing by their driveway, awaiting our arrival, and were extremely grateful that we'd come to their aid, especially on a Saturday evening. As we entered the barn, there she stood, undeniably the smallest Hereford first-calf heifer that I'd ever seen! That diminutive little girl had C-section written all over her, no doubt about it.

"What was she bred to?" I asked.

"A Hereford bull," The man replied.

Oh joy! Hereford bulls usually produce big calves, and that could create some problems. I got all my buckets, disinfectants, medications, and surgical instruments prepared and organized together for a C-section. First I needed to examine the heifer and check the position of the calf and also see if the calf was still alive. As I inserted my arm into the birth canal, I palpated (felt) a very small hoof. It was tiny, like that of a fawn.

"That's strange," I thought. Then the little hoof pulled back. "It's alive and small!" I announced. "I might be able to deliver this little guy."

I aligned the little calf's legs, and as I applied steady, even traction, the heifer strained and forcefully contracted her abdominal muscles, groaning with each heavy contraction. I grabbed ahold of the hooves and synchronized my pulling with her contractions. First came the tiny hooves, then the nose appeared, next, the head popped out of the birth canal, and finally the body was exposed. It took only a bit more traction, and the little fella was delivered. At first the calf laid motionless, but after some vigorous rubbing and tickling its nose with a piece of straw, the little guy blinked his dark brown eyes, coughed, took a deep breath, then sneezed and forcefully blew fluid out of his little pink nose. When the calf belted out its first bleat, the little cow turned and immediately started vigorously licking her baby calf all over its head and body with her raspy tongue. She was a good mom, and she was sure proud and protective of that little calf too. As they say, "All's well that ends well." What could have been a disaster turned out to be something extra special and meaningful. We'd witnessed the miracle of birth and it's a wonderful experience each and every time.

"Hey, Sandy, we've still got some time tonight. Let's go home, get cleaned up, go out to dinner, and celebrate!"

PASTURE COWBOY

Secretly, I'd always wanted to be a rodeo clown. Having a two-thousand-pound animal charging you, intending to put your lights out, is an adrenalin rush like no other. Escaping unharmed and in one piece was definitely a thrill.

I had what might be called an easy farm call to go on that morning—just one bull calf to castrate at Mr. Corless's place. Heck, that shouldn't take any time at all, or so I thought. The directions were good, so it didn't take much time to get there. Instead of a farm, it turned out to be a thirty-acre pasture with a small herd of cattle grazing in the far corner and a little red barn sitting next to the road. I got out of my vet rig and looked around. No vehicles. Nothing. It was as quiet as a tomb.

I called out, "Hello, anybody here? Mr. Corless, are you here?" No answer. Where was everybody? Where was Mr. Corless? Did I screw up on the directions? I waited for a few more minutes and then decided to take off. Suddenly, just as I was about to leave, a short, pudgy, elderly gent dressed in bib overalls and wearing a long-sleeved red-and-black-colored plaid shirt, materialized out from behind the barn. It was Mr. Corless. He approached with a waddling shuffle, waving his arm in the air, letting me know that he was on his way. When he got within earshot, I introduced myself and asked, "Where's the calf that needs to be castrated?" I'd surmised that the calf was pinned up and waiting for me in the barn, but Mr. Corless motioned his arm in the direction of the pasture. "Out there?" I asked.

He nodded yes, not speaking, and seemingly out of breath. Mr. Corless looked to be in his eighties, and by the way he was breathing, not in the best of health either. Looking around, there didn't appear to be anything that resembled a corral or catch area for confining the calf. Nothing. Nada. Zippo! Mr. Corless then told me, "He's out there with the cows."

"What kind of cows do you have, and how many?" I asked.

"Simmentals, twelve cows and just one bull calf, about two hundred pounds," he replied. Now, Simmentals are an old breed of cattle that originated from Switzerland. They are big, heavily muscled, and were used primarily for milk production and drafting (pulling wagons and plows). Simmentals usually stand about five feet tall at the withers, and can weigh nearly 1,500 pounds when mature. They also have huge muzzles, about the width of a good-sized cantaloupe. Simmentals are a gentle breed of cattle, but they can be very protective of their young, which is normal.

Mr. Corless then popped the big question that I really didn't want to hear. "You got a rope?"

I had a lariat in the vet rig, and unfortunately, it looked like I'd be using my roping skills, which in all honesty, weren't very good. The challenge now was, how can I get to the calf that's way out there in the pasture surrounded by twelve protective cows? There I was, a stranger with a lariat draped over my shoulder, carrying a clanging bucket of surgical instruments, invading their territory. The cows immediately sensed danger, and with their heads raised in alarm position, they started stampeding from one end of the pasture to the other. The calf, all the while, was being surrounded by the protective cows, and my approaching moves caused the small herd to run off in panic mode. I noticed that the herd seemed to run in a circular pattern, so I strategically positioned myself, hoping for a closer run-by.

Suddenly and unexpectedly, the thundering herd came my way, and I got a glimpse of the calf. Here was my big chance. I swung the rope over my head, took a sizable lead, and blindly tossed the lariat in the general direction of the calf. Amazingly, as the lariat reached its full extension, the calf's head miraculously passed perfectly through the loop. I leaned back on the rope as the loop tightened around the calf's neck, you know, the way real cowboys do it. *Got him!* The calf lost his balance, fell to the ground, and let out a loud bellow alarm for help. The cows immediately answered the call and came rushing to his rescue, and at that very moment, I knew it was now or never! I had to get to the calf quickly, hold on for dear life, and hopefully not get trampled by those 1,500-pound cows trying to save one of their own. As long as I held onto the calf, I was semi-safe, because the cows didn't want to hurt their calf—just me! I tied up three of the calf's legs in a flash, grabbed the bucket containing the surgical instruments, and performed the fastest castration ever, probably record-setting time! All the while, the frantic, protective cows were literally on top of me, bellowing directly into my ears, and flinging slobber from their huge muzzles all over my head and shoulders. As I untied the rope, the calf made his great escape, and the cows reassuringly followed.

My ears were still ringing as I stumbled to my feet. Out of the corner of my eye, I noticed Mr. Corless shuffling along through the pasture in my direction. Although visibly tired and out of breath, he still managed to ask, "Doc, you need any help?"

I replied, "Nah, my rodeo cowboy routine is over with. I only wish somebody could have timed the calf roping and castration and given me a score."

HE OR SHE?

The phrase "one in a million" usually conjures up thoughts of winning the lottery or having someone ring your doorbell announcing that you'd just won the big sweepstakes. Well, this one particular day would be a "one in a million" day, but not the kind where money was involved.

"Doc, a lady just called, and she wants you to check out something that's growing by her dog's private parts," Roberta, the receptionist, loudly announced from the front desk. "She said it looks weird and just noticed it yesterday. What do you think it is?"

"I don't know. It could be a lot of things. We'll just have to wait and see," I replied. We didn't have to wait long because the owner considered the growth to be an emergency and was rushing right in.

The fifteen-pound, brown-and-white, intact female Terrier cross named Lilly arrived and was quickly placed on the exam table. She was visibly nervous, very wary of the surroundings, and was repeatedly licking at her "parts."

"Let's take a look," I said while lifting her tail. There it was, for all the world to see. The owner was right. A cylindrical shaped growth, the size of a person's little finger, was protruding from Lilly's vulva. The tissue appeared to be pink and healthy, but definitely in the wrong place. Upon closer examination, the unusual growth appeared to be a vestigial (rudimentary, undeveloped, nonfunctional) penis. "We could have a little hermaphrodite or pseudohermaphrodite here," I told the owner. "I'll need to surgically remove that growth and also perform a spay at the same time because there could be some associated ovary problems as well." I then asked the owner if she had ever noticed Lilly acting more like a male than a female. "Does Lilly squat or hike her leg when she urinates?"

The owner said, "She always hikes her leg and humps the pillows too. Isn't that bizarre for a female?"

"Yup, and it could indicate that there might be some additional problems inside of her too. You see, the sex of an individual, whether they're male or female, is determined by the gonad (ovary or testicle) that is present, not the external plumbing. Lilly could have one or the other, or both, as is the case with a true hermaphrodite. We'll see," I said.

The surgery was quickly scheduled. The vestigial penis was removed and an ovariohysterectomy (spay) was performed. Lilly did have a normal uterus, but instead of ovaries, she had testicles in the place where the ovaries should have been. So Lilly was technically a male! Following the surgery, I delicately dissected the surgically removed vestigial penis, and it did contain the bony structure called the os penis, which is a normal structure found in male dogs. I cleaned it real well and took it home, hoping to someday make it into a tie tack. That would make a conversation piece like no other!

When Sandy saw my souvenir, she couldn't believe that I'd actually brought that "thing" home, and she thought my tie tack idea was gross and weird. So she threw it in the garbage without me knowing. When I found out that my little trophy was long gone, I was bummed out because I'd most likely never see another case like that ever again in my lifetime. It was an extremely rare, one-in-a-million find, now gone. Oh well, c'est la vie.

Lilly had to be renamed because she turned out to be more of a boy than a girl So, instead of Lilly, *he* became Lawrence, even though he still had female/girl external plumbing.

THE FORBIDDEN FRUIT

Stan Winslow, a commercial airline pilot who flew out of Seattle's Seatac Airport, loved the Pacific Northwest and had made Enumclaw his home base. His small ranch of fifty acres served as his retreat from the hectic demands he routinely faced, and he found solace working with his small herd of twenty purebred Angus cows. He was, what you might call, a weekend rancher. Mr. Winslow dearly loved his cows, providing them with the best feed available and plenty of other goodies, including whole apples. The caseload was comfortably slow that morning at the veterinary clinic. It was, undeniably, a welcomed change of pace. Everything was going along well, fairly routine cases, until the phone rang, and Roberta said, "Doc, we've got an emergency! Stan Winslow is on the line, and one of his cows is choking. You've got to get out there *right now*!" I quickly grabbed my stuff, and as I was racing out of the building, I yelled back to Roberta, "Reschedule whatever you can. I'm outta here."

On the way to an emergency, I usually put the pedal to the metal, hoping not to get stopped by the police and having to explain myself. As I turned onto the lane leading up to Mr. Winslow's place, I could see him standing there with the choking cow in a small pasture next to the house. The cow had her head extended down and forward, thrusting her tongue out as far as it could possibly go. She was heaving her chest and abdomen in a frantic attempt to dislodge whatever was in her throat, and it appeared that she wasn't getting any air either. No time for trying to find the mouth speculum that would keep her from biting me. I jumped out of the truck, ran over to the cow, and thrust my hand and arm into her mouth and down her throat, hoping to grab or dislodge whatever was causing the obstruction problem. All the while, this big panicking animal was chewing on my arm. At first I couldn't feel anything in her throat, but then as I thrust my arm deeper, to the point where the cow's muzzle was almost up to my shoulder, the tips of my fingers contacted a hard round object. It was positioned at the junction between the trachea and the esophagus, essentially shutting off the air flow. It was too far down and too tightly wedged for me to grasp with my fingers, so my only option was to attempt to push it forward, hoping she would swallow it. I flicked my fingers at the object while trying to thrust my chewed arm even deeper. Suddenly, it moved forward, the cow swallowed hard several times, and then she took in a huge deep breath of air. That had to be one of the most beautiful sounds I'd ever heard. I quickly jerked my slobbery, bruised, chewed-up arm out of that chomping cavern and was thankful to see that I still had an arm. No more straining or choking as the cow wandered off. The cow and Mr. Winslow were both relieved, and believe me, so was I. Honestly, I couldn't have taken much more, and neither could the cow.

"We dodged a bullet, Stan," I said. He nodded in agreement. "You know, those whole apples are forbidden fruit to those cows, but if you're going to give them apples, cut them up into smaller pieces, okay?" Mr. Winslow nodded sheepishly. Oh yes, Mr. Winslow's cows were fed *cut* apples in the future, and it took several days for my arm to heal.

THE DEVIL'S ROPE

The expression "good fences make good neighbors" is basically true, but fences are often like a two-edged sword in that they can either be a blessing or a curse. I've seen both ends of the spectrum, especially where barbed wire was involved.

Barbed wire came on the scene in the late 1800s, drastically changed the Wild West, and adversely affected the lives of the nomadic Native Americans. They aptly called those thin, spiked, twisted strands of metal, "The Devil's Rope". Today, barbed wire is widely used throughout the world because it is inexpensive and very effective at setting boundaries. The flipside, however, is much more sinister. Barbed wire is nearly invisible and can pose a serious physical threat to any unsuspecting animal or human who unfortunately runs into or through it. The Native Americans were right. Barbed wire truly is "The Devil's Rope".

I was scheduled to work that Saturday morning, and it was also my turn to be on call for any weekend emergencies. It'd been a wild week at the clinic. I was a little on the tired side and needed a lighter weekend so I could recoup. The cases at the clinic that morning had been pretty routine, and it looked like I'd actually get out of there on time for a change. Wow! Wonders never cease! When I got home, Sandy greeted me with a neatly written "honey-do" list. That wasn't what I'd envisioned for the weekend, but at least it was a change of pace from what I'd been through the previous week.

All was going well until that 3:00 p.m. phone call. "Hello! This is Bonnie Calvert out here on 416th. My horse just ran through some barbed wire. He's cut up really bad on his chest and legs. He's bleeding all over the place. Can you come out right now? Please!" I got directions, grabbed my stuff, kissed the honey-do list good-bye, then hit the road. The Calvert place was located just a few miles outside of town, so I didn't have much time to conjure up a game plan.

Usually I'd try to visualize what might be waiting for me and get mentally prepared for what I was in for. Most of the time, however, things turned out to be much worse and more complicated than imagined, and as I'd soon find out, that would also be the case in this instance. As I pulled into the Calvert's lane, there he stood, a big, red roan quarter horse, surrounded by four women. One on the lead rope, trying to control the fidgety, stressed-out horse, and the other three holding blood-soaked towels to the horse's chest and upper front legs. The first thing I heard when getting out of the truck was, "Boy, are we glad to see you!"

As the women repositioned the towels, I got a quick glimpse at the barbed wire injuries and instantly understood their reason for concern. The horse was ripped to shreds! Literally! This horse hadn't just been cut, he'd been dissected! The horse, named Sid, was in obvious pain and discomfort, so I immediately gave him an injection containing a strong sedative and pain killer before proceeding any further. Once he was in La-La land and feeling no pain, I gently lifted the towels, quickly clamped the active bleeders, and surveyed the extent of tissue damage. There were multiple traumatic lacerations to Sid's chest and upper front legs. The skin was savagely torn, and several lacerations had penetrated deeply into his chest muscles, completely severing some of the muscles, causing them to hang limply, almost halfway down to his knees.

I began by strategically injecting local anesthetic throughout the mangled mess, and then started the arduous task of cleaning, scrubbing, and disinfecting the surgical field prior to reconstruction. It was a challenge to identify what was what and what went where. I mentally visualized the normal anatomical configuration of the muscles and then began the painstakingly slow process of identifying and reuniting the muscles and reconstructing the severely damaged tissue. It took about two hours of intense surgery to put Sid back together, but when finished, I was confident that all the skin and muscles were successfully reunited, and I truly believed that he had a good chance of someday running again. Granted, Sid may have looked like an equine version of Frankenstein after the surgery, but it was now just a matter of time for complete healing to take place. Time would tell. When all the sutures were removed two weeks later, Sid looked and acted as good as new. He did run again, but had some permanent trophy scars as evidence of his untimely encounter with the devil's rope.

MOONSHINE

Black Diamond is a small town near Enumclaw, and an old mining cart is proudly displayed at one end of town. The town obviously derived its name from the mining of coal, which was once a thriving industry in the area. At one time, coal miners from the southeastern states ventured to the Pacific Northwest in search of work. Their immigration into the region gave rise to some neighboring villages and hamlets with names like Ravensdale, Carbonado, and Wilkeson. When the demand for coal decreased and the supply of the black fuel dwindled, many of the miners and their families left the area. There were some, however, who chose to stay and make these parts their permanent home. These honest, hardworking folks infused new skills and traditions into their chosen communities, and it was rumored that one such skill was the art of making some mighty fine moonshine.

I was on my way to Carbonado one summer day to check a steer that was down and, according to the owner, was very weak and couldn't stand. Carbonado was a small community with a population less than five hundred, located in a heavily forested area near the Mount Rainier National Forest. The written directions seemed fairly straightforward, but with all the twists

71

and turns on those hinterland roads, it took quite a while to find the place. I finally pulled onto a narrow dirt road that eventually led to an older mobile home that was partially hidden among the trees and other vegetation. It looked kind of spooky. This place was really way off the beaten path; there were no vehicles around, no movement—it appeared deserted. Was I at the wrong address? *Oh well*, I thought, *I'd better go up there and at least knock on the door.* I couldn't hear any movement in response to my initial knocking, but then the door suddenly opened, and this big, broad-shouldered, unshaven, suspender-wearing, brawny fella appeared right before my eyes and said, "Whata ya want?"

Looking up at this imposing giant of a man, I asked, "Are you Joe McKay?"

"Yup!" He gruffly responded.

I told him, "I'm the vet, and I'm here to check out the downed steer you called about."

Mr. McKay's facial expressions softened somewhat, but not much, as he said, "Oh yeah, he's out back."

I quickly grabbed my medical bags and followed Joe toward the steer. There he was, laying in squalor and looking very pathetic. Upon examination of this poor animal, he appeared thin, weak, extremely pale and anemic, acted as if he couldn't see very well, and had bloody diarrhea. His abdomen heaved as he struggled to breathe. It was a pretty sad situation. Looking around the little pen, I noticed the poor quality of hay that this animal was being fed, and the small adjacent pasture was loaded with bracken ferns. The handwriting was on the wall. "It looks like your steer has bracken fern poisoning, and the outcome doesn't look good at all," I told Mr. McKay. He looked puzzled. "Bracken ferns are poisonous, and when they're eaten by livestock, all kinds of problems can occur, like tremors, blindness, internal bleeding, anemias, secondary cancers, and sometimes even death."

Mr. McKay responded, "Eh, just put him out of his misery, Doc."

So I did the humane thing and gave the dying steer an intravenous injection of euthanasia solution and instantly relieved his suffering.

When the job was done, Mr. McKay told me to come inside, and he'd "pay up." Upon entering the dimly lit mobile home, I was surprised to find three more bruisers sitting there. They all looked rather surly and stared at me as if I were some kind of intruder. The silence was deafening, and honestly, I was becoming a little uncomfortable. There was tension in the air too, and I didn't feel welcome, or at least that was my perception. So in an attempt to break the icy silence, I blurted out with what had to be the dumbest thing I've ever said. "I hear they make some mighty fine moonshine up in these parts." As I heard those words come rolling out of my mouth and saw the blank stares on those guy's faces, I thought to myself, , *that was really a stupid* thing to say.

I felt myself sweating, and it seemed like an hour passed before Joe said, "You've never had any good shine before?"

"Nope, never have. I've always wanted to try some of the stuff though," I said.

Mr. McKay then motioned to one of the bruisers, his son, to go get some shine. It didn't take long for his son to return with a mason jar filled with what looked like water. Joe unscrewed the lid, poured a small glass half full of the clear stuff, and extended the glass toward me saying, "Here ya go. This here is some really good white lightnin'. Go slow now."

They all watched as I put the glass to my lips and took my first sip of that high octane concoction. "Holy cow! That stuff is strong, but smooth," I said, gasping. My mouth was burning, and it didn't take long before I couldn't feel my lips. I coughed and rubbed my now totally numb lips, and that brought welcomed laughs and smiles from all the guys. I thanked them for sharing and told them that they should be proud of their white lightning, and I could see how it got its name. They grinned and nodded their heads in approval.

As I was getting back into my truck to leave, Mr. McKay came sauntering up to the cab with a small brown paper bag in his hand. "Here ya go, Doc. A little somethin' to take home with ya. Now, take it easy with this stuff. It can be habit formin'. Oh yeah, you don't know where this came from either," he said with a wry grin. I thanked him, shook his hand, and took off. My lips were still numb by the time I got home. That really was some mighty fine moonshine.

THE NEIGHBORHOOD
STREETWALKERS

We lived in a nice, old home that was located two blocks from the veterinary clinic. It was a quiet little neighborhood, there wasn't much traffic, and it was relatively safe for dogs to freely roam about. While living at that location, I'd experienced firsthand that life can certainly be full of surprises and sometimes things may not be as they first appear. Susie and Jenny were prime examples of that.

Susie was a little geriatric cocker spaniel–cross female who lived at the house on the corner of the street. She was a sweet and gentle senior citizen with compromised vision and hearing. Her tongue constantly dangled out of the left side of her mouth through the space created by some missing teeth. She regularly patrolled the sidewalk, walking at a snail's pace, and sniffing the air, seemingly oblivious to any major sights or sounds—kind of in her own little world—surveying her domain. She had one very bad habit though, and that was her penchant for sitting smack-dab in the middle of the street. There she'd sit, tongue dangling, her eyes squinting at the cars, and giving them the evil eye as they maneuvered around her. It was quite the sight. That was her street, and she owned it. I told Sandy that little old Susie must have a serious death wish, because one of these days, she could get hit by a car and be seriously injured or even killed. That concerned me, so I kept telling her to get off the street and go home, but to no avail. She just squinted back at me and defiantly ignored my every word. Susie was very independent, stubborn, and wasn't about to move until she felt like it, so there!

Several weeks had passed, and one day as I looked at Susie, she had that certain glow about her. Her tiny tummy was getting a little rounder, and she had more of a swinging waddle to her stride. Could it be? I checked her over, and sure enough, I felt movement. No doubt about it. This little grandma was pregnant! Susie's owners didn't have a clue as to what she'd been bred to and didn't seem to care either. Heck, she'd been free to wander the streets, and when one is a street walker, some bad things can happen. I had some legitimate concerns about Susie because she wasn't a spring chicken, and older dogs can potentially have all kinds of problems with the pregnancy, delivering the puppies, producing enough milk, and even being good mothers.

Several more weeks had passed, and then one day, there she was, proudly waddling down the sidewalk with four little butterball puppies trailing behind. Susie was so proud of those puppies, and she was a good mom too. She even made sure that the little ones stayed safely out of the street. Wow! What a surprise.

Then there was Jenny. Jenny was an unkempt, undisciplined, hyperactive, gray-and-white, eight-month-old cockapoo. She was a friendly little dog, but a real ditz. Jenny was heavily matted, dirty, smelled, and even though they couldn't be seen, you knew she had to have a pair of eyes somewhere under all that hair. She'd run up and down the sidewalks and streets in hot pursuit of attention from anyone she could find. This hyperactive, frenetic, gyrating little dog would unabashedly jump up on people with her dirty paws, just trying to play and be noticed.

One Saturday afternoon I noticed a cute, little, well-groomed dog leisurely prancing down the sidewalk. *Hey, new people must have moved into the neighborhood, and this nice little poodle cross must belong to them,* I said to myself. The little dog seemed friendly and was actually very well behaved. There was something, however, that seemed odd.

The new dog appeared to be unusually familiar with our street and the surroundings. My lightning-fast mind was finally putting all the pieces together. The size, color, and age were about the same, and this little dog with the pink ribbons in her hair didn't really act like a stranger to the area either. Nah, it couldn't be. Getting bathed, trimmed, and all prettied up shouldn't make that much difference, should it? I called out, "Jenny?" This little princess slowly turned her head toward me with a regal, almost condescending flair, then she elegantly trotted off to her house, or should I say, palace. Jenny had unbelievably become a new person—er, dog. She had been transformed from a real ditzy ragamuffin into a beautiful princess, and she wanted everyone to know it too. Jenny was now a lady with style, and she walked the streets with pizzaz!

THE FEDORA
AND THE TRENCH COAT

I could tell by the clear blue sky that morning that all was well with the world, and that the coming day was going to be a good one. It was the weekend, the schedule on the books looked fairly light, and we had a day hike on Crystal Mountain planned for Sunday afternoon. I was really looking forward to getting out there and soaking in the beauty and majesty of God's creation.

It was around ten that morning when the clinic phone rang, and there was a very disgruntled lady on the other end of the line. Roberta sat there listening, looked back at me, and rolled her eyes. I always hated that because it usually signaled something rather serious and complicated was going on. Roberta suddenly swirled around in her desk chair, thrust her arm toward me while tightly gripping the phone in her hand, and with a voice filled with frustration said, "Here, *you* talk to this lady!"

"Hello, Doc Roloff here," I said.

The lady took off on a wild tirade. "You vets are all alike! Nobody wants to come out! My cow's got a dead calf in her, and damn, now she's gonna die too if she doesn't get some help. Nobody wants to help! All that you people want is the money!

You don't care about the animals! You're the fifth one I've called. Everybody says they're too busy and don't have time. Nobody is willing to help me, damn it!"

I had to hold the phone away from my ear because she was yelling and cursing so loudly. *Well, so much for the beautiful day*, I thought to myself. I had to wait for an opening in her diatribe, and when the moment presented itself, I quickly interjected, "Who am I speaking to?"

"Gertrude Rempher," she said. "I live over by Federal Way." Oh brother, that's about twenty-five miles away, and with her attitude, no wonder she couldn't find anyone to help her.

"Give me directions, Mrs. Rempher, and I'll be right out," I said.

"That's *Ms.* Rempher to you. I'm not married," she curtly retorted. I apologized and told her that I'd be out to help her in a flash. My ears were still ringing for a while after hanging up the phone. I guess the old saying is true, "Hell hath no fury like a woman scorned." I believed it now because I just witnessed it and was on the receiving end too.

I phoned Sandy and asked her if she'd like to go on a farm call over to Federal Way. I explained the dilemma and told her that I desperately needed her feminine help and moral support on this one, and I'd really appreciate it if she'd come along. Maybe Ms. Rempher would be a little more restrained with a woman present, maybe not. It'd be worth a try anyway. Thank goodness, Sandy agreed to go, and down the road we went. A verse of poetry came to mind, "Into the valley of death rode the six hundred."

Amazingly, the directions to Ms. Rempher's place were spot on, and it wasn't long before we pulled into her driveway on the outskirts of Federal Way. Just as I turned off the ignition, an imposing figure wearing a brown fedora hat, khaki trench coat, and black barn boots materialized next to the white farm house. At first I thought it was a man, but no, it was Ms. Rempher, and her size matched her booming voice.

80

"You the vet?" she gruffly asked.

"Yup, and I'm here to help, if I can. Where's this cow that's having problems?" I asked.

Ms. Rempher replied, "This way." And off she went. She led us around back of the house to a small red barn, and there stood a good-sized Brown Swiss cow, not looking all that bad or distressed.

I started to examine the cow, whose name was Mabel, and she contentedly chewed her cud throughout the whole ordeal. Next, I had to do a vaginal exam to see if, in fact, there was a dead calf inside, as Ms. Rempher had expected. As my hand and arm entered the uterus, I felt a small muzzle, and when that little muzzle mouthed my fingers, I instantly knew that we had a live one. I looked over to Sandy, gave her a wry smile, winked, and then cheerfully announced, "We've got a lively little one in here!"

Ms. Rempher's face, peering out from beneath the brim of the fedora, underwent a facial expression transformation—from one of extreme skepticism and gloom to downright elation—in the twinkle of an eye. That hard-nosed doubting Thomas, or Thomasina, actually chuckled, and I could see glimpses of a compassionate person hidden deeply in there somewhere under that stern bravado exterior. She was overjoyed when I managed to free that little live calf from its dark, warm sanctuary. I took a small blade of grass and gently tickled the calf's nostril with it in an effort to make the little guy sneeze.

Achoo!

It worked! Snot flew everywhere. A deep breath and loud bellow soon followed. Ms. Rempher was one happy camper and very appreciative too. Ms. Rempher was a very interesting person—extremely defensive and distrusting. She'd probably been taken advantage of over the years and experienced more than her share of rejection and persecution. Her tough talk and rugged attire definitely distanced people and surely didn't make her a candidate for Miss Congeniality. Anyway, she was happy and smiling now, seeing that her beloved Mabel was alive, and that she had a beautiful, healthy calf to boot. As they say, "All's well that ends well." Perhaps Sandy and I helped restore Ms. Rempher's trust and confidence in veterinarians—I sure hoped so.

Our paths with Ms. Gertrude Rempher would never cross again, but the image of that stern, imposing woman, wearing a brown fedora, trench coat, and black barn boots, will be forever etched in my memory. Oh yeah, we did manage to go on that hike up on Crystal Mountain. The sky was clear, the sun was shining, and the view was absolutely breathtaking. The thought crossed my mind, *I wonder if Ms. Rempher has ever seen such beauty? Maybe we should bring her up here sometime...nah!*

THE LUMBERJACK COOK

The timber industry was big business in the Pacific Northwest and especially in Western Washington. Weyerhaeuser, one of the world's largest wood and paper companies, had its headquarters located not too far from Enumclaw. Weyerhaeuser was a major employer in the area and directly affected many communities, including Enumclaw. Logging trucks were everywhere, and you needed to watch out for them at all times. They were big and fast, and they owned the roads. When passing them on some of those narrow roads, my heart would always beat a little faster and my palms would become sweaty because those monsters had a lot of weight behind them, and they were really moving too. Time was money for those drivers, so you'd better get out of their way. No problem!

It wasn't hard to identify the lumberjacks around town either. They usually wore red suspenders, rugged logging boots, black high-water pants, and drove pickups with chainsaws, gas cans, and other logging equipment in the truck beds. No matter who you met, they often seemed to have connections with the lumber industry in one way or another. Such was the case with Emma Doyle.

It was late in the day, and there weren't anymore appointments scheduled. *Great! Maybe I'll get home at a reasonable hour today*, I thought to myself. It would be nice to have dinner with the family for a change. Then the phone rang, and there was that dreaded pause. Roberta wrote down some things, hung up the phone, and chimed out, "You've gotta go out to Emma Doyle's place. She's gotta steer down. It's just outside of town on 264th. You should still make it home on time for dinner." Oh brother, I'd heard that line before, and most of the time, things usually didn't work out that way. Oh well, like the saying goes, "Duty calls, and you must attend."

Roberta's directions were right on the money, and it didn't take any time at all to find the place. There it was, an old two-story farmhouse needing paint, hidden among an untended windbreak of trees, shrubs, and overgrown, tangled blackberry bushes. I pulled into the short lane and stopped the truck. It looked like a scene taken right out of an Alfred Hitchcock movie—dark, no movement, and eerily silent. I sat there for a moment, surveying the eerie setting. Suddenly, a short, portly, mustachioed gent, dressed in a tweed sports coat and Irish driving cap, came sauntering up to the truck. He paused, smiled, and with a sweeping motion of his arm, gestured for me to follow him. It was kind of spooky. I got out of the truck and introduced myself. I wasn't prepared for what happened next. I'd heard people talk fast before, but not like this guy. When he opened his mouth and spoke, it sounded like a rapid fire, verbal machine gun. I couldn't understand a single word that he said. I repeatedly interrupted him by asking, "What?" But he wasn't fazed and kept on launching the verbal volleys. Finally, I waved my hands and arms in the air as if surrendering and pleaded, "Whoa, *slower!*"

He smiled apologetically, realizing that he had a communication problem. He then forced himself to speak slower. His speech was still fast, but now I could understand some of what he said—at least I got the gist of it.

He said, "Come with me to the barn. Mother will be coming." I nodded that I understood, and then we were on our way.

We hadn't walked more than a few steps when out of the shadows came a slight framed, petite, elderly, sneaker-wearing dynamo, charging down the steps of the old rickety house. She had her gray hair pulled back in a bun, and together with the black dress, she strangely resembled the farmer's wife in the famous painting entitled *American Gothic*.

"I'm Emma," she said. "You must be the vet. Follow me." So with long strides and her arms a-swinging, Emma left us in the dust. The little gent looked at me, raised his eyebrows as he cocked his head, and forced out, "Mutter!"

I got to the barn and started to examine the steer. He was weak, had pale mucous membranes, and the sclera of his eyes were also whiter than normal. The steer had labored breathing and was unable to stand. I found thousands of lice and nits (lice eggs) all over his body. They were sucking lice; meaning, they fed on the steer's blood. The poor animal was essentially being drained dry, and his chances of surviving weren't good. I placed an IV catheter and started the IV fluids, gave vitamin injections to stimulate red blood cell production, and applied pesticides to get rid of the lice that were robbing the poor creature of its life-sustaining blood. I told them that nothing more could be done, and we'd just have to hope for the best. I then gathered up all my medical things, and Emma's son accompanied me back to the truck.

When I opened the door of the truck, there on the seat laid a beautiful handpicked bouquet of flowers. It was Emma's way of thanking me for at least trying to save her steer. That thoughtful act of kindness really touched me. As I was writing up the bill, Emma's son, struggling to talk slower so that I could understand, said to me, "She wants you to come inside for something to eat." I glanced at my watch, and since this was my last call of the day and I was already late for dinner, I thought that it wouldn't hurt to go inside for a little while.

Upon entering the dimly lit house, Emma's son ushered me to the dining room, where a huge dark oval oak table was filled to overflowing with wonderful smelling food. It looked like a feast fit for a king, or a lumberjack crew. It turned out that Emma had been the cook for a local logging crew for many years, and she'd retired only recently. I sat down to eat, and boy did I ever eat! The food was unbelievably good, and there was lots of it too. Emma's son, still wearing his tweed sports coat, brought out his favorite Irish beer, and we indulged. It was fantastic! I was in hog heaven. Emma didn't say much; she just sat there smiling, simply finding pleasure in having a guest thoroughly enjoying her cooking. I'd become totally stuffed, to the point where I couldn't eat another bite. I actually had to loosen my belt as I headed out the door to my truck. Wow! What a meal!

The steer eventually recovered, and Emma made sure to watch out for the lice. I'd learned that those lumber camp cooks could serve up some very tasty food. The only problem was, Emma's recipe books didn't show how to cook for just three people. When I finally got home, I had some explaining to do because I couldn't eat the dinner that Sandy had prepared—no room left. Sandy graciously understood, wrapped up the meal, and said with a smile, "That's okay, we'll just have it tomorrow night." That was just hunky-dory with me.

WHY ME?

We've all had moments in our lives where we've asked the question, "Why me?" How do we respond? Alfred Lord Tennyson provided us with an answer in one of his poems. He wrote, "Theirs not to reason why, theirs but to do and die." I prefer the vernacular, "Suck it up, stop the whining, and just do it."

I had many opportunities to apply that philosophy. One such opportunity was being designated the veterinarian on duty at the King County Fair. A veterinarian was needed to examine the incoming livestock, making sure to permit only healthy animals onto the fairground premises. Unfortunately, there were a few overzealous parents who attempted to slip their kid's sick animal into the fair. Since the animal was sick, it had to be disqualified, denied entry, and sent home. As a consequence, I was called every derogatory name in the book and even had my ancestry questioned. On top of that, there were several occasions where I was called upon to treat some horses and ponies who were colicky because they'd been fed pizza and cotton candy by their adolescent owners. It really was a thankless community-service job, and more than once, I asked myself the rhetorical question, *Why me?*

• • • • • • • •

Charlie Windslow was a master of understatement. It was a day packed with appointments, and time management on farm calls was paramount. Simply put, the day was crazy! I had previously been tipped off to Charlie's antics of slipping stuff in on farm calls, but I had somehow let that bit of info slip my mind. Charlie had initially scheduled six Holstein calves to be castrated. I figured that shouldn't take too long to accomplish and I'd still stay on my time schedule. When I arrived at Charlie's dairy, instead of six calves, as I'd erroneously assumed, he had forty big Holstein calves, each weighing close to seven hundred pounds, milling around, needing to be castrated. My first thought was, *Charlie pulled it off again. This will really screw up my time schedule, and now the rest of the day will be a game of catch up.* I really had to hustle! I managed to get the job done pretty fast and even remembered to save the testicles for Dave Bishop. Dave often asked me to save bull testicles for him because he liked to put on Rocky Mountain Oyster feeds for all his friends. Trying to be all things to all people wasn't easy, and once again I asked myself, *Why me?*

Now Dave Bishop was one of a kind. He was a shrewd, wheeler-dealer type businessman, socialite, and a self-appointed food critic, who thoroughly enjoyed well-prepared food, and oddly enough, was very fond of rocky mountain oysters. On one occasion, he asked me if I'd ever eaten rocky mountain oysters. I told him I hadn't, and probably never would, because the mere thought of eating a bull's testicles was, to say the least, very repulsive to me.

Dave remarked, "Oh, Doc, if they are prepared properly, they're *good* eating. They taste exactly like regular oysters. I'll bet, if you ate some, you wouldn't be able to tell the difference."

I told Dave that I'd definitely be able to tell the difference and surely wouldn't eat any on purpose.

Dave just laughed and said, "Okay, Doc, we'll see."

Several months had passed since I'd last talked to Dave. It was sometime in July when Sandy and I received an invitation to attend a get-together at the Bishop's home, which was located on the outskirts of town. It was to be a casual and relaxed evening of dining and socializing. Dave would be preparing most of the food, and the rest of the menu would be catered. It sounded wonderful, and it provided Sandy and me with an opportunity to do something extra special together. It was a fabulous evening— delicious food and a chance to meet some very interesting and influential people.

Dave made his way through the crowd to personally thank us for coming and reminded us to sample some of the dishes he'd prepared, especially the oyster fondue. Sandy and I assured him that we would, and eventually we did try the oyster fondue. Dave was right. It was very tasty. Sandy and I thoroughly enjoyed ourselves. It really was an evening to remember.

On the following Monday, Dave stopped by the clinic and greeted me with, "Doc, glad to see that you and your wife could make it to the dinner. Did you have a good time? The food was great, wasn't it?" "Dave", I said, "Everything was simply outstanding, and thanks again for inviting us. We had a wonderful time." How'd you like the fondue, Doc? He slyly asked. "It was actually very good, and that was the first time I'd ever eaten oyster fondue." I replied.

"Gotcha, Doc!" Dave said with a big grin on his face. "Those weren't mere oysters, Doc, they were rocky mountain oysters, and *you* ate 'em and thought they were good! See, I told you that you wouldn't be able to tell the difference."

The thought then flashed through my lightning-fast mind. *I'd been had! I'd been set up! Why me?*

• • • • • • • •

Another opportunity was a Palomino gelding named Apache. He needed to be tube-wormed, and tube worming wasn't one of my most favorite procedures, and the horses didn't exactly care for it either. You see, a long rubber tube had to be inserted into the horse's nose, then slowly and carefully passed down into the stomach where the liquid wormer would be placed with the use of a small hand pump. Most horses tolerated the procedure pretty well, but Apache absolutely hated it with a vengeance! He'd rear up and strike out with his front hooves, intending to plant one or both squarely between a person's eyes. He was ultra quick and had pinpoint accuracy too. Believe me, this boy knew what he was doing, and he had the ability to seriously injure someone. Apache had to be heavily sedated before attempting to pass the tube, and even then, with his head almost touching the ground and his lips floppy limp, he'd still try to strike with his hooves. Additional hobbles had to be placed on the guy's front legs before the procedure could be safely completed. The whole thing turned out to be a real rodeo, but I got it done. I once again asked myself the proverbial question, *Why me?*

• • • • • • • •

Frank Amsdon was something special. He called the clinic one day, and Roberta answered the telephone. I saw her smile, and while struggling to keep from laughing out loud, she handed me the phone and said, "You really won't believe this. You gotta talk to this man."

"Doc Roloff here, what can I do for you?"

Mr. Amsdon chimed out, "I've got a bull calf here with three testicles, and he needs to be cut."

I was, quite honestly, caught off guard, and chuckled as I told him that it would be extremely rare and highly unlikely for a bull calf to have three testicles. I wasn't prepared for his curt response.

"Are you new? Now listen here, sonny, I've been rais'n' calves for a lot of years, and I've probably seen a lot more than you have, and what I got here is a calf with three testicles! And I want him cut!" It was glaringly obvious that I shouldn't have chuckled, and I needed to be more diplomatic with this guy, so I said, "Mr. Amsdon, I'll be right out to check the calf, and maybe you're right. It would be a first, at least for me.

I made it to Frank Amsdon's place to check out the calf. Lo and behold, there were only two testicles, and everything appeared normal. I castrated the calf and then gave Mr. Amsdon a short anatomy lesson. I showed him the two testicles, and what he thought was a third testicle was actually the scrotum, where the testicles resided. He wasn't totally convinced though. He looked at me with a skeptical expression, and while squinting his eyes, he said, "You sure you're not miss'n somthin'?"

I said to myself, *Why me?*

A CLOSE CALL

The ten o'clock appointment on the schedule simply stated, "Dehorn and place nose ring in bull." That didn't sound too tough. I'd done lots of dehorning, but not too many nose ring placements. Those procedures usually aren't that difficult when performed on young calves, but doing them on older and bigger cattle can present a whole new set of challenges. The main concerns with the dehorning procedure are getting adequate anesthesia around the base of the horns to minimize pain and controlling the bleeding. There usually isn't too much bleeding with younger calves because the horns are smaller and there's more limited blood supply at that age.

I got the truck stocked with all the medications and supplies I thought were needed for the day's upcoming calls. The schedule said that I'd be going out to Ralph Petre's place for the bull dehorning. I'd never been to his farm before, but Dr. Wagner had mentioned that Ralph had a very upscale Hereford operation. I was looking forward to the farm call and working with some beef cattle again.

It wasn't hard to find the farm because of all the red barns, white corrals, and the herd of white-faced Hereford cattle peacefully grazing on the lush pasture. There was no doubt about it; this was the place. I drove up the fence lined lane to one of the barns where Ralph Petre was patiently waiting.

"Mr. Petre, I'm Dr. Roloff, Dr. Wagner's associate. I understand you've got a bull that needs to be dehorned and have a nose ring inserted, right?"

Mr. Petre responded, "Yup, and I've got him tied up in the big barn for ya."

I thought to myself, *This is great! He's got the calf all tied up and waiting for me. This should be a piece of cake.* We went inside the big red barn, and Ralph nonchalantly said, "There he is."

I was dumbstruck! This wasn't a small calf of a hundred to two hundred pounds I'd be dealing with. This was a massive, mature Hereford bull who weighed at least two thousand pounds, and his *huge* curved horns ominously extended forward and slightly downward from his head. He turned his gigantic, powerful neck and head toward me, stared directly at me, then snorted as if saying, "Make my day!" This proud, defiant, and imposing creature could seriously hurt somebody, and that included me. I looked right back at this enormous bruiser and let him know by my body language that I wasn't about to be intimidated by him. My experience of being raised around beef cattle and having worked with bulls throughout my youth had taught me a lot about their body language and how it related to their will and behavior tendencies. This bull was formidable, and I immediately knew that I had to be on my A-game when dealing with him.

"Ralph, why are you dehorning this guy now at this age?" I asked.

"Because he's tearing up all the other cattle with those weapons of his. He really knows how to use those things, and I've had enough of it. He's stubborn, and he's dangerous too. I need a ring put in his nose so that I can, at least, have some control with him," Ralph said.

That was good enough for me. I told Ralph, "Okay, let's do it." He nodded his head in agreement. It was then that I made, what could have been, a fatal mistake. I wrongly assumed that an experienced cattleman, such as Mr. Petre, would have securely tied and properly restrained such a powerful animal. I'd always reminded myself to never assume anything, but this time, I disobeyed one of my tenets, and that error could have gotten me killed. As I approached the bull to assess the size of the horns and the amount of local anesthetic I'd need, the bull suddenly whipped his powerful neck, head, and curved horns at me with a determined, sweeping motion.

There must have been about three feet of slack in the rope, and that extra freedom of movement allowed him to get a good swing at me. His left horn came in toward my abdomen in much the same way that a boxer would throw a hard left hook shot to an opponent's midsection. He connected! I flew at least twelve feet across the barn runway, dazed and stunned by the fact that I had narrowly escaped being gored by the bull. I slowly got back up on my feet and checked to see if I was bleeding or injured. I wasn't, but the right side of my pelvis was totally numb. The bull's sweeping hook move had allowed the point of his horn to hit me just below the brim of my pelvic bone. I had survived only by the grace of God. If that horn would have been an inch higher, it would have passed directly through me, —- in one side and out the other. I would have been completely eviscerated and dead! As I regained my senses, I noticed Ralph's face had turned pale as if he'd just seen a ghost.

"You all right?" He asked.

I answered, "I think so." Now I started to become perturbed. I pointed my finger at Ralph and told him, "You go tie that guy up really tight this time, the way he should have been tied in the first place. That's going to be the *last* time that bull's ever going to use those horns on anybody, and I mean it!"

Mr. Petre promptly got the bull's head tightly secured to a support beam. I went up to the bull, looked him in the eye, and said to him, "Hey, buddy, you remember me? If you don't, you will!" I anesthetized the area as best I could and then proceeded to saw off that bull's weapons. Once that bloody job was finished, I grabbed the nose ring and plunged it through the septum of his nose, making sure that it was firmly in place. Finally, the ordeal was over. Actually, the whole fiasco was a real adrenalin rush for me. It was exciting! I guess it was the thrill of dodging a bullet and getting away relatively unscathed, and honestly, I'd be willing to do it all over again. The critical key elements in this situation were maintaining my self-confidence, keeping my composure, not allowing myself to be intimidated, and never showing fear.

I had a very bruised hip and sore pelvis for several weeks, but I was thankful to have escaped such a close call. The incident, however, didn't tarnish my fondness of cattle one bit. Heck, I'd grown up on a wheat and cattle ranch, where feeding and caring for the cattle was a daily routine. Although I'd been stepped on, kicked, butted, run over, and chased by cattle, I still enjoyed working with and being around them, even if it did involve a close call now and then.

DALE THE CHIPMUNK

One of the best things about being a veterinarian in a mixed practice was that no two days were ever alike. It made life very interesting and fun. You never knew what kind of animal or medical condition you'd be facing next, and a person had to be mentally prepared for just about anything, anytime, day or night. It definitely wasn't boring.

I had just finished performing a spay (ovariohysterectomy) on a cute little cockapoo named Susie and was in the process of placing her in the recovery room when Roberta stuck her head around the corner. "Doc, there's someone up front who wants to talk to you." I replied, "I'll be right there."

As I entered the waiting room, the man standing by the front counter said, "Hello, Doc, I'm Bill Carter from the Weyerhaeuser Company. Do you know anything about chipmunks?"

I sure wasn't expecting that type of question, but I told him, "Honestly, not much!"

Mr. Carter smiled and responded, "That's more than I know. You see, we're trying to make a promotional commercial for television that incorporates a chipmunk peeking over a log. The problem is, we can't get the little guy to hold still. He's always moving or tries to escape just as we're about to film. Do you have a sedative or something that would slow him down? That's what we really need."

"My concern," I said, "is that I don't know how a chipmunk would respond to the sedatives I have, and I'd have to estimate a dosage. That could be tricky. Sometimes those tiny forest creatures can even have adverse reactions to the drugs and die."

"That's okay, Doc," Mr. Carter responded. "See what you can do. I'll tell you what, I'll leave him here with you for a couple days, do what you have to do, and then we'll just go from there. Okay?" I couldn't believe that I'd agreed to do it, but I did.

· · · · · · · ·

Dr. Wagner noticed me carrying the small cage and its passenger back to the treatment room. He asked, "Hey, Doc, whata ya got there, some ferocious, rabid, forest creature?"

"Nah, a chipmunk that some guy from Weyerhaueser wants sedated for a TV commercial," I said.

"Good luck. That should be interesting," Dr. Wagner responded with a laugh. "Don't kill him."

I told Dr. Wagner that I'd do my best not to. The little guy was cute and actually pretty good sized for a chipmunk. He was bright eyed, a little on the pudgy side, but still very quick. I managed to find sedative dosages for gerbils and rats, but nothing for chipmunks specifically. Chipmunks weren't all that much different though. They were all rodents, so I thought I'd give it a try. Giving a tablet orally to this little speedster was definitely out of the question, so my only option was to administer a subcutaneous injection of the sedative. I calculated the dosage, essentially for a rat, then reduced it by 30 percent. It took some coercion to get Roberta to assist with giving the injection to "Dale" the chipmunk, but we got it done. Within moments, Dale fell fast asleep. Oops! That dosage won't work for filming. It took a while for him to sleep it off, so later in the day I adjusted the dosage and tried again. This time it worked, sort of. Dale got pretty drowsy and his little eyes got squinty, but now he could be easily handled. I positioned him up on a rolled up towel that substituted for a log, and he didn't move. He sat there as if he'd just tied one on. His little head gradually sank down, and his eyelids began to close, but when I snapped my fingers, his head came back up and his eyes were wide open for a few seconds, then they slowly closed again. Voila! This dosage should work!

· · · · · · · ·

Bill Carter showed up at the clinic the following day as he said he would. I explained what I'd come up with for a workable sedative dosage, and the timing of the finger snap to get the eyes to open for filming. I gave little Dale the chipmunk his happy shot, then off he went with Mr. Carter. I never heard back from Mr. Carter about how things worked out. I thought the commercial had probably been scrapped for one reason or another. Anyway, it had been a fun case.

Then about a month later, while Sandy and I were watching television one Sunday afternoon, a Weyerhaeuser commercial appeared on the TV. At the end of the commercial, there was a short clip of a little chipmunk peering over a small log. It was Dale! I knew it was him because I'd recognize those squinty little eyes anywhere. I said to Sandy, "Hey look at that. I helped make Dale a TV star."

UNBELIEVABLE

It was late summer, the days were longer, and the sun didn't set until about 8:00 p.m. It had been a good day, pretty routine, and I was even getting home at a decent hour. Time to pull out the ole barbeque and grill some of that fresh salmon I was given by a client earlier in the day. I was really looking forward to spending some quality time with Sandy and our young son, Eric. Veterinary medicine can definitely cut into family time, and a person needs to take advantage of every opportunity that comes their way.

The barbecued salmon was, without a doubt, outstanding! We were having fun and thoroughly enjoying the evening together— until the dreaded phone rang at 7:30 p.m. Sandy answered the phone and handed the receiver to me. I listened to the concerned individual on the other end of the line and said, "I'll be right out. Put some pressure on it until I get there."

Sandy asked, "What is it?"

"A horse got shot with a rifle, right through the front leg," I said. At least we had a little time together as a family and a fantastic BBQ salmon dinner to boot.

On the drive out to the farm, I pondered over how the horse got shot, especially at this time of day, at dusk. It didn't take long to get to Mr. Hume's farm, and it was obvious that I'd found the right place because there was a rather large group of people standing around a horse, and one of the guys was holding a rifle. Something really weird was going on here. I got out of the truck and promptly went over to the horse to examine its injuries. He was a Morgan gelding, a smaller-statured breed of horse, and was quietly standing there, acting very nonchalant about the whole incident. There was no active bleeding, just some passive blood trickling down the back of his right front leg. The bullet had passed completely and cleanly through the flexor muscles located between his knee and chest, miraculously missing the radius bone and any of the major arteries, veins, and nerves. This horse was, without a doubt, totally graced out! I cleaned, medicated, and bandaged the wound and also started him on antibiotic therapy.

I then told Mr. Hume, "I'll be back in a couple days to recheck the horse. You know, —- your horse was really very lucky. He literally dodged a bullet. That comment brought a few chuckles and helped lighten the atmosphere a bit. Well, the show was over, and most of the onlookers took off. The fella I'd seen with the gun turned out to be Mr. Hume, and he confessed that he'd accidently shot his own horse. I looked him straight in the eyes and asked, "How in the world could you ever do that? What were you shooting at? A bear, a coyote, or what?"

He sheepishly looked down at the ground and shook his head no. He then looked up and said, "You may not believe it, but I was trying to scare off a Bigfoot with a shot, but I hit the horse by mistake. Can you keep a secret and never tell anyone about this place? I don't want people running all over my property looking for Bigfoot."

I assured Mr. Hume that I wouldn't tell anyone. I wasn't prepared for his next question, "Doc, do you believe in Bigfoot?" The look in his eyes left no doubt whatsoever that this man had indeed seen a Bigfoot, or some creature that resembled one.

I said, "Honestly, I have no basis for making a judgment either way."

"When you come out to check the horse in a couple days, Doc, I want to show you something, and then you can decide for yourself if you believe or not," he said.

"Okay, that's a deal. I replied.

I'd scheduled the recheck on the horse for Saturday afternoon because I had the afternoon off, and there'd be more time to spend with Mr. Hume. His property was located adjacent to the Mount Rainier National Forest, a huge forested area. If there was such a creature as Bigfoot, and if he did roam in this area, he'd have ample cover to go undetected. I still secretly had my doubts, but I kept an open mind.

Mr. Hume had the horse waiting for me when I arrived at his farm. The wound was healing nicely and no longer required bandaging. Mr. Hume was pleased and relieved because he was fond of that horse and felt awful about the shooting incident.

He then began to share with me his experiences involving Bigfoot. He'd owned the property for only five years, but the previous owners told him many stories about Bigfoot encounters. One of the stories was extremely interesting. The previous owner was an eighty-eight-year-old woman. She told Mr. Hume that as a child, she played with her big hairy friend many times. Her friend would come to her bedroom window at night, she'd slip out the window, and they'd play together in the small orchard nearby. The elderly lady always spoke fondly of her big hairy friend.

I asked Mr. Hume if he'd ever seen a Bigfoot or Bigfoot tracks. He said he'd found footprints and bedding areas. He'd sent hair and fecal samples to research facilities for analysis, and the results came back: species unknown! I asked Mr. Hume if he could show me where he had found a Bigfoot footprint. He was more than willing to oblige.

We then proceeded to the edge of the pasture that abutted the Mount Rainier National Forest, climbed over the fence, and entered a heavily wooded area. There was heavy undergrowth and a nearby low area where water had collected, making the ground soft and moist. As I was parting some of the grass to expose the earth, there it was, a huge footprint! We also found a resting area, an impression of where the creature laid down, and some hair that really smelled foul. Suddenly, I had this overwhelming sensation that we were being watched. The hair on the back of my neck began to stand up, and I froze. I slowly turned my head toward Mr. Hume, who was about twenty feet to my left. He was also motionless and had an alarmed expression of on his face. He then slowly motioned with his head that we'd better leave. We slowly and carefully withdrew from the area, and then Mr. Hume said to me, "Did you feel that? —- We were being watched by something." I told Mr. Hume, "I felt it too. —- That was really weird!" Was it Bigfoot? I don't really know.

That was an incident I'll never forget! Two men, simultaneously sensing imposing danger, the finding of a very large footprint, about fourteen inches long, under some pressed down grass, and collecting some very unusual looking, and stinky hair. I'd become less of a Bigfoot skeptic. Some people may think Bigfoot is a hoax, but I know what I saw and the feelings I'd experienced. I've held true to my word as well. I've never divulged the exact location of that unbelievable encounter.

GOOD TIMING

We've all experienced serendipitous moments in our lives, especially when things unexpectedly worked out to our benefit. Sometimes those spontaneous moments of good fortune can even rescue us from difficult and unfavorable circumstances. A case in point, the surprising downpour of rain that positively impacted the outcome of one particular farm call.

Clayton Zuker was a conscientious cattleman, and his registered Hereford operation exemplified that fact. He was very attentive to the health and welfare needs of his cattle, so it was not surprising that he quickly detected a problem with one of his prized bulls. The bull had been favoring his right front leg for several days, and Mr. Zuker suspected that the bull had somehow sprained its leg. When the limping got worse and traces of blood appeared where the bull had been walking, it was time to call the vet! Lucky me!

It was that season of the year when the sun didn't shine. If the sun did peek out, you'd wonder what you did wrong. Day in and day out, the sky was cloudy, rain fell almost constantly, ranging from light drizzles to heavy downpours. Some people called it liquid sunshine, but that was certainly a matter of opinion. The flip side to all of the moisture was the beautiful scenery of lush pastures, dense green forests, and all the rivers and streams. It was a good trade off, at least that's the way I rationalized it. One thing for sure, rain slickers and rubber boots were very much in vogue, and the standard attire of the day.

Mr. Zuker had the bull secured in the squeeze chute when I arrived. The bull's hooves were encased in mud, so it needed to be thoroughly washed off before the problem could be assessed. Once the hooves were clean, the source of all the limping stuck out like a sore thumb. There, deep in the web of the cloven hoof, was a bloody, firm, tumorous mass, about two inches in diameter, and it was forcing the digits of the hoof to spread wider apart than normal. The growth was an interdigital fibroma, and sometimes they're loosely referred to as "bovine corns". That type of fibroma tended to be firmly attached, grew around and entrapped arteries and veins, which in turn resulted in making the surgical removal of the mass a rather difficult, time-consuming, and very bloody procedure. I knew what I was up against, but there were no other options. The tumorous mass had to be surgically removed.

The two-thousand-pound bull had to be immobilized in order to eliminate pain and constant leg movement during the operation. The absolute last thing I needed was to have a two-thousand-pound patient thrashing his legs all over the place during surgery. We found a suitable soft, grassy area where the bull could be safely laid down, and then I proceeded with the anesthesia. So far, so good. Just as I was preparing the surgical site, a few raindrops began to hit my slicker, but I continued in spite of the drizzling rain. As I'd expected, the fibrotic mass was firmly attached and had grown extensively around the blood vessels in that area. Unfortunately, many of the arteries and veins had to be severed in order for the mass to be completely removed, and that resulted in substantial bleeding. Blood quickly filled the surgical field and obscured my view of the arteries and veins that desperately needed to be located and ligated (tied off) to stop the hemorrhaging. A tourniquet and gauze sponges were totally ineffective. Then suddenly, as if an answer from above, the rain increased from a slight drizzle to a heavy downpour. The intensity of the rain flushed the blood from the incision site, and made the severed arteries and veins clearly visible. They could now be easily identified, clamped, and ligated. Man, was that perfect timing or what! Now I could see what I was doing, and it didn't take long after that to successfully remove the fibrous mass. I bandaged the hoof, the bull woke up, and the ordeal was over.

Thank you, Lord, for the rain! That downpour of rain came at the right time, and was a true blessing. It really was a serendipitous moment.

A DAY IN THE LIFE

It has been said that "variety is the spice of life." If that saying is true, and in most cases it is, then the life of a veterinarian is very well seasoned.

The first order of business each day was to take a look at the appointment book, see what was on the schedule for the day, and get mentally prepared for the onslaught. The schedule always looked so organized and manageable on paper, but we all knew that after the first appointment, things would invariably change, and the rest of the day would be a wild ride, but it was still fun. The reality was that the term "typical day" didn't exist in our vocabulary.

The day began with well-check exams and vaccinations on two cats and a dog named Skippy. They were all healthy, except for the occasional fast-moving little brown guy scurrying in, around, and through the hair, attempting to make its great escape. Fleas! Fleas were a common finding in that part of the country, and the pesky, little, annoying opportunists were a relatively easy problem to deal with, except when they jumped off the animal and got on you. The patients were vaccinated, treated for fleas, given snacks for being good, and were then ready to go. Now, on to the next case.

· · · · · · · ·

I was scheduled to vaccinate two calves just a couple of miles south of town. These calves needed to be vaccinated against bacterial and viral diarrhea, rhinotracheitis and parainfluenza virus of the respiratory system, and pinkeye, a type of conjunctivitis of the eye. They also needed to be wormed against internal parasites and checked for lice. Once that was completed and I was about to leave for my next scheduled appointment, Mr. Ensor, the owner, came running up to the truck. "My wife wants to know if you could take our dog Lucy back to the clinic with you, check her over, and I think she needs some vaccinations too. We'll come in later in the afternoon and pick her up."

I asked, "Sure, what kind of dog is she?"

"A Doberman, but she's nice. She just looks mean. She rides well, and she should be good with you."

I thought to myself, *Should be good!* What happens if she *isn't* good with me in the truck?

Then Mr. Ensor hollered, "Lucy!"

Bounding around the corner of the house came a big red Doberman with head held high and ears raised in full alert position. Mr. Ensor managed to grab her by the collar, quickly got her attention, and immediately commanded her, "Lucy, now you be nice to this man!" Oh joy! Now he's telling her to be *nice*.

I asked myself, "*What have you gotten yourself into?*"

Mr. Ensor then opened the passenger door and ordered, "In."

Lucy hesitated at first, but with the second command, up and in she jumped and promptly situated herself as close to me as she could possibly get. I swear, we must have looked like we were joined at the hip. As I drove down the road back to town, any oncoming driver probably couldn't tell who was actually driving the truck, me or Lucy. In fact, she had nudged so close that I asked her several times, "Lucy, do you want to drive?"

We made it back to town, and I stopped by the local grocery store to pick up a can of pop, and when I came out of the store, there she sat, smack-dab behind the steering wheel. This big mean-looking dog, head up and ears alert, appeared to be guarding my truck. People gave my truck plenty of room. No one was going to get close to that truck except me. As I got into the truck, Lucy acted like I was her long lost friend whom she hadn't seen in years. She yipped and licked my hands and face in sheer delight. Lucy may have looked tough, but she was a real cream puff. From that day on, red Dobies and the name Lucy would always produce fond memories. I dropped Lucy off at the clinic, and was off again to the next case, an emergency, a horse with a stick through its ear.

• • • • • • • •

As I pulled into Virginia Cumming's pasture, I could see several people standing with a sorrel quarter horse whose name turned out to be Buck. Buck appeared to be mildly agitated and intermittently flicked his left ear in an attempt to dislodge the one inch by twelve inch wooden stick that had impaled the lower part of his ear. Each time Buck flicked his ear, the stick moved past his eye, causing him to react by jerking his head in an effort to avoid being hit by the object. That only made things worse because he'd now become very head shy. I quickly grabbed a towel and placed it over Buck's eyes in an attempt to calm him down. It worked!

I was now able to assess the situation. The stick couldn't be pulled through; instead, it had to be cut close to the ear and removed in two pieces. The procedure was fast, effective, and with minimal bleeding. The only problem was that the one-inch puncture hole left by the stick near the base of the ear didn't lend itself well for closure with sutures (stitches). It would heal fine as an open wound. Buck now had a permanent identification mark—er, hole, a real topic of conversation. A couple antibiotic injections were given, and on to the next case.

• • • • • • • •

The last farm call of the day was to Bill Talbert's place. Bill was a very big man who played professional football in the NFL for a number of years. When his playing days were over, he bought himself a small ranch, and settled into semi-country life. He didn't have much acreage, but enough for a couple cows and a pig named "Clarissa". Mr. Talbert had been a tough interior lineman during his glory days of pro-football, but it was his pet pig "Clarissa" who stole his heart.

Bill met me at the truck as I pulled into the driveway, and he proceeded to emotionally explain that Clarissa had injured her eye, and that now she was in severe pain and unable to open her eye. I told Mr. Talbert, "Let's take a look. Where is she?"

Mr. Talbert told me, "Out back." I grabbed my medical bags, and we were on our way. What I saw next was definitely not what I had expected to see. Mr. Talbert had led me to an extra large doghouse with the hind end of a pig sticking out of the doorway. "There she is, the poor girl. Please do something to help her," he pleaded.

I had to get her out of there in order to examine her eye, but all of Bill's coaxing hadn't budged her an inch. Every time he touched her, she grunted defiantly, and then Mr. Talbert stopped. I suggested that maybe we could pull Clarissa out far enough so I'd be able to check her eye. Nope!

Each time we'd attempt to grab ahold of her legs, she'd scream bloody murder, and the idea of dismantling the doghouse wasn't an option to Mr. Talbert. I noticed that there was a small space on her right side and thought that maybe I'd have enough room to slide in beside her, and with the aid of a small flashlight, I might be able to check out her eye. Vet school hadn't prepared me for this maneuver. Anyhow, there I was, wedged between a pig and the doghouse, in ultra tight quarters, attempting to examine a pig's eye. If she had attempted to bite me, I had nowhere to go. Heck, I could barely move, let alone get out of her way. Somehow, I managed to apply a local anesthetic to her eye, and once the pain was gone, she opened her eye, and it could finally be examined. The cornea of the eye was swollen, edematous, cloudy, and ulcerated. Corneal ulcers can be very painful and are extremely sensitive to light. No wonder she was holding her eyelids shut and in so much pain!

During the eye exam, I found a piece of barbed plant material wedged between the lower eyelid and the eyeball. That little thing was the culprit! It was a cheatgrass awn, sometimes called a foxtail. It scratched her cornea, and it hurt. Clarissa was rubbing her eye in an attempt to get the thing out. Unfortunately, there was more harm done than good. I removed the cheatgrass awn, medicated the eye, and began my Houdini moves in an attempt to dislodge myself from the confines of that doghouse. When I finally emerged and showed Mr. Talbert what I'd removed from Lucy's eye, he was so overwhelmed with relief and appreciation that he actually started to cry tears of joy. That man really did love his pig. All's well that ends well.

· · · · · · · ·

The day had finally come to an end. Time to go home and have a beer. After that day, I really needed and deserved one. I was tired but happy, knowing I'd helped some animals and their owners as well. A good night's rest was really needed because the next day was guaranteed to be more of the same, but I loved it!

OUT ON MY OWN

A NEW BEGINNING

Owning my own veterinary clinic somewhere in Eastern Washington had always been my ultimate goal. While attending a veterinary conference in Seattle, I'd heard that the area in and around Four Lakes, a small rural community near Spokane, was ideal for and in need of a veterinarian. So Sandy and I decided to take a weekend excursion to Eastern Washington and check it out. As we approached Spokane on Highway 2, I took an errant turn onto Brooks Road, which led us directly to a charming little town with a lake actually located within the city limits. The town had a very unique and interesting history that involved the healing properties of the lake water, so that's where it got its name—Medical Lake. We drove around and explored the little City of Medical Lake, liked what we saw, and thought that this quiet little town definitely had possibilities! Sandy and I both felt that this was a good place for us to risk it all and step out on our own. Now, the town of Four Lakes was just five miles further down the road, but fate had stepped in, and we never did make it to our original destination.

We knew that it would be a bittersweet relocation process for us. The decision to leave Enumclaw was very difficult because we'd made many new friends and thoroughly enjoyed the beautiful surroundings with Mount Rainier nearby. I also greatly appreciated the opportunity to practice veterinary medicine with Dr. Wagner, and I had learned a lot from him, but I still had that unquenchable desire to pursue my dream of someday owning and operating my own veterinary practice. It was a huge step of faith, but Medical Lake would eventually become our new home, and the place where I'd hang my veterinary shingle for many years to come.

When we saw an unsightly, abandoned service station littered with vintage posters and smelly empty oil cans, located in the center of the city of Medical Lake, we thought that it had the potential to be resurrected as a new veterinary clinic. It was truly, without a doubt, a diamond in the rough—real rough! Not only would we be removing a perennial eyesore from city center, but we'd be providing a new business to the community. A win-win situation that was enthusiastically welcomed by the townspeople.

A future client, Mel Holmes, handcrafted and donated a large wooden veterinary sign as a welcome gift. He'd painstakingly chiseled out the letters Medical Lake Veterinary Clinic into one massive timber, and James A. Roloff, DVM into another massive timber. Then he proudly mounted the timbers onto the front of the building. It looked great!

Word of a new veterinarian in town spread like wildfire throughout the community and the surrounding area. The renovation project had not yet been completed, but that didn't stop people from coming to our residence, seeking veterinary services for their pets. Necessity truly is the mother of invention, so I modified our little, used RV into a makeshift mobile veterinary clinic, and it sufficed for the time being.

Sandy and I had scheduled an open house for the clinic on a Sunday afternoon in October. It was intended as a time to meet and greet the townspeople of Medical Lake, but it didn't turn out that way at all. You see, many people seized the opportunity to get long overdue veterinary care for their four-footed family members. I finished seeing patients at nine o'clock that evening. We were tired, but happy with our new hometown and its friendly people. It really was a new beginning and a dream come true.

BRUTUS

Dogs are often referred to as man's best friend, and rightly so. Dogs tend to be loyal and faithful companions who shower us with sincere devotion and unconditional love. As a general rule, they view their people as consummate masters and providers. However, there are always exceptions to the rule, and Brutus was a prime example of a dog who didn't get the memo.

Brutus, a stout Norwegian elkhound, was an independent, self-serving guy who operated outside the box. He considered himself the center of the universe, and all of life revolved around him. In addition, he had a checkered history of unabashedly expressing his disdain for veterinarians and veterinary hospitals. His owners alerted me to that fact before he arrived at the clinic. I cautiously introduced myself to Brutus and proceeded to examine him.

It didn't take long to see that Brutus had a serious problem. He was unable to urinate, and the urinary bladder had become extremely distended, causing him to experience intense pain and discomfort. X-rays revealed a urolith (bladder stone) lodged behind the os penis structure, totally occluding the urethrae and preventing the passage of urine. That resulted in the over distention of the bladder. Death could result if this condition were to go untreated. Brutus had experienced a similar problem previously, but the urolith was smaller and passed successfully, but not this time. The urolith was too large, and it would be impossible to pass without surgical intervention. I immediately performed an emergency surgery called a urethrostomy, removed the offending urolith, and reconstructed a new permanent opening for Brutus so that he'd never have the problem again. The delicate surgery was successful, and Brutus was then placed in a nice warm recovery cage where he'd slowly wake up from his slumber. When he awoke, he was much more comfortable, the intense pain was gone, he was in a nice warm place, and to him, life was good again.

From that moment on, in Brutus's mind, that was *his* feel-good cage, and I was his good buddy. He actually liked coming to the clinic after that day. He'd barge through the door of the clinic and make a beeline to the recovery room where he'd check out his special cage. He'd give it a few sniffs, making sure that all was well and that it was still there. It was to be an expected routine with Brutus that would be repeated many times for years to come. Oh yeah, he never experienced another blockage after that surgery was performed.

A KITTEN NAMED ARROW

Some idioms are strangely true. "A miss is as good as a mile," "close but no cigar," and "stranger than fiction" are three idioms that perfectly describe the case of a very lucky kitten.

A young boy burst through the front door of the clinic with a calico kitten cradled in his arms. He exclaimed with panic in his voice, "I found this kitten by my house. Somebody shot it with an arrow. Can you do something to help it?"

The kitten, about four months old, with big green eyes, was resting nonchalantly in the boy's arms, and there was an arrow lodged in its face and sticking out the other side of its back. I'd never seen anything like that before. The kitten didn't appear to be overly distressed except for when she attempted to move her head. It was then that the shaft of the arrow wiggled slightly, and it greatly impeded her lateral head movement.

The kitten's vital signs appeared to be normal, there was no active bleeding, and her lungs sounded clear. She was understandably somewhat apprehensive, but who wouldn't be, with an arrow lodged in their face. The kitten needed to be placed under a general anesthetic and the situation evaluated before attempting the removal of the arrow. The point of entry of the arrow was on the left side of the kitten's face, near the corner of her mouth. It bounced off her cheekbone and exited by the back of her jaw. It then reentered by her left shoulder blade (scapula), passed between the vertical processes of her thoracic vertebrae, and exited on her right side. This sweet little kitten had been literally skewered by an arrow. In the process, all the major arteries, veins, and nerves had been missed. It was basically a miracle! The wooden shaft of the arrow needed to be cut in order for it to be removed. I then cleaned, medicated, and sutured the traumatized entry and exit holes. We were done.

The kitten awoke from the anesthesia uneventfully and moved her head around in all directions as if nothing had happened. It was pure joy, watching her jump and play like a normal kitten again, especially so soon after surgery.

As it turned out, the kitten was a nameless stray without a home. I wasn't going to let that continue, so I named her "Arrow," gave her all the necessary vaccinations, and found her a home where she would be safe and loved. Arrow's case really did turn out to be stranger than fiction.

TEMPTING FATE

One of my mother's favorite sayings was "Haste makes waste." I should have been a better listener because on one particular occasion, my overconfident haste almost resulted in me getting permanently wasted.

A cow with a sore on her tail was my first farm call of the day. It was a short five-mile drive to Frank Slind's place. Frank was essentially a hobby rancher with limited acreage and a herd of three Shorthorn-cross cows. Mr. Slind wasn't much of a talker. Actually, he was a very quiet, reserved man. So when asked where the cow was located, he simply pointed out in the direction of the small pasture. There, standing quietly and tied to a lone tree was a compact roan-colored cow, rhythmically swishing her tail. I asked Frank, "Do you have a squeeze chute or something where we could restrain her movement?"

He curtly responded, "Nope."

Well, that answered that! Wow, this case was going to be more difficult to treat than I thought.

The swollen, bloody, foul smelling sore was located high up at the base of her tail, and her feeble tail swishes weren't effective at keeping the annoying flies away. As I approached the cow to check out the sore, she instinctively knew that something was up and began frantically pivoting around the tree in a vain attempt to escape. This case had become a real challenge and was getting more dicey by the second. The cow was now in survival panic mode, and her constant movement made it nearly impossible to give her a tranquilizer injection.

I was running out of ideas, but then I remembered a seldom-used barrel-roll rope restraint technique. The rope would be tied around the cow's neck, then maneuvered round her shoulders and flank, and when pulled it would apply pressure to the nerves, which in turn would slow the cow's movements and also prevent her from kicking. That seemed like a good plan! Just as I was getting the rope readied, a big black fly suddenly landed on the cow's right ear. Instantly, and with lightning-fast speed, she kicked off the fly with her hind hoof. It was a blur of motion! Boy, was she good, ultra fast and accurate too! That was a wakeup call for me to be very cautious. I carefully proceeded to tie the rope around her neck, and then placed the rope over her back.

The next step was to reach under her belly and grasp the dangling end of the rope and pull it toward me. Hindsight is always twenty-twenty and suggests that I should have used a stick or broom handle or something to reach the rope, but I was in too much of a hurry. Knowing full well that the cow had a very fast kick, I nevertheless thought I was faster. I mistakenly thought that I could quickly grab the rope and move my head out of the way before she could kick. WRONG! The moment I reached under her belly—*pow!* She caught me flush on my left jaw with a right hook, or should I say a right hind hoof. I'll never forget the sound of the impact inside my head. It sounded like a baseball bat hitting a telephone pole. My eyeglasses flew about twelve feet, and my head must have spun around because I later found hoof scrapes on my right shoulder. The amazing thing was that I was still standing after getting nailed by that powerful knockout blow. I saw a few twinkling stars, and my ears were ringing, but she didn't knock me out! I took a lickin' but kept on tickin'. After regaining my senses and composure, I went at it again, only more carefully this time, and completed the rope restraint. I was then able to successfully clean, treat, and medicate the sore on the tail.

It goes without saying that I was very fortunate and truly graced out. I could have been seriously injured by tempting fate with my overconfident haste. I'd learned my lesson the hard way, and as usual, Mother knew best!

DOUBLE TROUBLE

The odds of lightning striking twice in the same place are, quite honestly, slim to none. Likewise, the odds of saving a client's two animals from near death conditions is also pretty remote. However, sometimes things just happen to work out in a way that totally defies the odds. Such was the case with a cat named "Hoss" and the family cow.

Phone calls to the vet clinic usually involved the scheduling of appointments, animal care questions, or salespeople pitching something or other. Then there were the emergency calls—they'd really get the juices flowing. Like the time when our receptionist hung up the phone and chimed out, "A lady just called, and she's on her way in with a cat that just got caught in the fan belt of her car." A statement like that would always conjure up all sorts of macabre-like mental images. When cats tangle with fan belts, cats never win! Severe and often life-threatening injuries invariably result. A bona fide emergency case was on its way. Staff members knew what to do and immediately began preparations for the cat's arrival.

It wasn't long before Christine Anderson stormed through the clinic door with a large, brown tabby farm cat named Hoss draped over her bloodstained arms. Hoss had sustained some major injuries from getting caught in the fan belt. He was really messed up and in serious trouble. There were lacerations on his head, ears, legs, and back, plus severe bruising around his left eye. But the worst injury was to his abdomen. The skin from his ribcage to his groin had been torn away, exposing the detached abdominal muscles along the ventral midline. His intestines and other internal organs could be clearly seen moving beneath a tissue-thin structure called the peritoneum, which lines the abdominal cavity. That extremely thin, delicate, transparent structure was the only thing preventing total evisceration (disembowelment) from taking place. Hoss was also in a state of shock, and his chances of surviving didn't look good. Intravenous catheters were immediately placed, and medications were given to counter shock. Once Hoss was stabilized, I turned to Christine and tried to explain that animals with injuries as severe and extensive as Hoss's usually didn't survive, but she didn't seem to grasp what I was saying. Instead, she stood there very composed and calmly said, "Oh, Doc, I believe in you. You'll save him."

I thought to myself, *How can she be so sure? She's either in a total state of denial or doesn't understand what's going on here.* Anyway, I told her that I'd do my best to put Hoss back together, but I couldn't make any promises. She just smiled and seemed to understand *that!* Hoss was carefully placed under a general anesthetic, and we got the show on the road. It was a team effort involving me and the veterinary assistants—shaving, cleaning, debridement, medicating, and the actual surgical reconstruction. Rebuilding that little guy was a long, painstaking procedure. Hoss had a strong will to live, and that was critical to his survival. Everything went well, and he made it through the surgery with flying colors. Granted, he looked a little Frankensteinish, with stitches everywhere on his body, but his mucous membrane color and respirations were good. As I placed him gently into the recovery cage, I told him, "Hoss, little buddy, you did good.

You hung in there and made it through this time. Now, stay away from those fan belts because I don't want us to keep meeting this way, okay?"

Christine brought Hoss back to the clinic several weeks later for a recheck. He'd made a remarkable recovery and looked almost as good as new! I told Christine that when I first saw Hoss's torn and beat-up little body, I didn't think he'd make it. I really had my doubts. He'd beaten the odds, but it cost him eight and a half of his nine lives to do it. He was, plain and simple, lucky to be alive. Christine smiled and said, "Doc, I never doubted for a moment that you could save him."

I thought to myself, *At least one of us did.*

It was later that year when Christine again called the clinic with another doozie of a problem. It didn't involve Hoss this time, thank goodness. Hoss was just fine, but her cow wasn't. She explained, "I think my cow has a dead calf inside of her. She's been out there in the pasture for several days, not moving much, and really stinks! I don't know how long she's been trying to have that calf, but I think she needs some help." I told Christine, "Cases like that are generally bad news. A cow with a dead calf inside for an extended period of time usually results in the cow becoming septicemic, developing blood poisoning, and in most cases, the cow dies. It's not a pretty picture! Sometimes it's more humane to put the cow out of her misery instead of letting her continue to suffer." Christine replied, "Doc, I know it's a long shot, but could you at least take a look at her and see? Maybe you could help her like you helped Hoss."

I couldn't believe what I was hearing. I said, "Christine, you don't understand. There's a 99.999 percent chance that this cow of yours is going to die from the advanced septicemia."

"That's okay, Doc", she said. "I have confidence in you because you saved Hoss, and he was almost a goner."

I told myself, *Oh brother, just go and check the cow out. She'll probably be dead by the time I get there.*

It was a twenty-mile drive to Christine's place, and she was waiting by the outbuildings when I arrived. As I was getting out of the truck, Christine asked, "Can you smell that?" The nauseating stench of rotting flesh permeated the air. It was bad!

"Where is she?" I asked. Christine pointed toward the open pasture. Way out there in the distance laid a black, white-faced (Hereford-Angus cross) cow. "That's her," Christine said. I had a bad feeling about this one, especially when you could smell her that far away. Someone once told me that a good way to counter foul odors was to place some Vicks Vaporub in your nose. I always carried a small jar of the stuff in the truck for moments like this, and believe me, *now* was the moment to give it a try! Pack those nostrils full! So with trusty Vicks stuffed up my nose and my stout rubber shoulder-length obstetric gloves on, I proceeded to examine the cow. Her mucous membranes were pale and tacky to the touch, and her respirations were weak and shallow. This poor gal was septic, dehydrated, and in big trouble. Not a good sign! As I inserted my arm into the pelvic inlet and uterus, it felt abnormally warm, actually hot, due to the infection, inflammation, and decomposition of the dead calf that was taking place inside of her. The rotten stench was almost overpowering, even with all that Vicks up my nose. I felt a hoof, grasped ahold of it, and as I began to position it into the pelvic inlet, it pulled loose. It was one of the dead calf's legs, and when I pulled it out, it looked bad. The hair was falling off, and the muscle tissue looked pale and resembled boiled chicken, only worse. It stunk to high heaven too! Christine surveyed the scene and said, "It looks really bad, doesn't it?" I told her, "If this cow lives, it will be a miracle. Downer cows with dead, rotting, decomposing calves inside rarely survive. They die!" I continued to remove the dead calf, one decomposed piece at a time until, finally, the entire corpse was removed, and laying on a stinking pile. I then flushed out the uterus with disinfectants, instilled antibiotics, and gave her a couple potent antibiotic injections. I told Christine that I was going to attempt to get the cow to stand up, but cautioned her not to expect much because the cow was so weak and septic. I then kneed the cow in the hindquarters and simultaneously hollered, "Come on, get up!" No response. I kneed her a second time, and this time she staggered to her feet, a little wobbly, but she was standing and looking around. Unbelievable! A few moments later, she sauntered off a short distance and started to eat grass! Christine started to laugh, cheer, and clap her hands. I just stood there smiling, amazed and speechless. "You did it again, Doc. You did it again!" Christine said while smiling ear to ear.

That cow had defied the odds too. She steadily improved, and yes, she lived. The rotten stench had penetrated the rubber gloves and had gotten into the pores of my skin. I washed my hands and arms with everything imaginable, but to no avail. It took several weeks to wear off, and during that time, I was referred to as "Stinky Doc" at the clinic. Looking back, lightning did strike twice in the same place for Christine. Hoss and her cow were living proof.

BABY HUEY

The original Baby Huey was a lovable cartoon character. He was a large, clumsy, goofy baby duck in diapers. The Baby Huey I knew as a patient fit the description perfectly, except for one minor detail—instead of being a baby duck in diapers, he was a huge, happy-go-lucky Great Dane.

I'll never forget the first time I met Baby Huey. He was scheduled for a routine physical exam and vaccinations, and his grand entrance into the clinic was an event not easily forgotten. This enormous fawn-colored Great Dane, weighing in excess of two hundred pounds, came bounding through the door, knocking over tables and chairs, with his owner flailing on the end of the leash like a lure on the end of a fishing line. The expression "Bull in a china closet" was appropriate in his case, except that Baby Huey had more of a Ferdinand-type personality. He was a very friendly, clumsy goof who loved everything and everybody— "happy, happy, happy," "Oh boy, oh boy," "can I sit on your lap?" type of guy. He really was a fun patient and could easily cheer up someone's day, if he didn't bowl them over first. Physically, he looked more like a small horse than a dog. He had a huge head, long legs, and enormous paws that resembled ping-pong paddles.

Baby Huey was, without question, one supersized hunk of love, very appropriately named, and a real kick in the pants!

Several months later, the owner called the clinic and frantically told our receptionist, "My dog just ran in front of the hay mower and got his legs cut real bad. Is Doc gonna be there?" It was Baby Huey, and it didn't sound good! When Baby Huey arrived at the clinic, he was unable to stand, let alone walk. He was placed on a stretcher, and four people struggled to carry him into the clinic, where he was immediately transferred to the surgery table. Pressure bandages had been placed around his left front and left rear paws in an effort to slow the hemorrhaging, but they were now totally soaked with blood. The bleeding had to be stopped soon, or Baby Huey could die from loss of blood. He was quickly sedated and anesthetized, the blood-soaked towels were removed, and the spurting arteries were located, clamped, and ligated (tied off). Once the bleeding was under control, the extent of tissue damage could then be more easily seen. There were severe lacerations just above the paws, in the metacarpal area of the left front leg and the metatarsal area of the left hind leg. The rapid back-and-forth motion of the hay mower's sharp sickle blade had made two very deep transverse lacerations, about four inches apart, on both of his legs, cutting arteries, veins, tendons, and nerves. It was a mess! Four tendons on each leg had been severed in two places, making a total of sixteen separate tendon cuts. One would have been bad enough, but sixteen! The four-inch pieces of severed tendon had shifted from their original positions, and that further complicated the situation. The nightmare would be trying to figure out where each piece had to go, and it essentially resulted in comparing the sizes of the severed ends. Tendons are notorious for being slow to heal, and sometimes they don't heal properly. Without adequate tendon support, Baby Huey might never be able to stand, let alone walk or run. His odds of recovery were not good at all, and his owner knew it. They were devastated, and even considered putting Baby Huey down. I didn't want to see that happen.

It's been said that necessity is the mother of invention, and I had an idea that might help Baby Huey. I told the owners that perhaps using a non-absorbable permanent suture to reattach the tendons might work. Baby Huey's tendons were pretty good-sized, which would allow the sutures to be more securely anchored, and that would provide a better chance of holding and increase the probability of healing. I also told them that I'd never performed a surgery like that before. I'd be essentially "venturing outside the box," so to speak, but if everything went well, then Baby Huey might, just *might*, have at least a chance of walking again someday. I couldn't make any promises, but making an effort to help him would be far better than putting him down. The owners, with tears in their eyes, didn't hesitate for a moment before they chimed out, "Let's go for it!"

Baby Huey was immediately taken to surgery, and the reconstruction process turned out to be a very intricate, tedious, and painstakingly slow procedure. Finding the displaced severed tendons, properly matching them up to their respective ends, and delicately reuniting each one was repeated sixteen times. Closing the skin lacerations was the final step. When the surgery was completed, I was totally spent, both physically and mentally. I was confident that the tendons had properly reattached and was hopeful that the sutures would hold. Time would tell.

Baby Huey spent the next several weeks under house arrest, with his left front and rear paws heavily bandaged in an attempt to restrict movement at the surgical sites. The "happy" pain pills also helped relieve some of the discomfort and slowed him down somewhat too, but he was still a handful for his owners. When he began moving his paws, that was an encouraging sign, but when he walked several steps, his owners were absolutely elated! The sutures held, Baby Huey eventually was able to run, and he became his ole clumsy, lovable self again.

The procedure was a long shot. It probably shouldn't have worked, but it did. Baby Huey was one of the most challenging and rewarding cases of my veterinary career. I'm thankful that I went outside the box with an idea, and it worked to save a friend's life.

IMPRINTING

Zoological imprinting is defined as a behavioral condition wherein a young animal can come to recognize another animal, person, or thing as a parent or object of habitual trust. Bugsy, a little six-week-old buff-colored cocker spaniel puppy was a prime example.

A man stepped up to the reception counter, plopped down a small puppy, and said, "Something's wrong with this pup. He doesn't look right, and the mom keeps pushing him away. He's the runt, and he doesn't get around like the other pups. I don't have the time to mess around with him, so I want you to just put him down." Melanie, our receptionist, ushered Mr. Torkel and his puppy into the first exam room. As I started to examine the tiny puppy, Mr. Torkel remarked, "I don't want him examined, just put him down!" I looked Mr. Torkel straight in the eyes and told him, "I won't do that without examining him first. Mr. Torkel, the *only* reason I'll ever consider euthanasia is to relieve the pain and suffering of an animal who is incapacitated or terminally ill, for humane reasons, not for convenience."

Mr. Torkel responded, "Well, forget it then. I'll take him somewhere else and have it done."

Somebody else might do it, but not me. I felt that this little guy at least deserved a chance at life, so I said to Mr. Torkel, "I'll tell you what, Mr. Torkel. You sign ownership of this pup over to me, and then he'll be mine. I can then give him a fighting chance on my dime, and it won't cost you a cent." Mr. Torkel thought for a second, but no more than that, and said, "Done!"

He turned around, walked out of the clinic, and I never saw or heard from that man ever again. I was now the proud owner of a malnourished little runt of a dog who just happened to be a hydrocephalic, with an enlarged head and protruding eyes. He was, without question, sitting squarely behind the eight ball. I gently placed the little guy into the pocket of my light blue smock, patted him delicately, and told him, "Little buddy, now that you're mine, let's see what we can do for ya." I walked out front and showed the staff my new little pocket pet.

"Whatcha gonna name him now that he's yours?" Melanie asked.

I looked down at the little bulgy-eyed puppy in my pocket and said, "Bugsy, that's what I'm going to name him. Yeah, Bugsy, because his eyes kind of bug out in a cute sort of way."

Bugsy was definitely exhibiting the signs associated with a hydrocephalic case. Hydrocephalus is a condition where there is excess fluid in and around the brain, causing the eyes to bulge and the head to become more dome shaped. The bones of the skull are softer and more flexible at this age because the fontanels (junction spaces) between these bones haven't yet ossified (hardened) and become fused. So the excess internal fluid puts pressure on these bones and causes them to spread somewhat, and that makes the head look bigger. Sometimes the fluid absorbs and the condition resolves; sometimes it doesn't, which could then result in seizures and possibly even death of the individual. Shunts were not a treatment option in Bugsy's case. His condition was not as severe as some, so there were possibilities that the problem might normalize with "tincture of time."

Over the next few weeks, Bugsy spent a lot of time riding in my smock pocket. I guess you could say that he was my sidekick. The bulginess of his eyes seemed to be resolving somewhat; he was eating well, more playful, and becoming a pretty spoiled little guy too. No doubt about it, Bugsy was improving, and it was also becoming increasingly apparent that he thought I was his *mom*.

It was around that time frame that one of our clients named Vi had lost her old cocker spaniel to cancer. She'd visited the clinic several times, saw Bugsy, and was totally smitten with him. I noticed how Vi's eyes would light up with joy when she saw the little guy, and there was definitely a mutual attraction between those two. I'd come to the realization that I wouldn't be able to carry Bugsy around in my pocket forever and that he needed a home where he'd be loved and cared for 24/7. Vi lived only three blocks from the clinic, so I'd be able to see him quite often. That was important to me because I'd become very fond of Bugsy as well. Vi and Bugsy seemed to be made for each other, and it was beginning to look more and more like a match made in heaven. As time passed, Bugsy's medical condition totally resolved, and he'd become very handsome and healthy. He was one happy camper! Every time Vi took Bugsy for a walk and passed by the clinic, he'd pull on the leash toward the door, wanting to come in to visit.

Vi often laughingly said, "I have this dog at my house who I feed and care for, but you know what, he's not really my dog, he's yours! He thinks you're his mom. He'll always feel that way, but I still love him. I can deal with that."

I smiled, gave Vi a big hug, and told her, "That's what's called imprinting, Vi. Bugsy's a doubly blessed boy because he's got something that most dogs don't have—two moms."

THE UNEXPECTED

Ray Winston and his wife, Vivian, lived on a small ranch located a few miles south of town. They enjoyed country life and of course accumulated an assortment of farm animals.

Vivian had become interested in showing dogs and selected a purebred Pekinese male from a very reputable breeder, hoping that someday he'd become a champion. The dog had a pedigree name that was a mile long, but they just called him "Howdy". He had perfect body conformation and an outstanding lineage, but unfortunately not the mind-set. Howdy thought he was a herding dog, like a Blue Heeler cattle dog, that somehow got morphed into a Pekinese body. He just loved to get out there, down and dirty, and to him, the barnyard was his show ring. His favorite sport was herding the cows, and he was fearless. At times, he'd come dangerously close to being kicked, but his low profile served him well. As the cows kicked in response to Howdy's annoying heel biting, their hooves sailed harmlessly over his little head. He was quick for such a short-legged little guy, and his timing was usually spot on.

Overconfidence can often lead to disaster, and one can go to the well just so many times before coming up empty. Such was the scenario with Howdy. Vivian called the clinic one day with a voice beset with dreaded concern and relayed to the receptionist that she was on her way to the clinic with Howdy, because his eye had been badly injured. Vivian didn't exactly know what happened, but she had a good idea. After examining the type of injury and the extent of tissue trauma, it was obvious that Howdy hadn't ducked fast enough, and a cow's hoof connected squarely with his left eye. There was considerable damage. Unfortunately, Howdy's left eye was prolapsed (moved forward and downward) out of the socket, and the optic nerve had been severed. Regrettably, Howdy's eye could not be saved.

I will forever be amazed at the will and resolve of some animals. We could all learn some valuable lessons from them. Howdy was undaunted with the loss of his eye. To him, having just one eye was nothing more than a minor inconvenience. The possibility of him ever entering the show ring had evaporated, but his love of life hadn't diminished one iota. He was the same happy-go-lucky, fun-loving barnyard dog, but now he was sporting a permanent wink. He didn't stop herding cows, but he did learn from his mistake. Howdy now had a very healthy respect for a cow's kick, and from that time on, he gave the cows a wider berth and made sure to duck a little faster.

ASSUMING

One of the meanings of the word *assume* is to suppose something to be the case without proof. Sometimes assuming can be advantageous, but on the other hand, incorrect assumptions can result in a bucketload of regrettable consequences.

Ron Winston called the clinic and told our receptionist that he had a pig that needed to be castrated. No problem! Most male pigs are altered at a reasonably young age, and since Mr. Winston didn't specify the age, it was assumed that he was referring to a younger animal. Such procedures are relatively quick and easily performed on the young ones.

Upon arrival at the Winston place, Ron told me that the pig was caught up in the barn. I appreciated that because now we wouldn't have to go through the "greased pig chase" routine. I grabbed my equipment, and together we headed to the barn. Once inside and seeing the pig that I was supposed to castrate, my facial expression must have resembled the dead fish look, mouth gaping and eyes opened wide. This wasn't a thirty pound pig! Standing right there before me was a five hundred-pound Landrace boar, with testicles the size of eggplants, and he didn't appear too keen about the idea of being transformed into a eunuch. There were no

stanchions around to help confine him, so Mr. Winston came up
with the brilliant idea of putting a rope around the boar's neck and
tying him to the massive three-inch thick wooden cow manger.
I had my reservations about doing that, but there weren't many
options—in fact, none! This huge boar was not about to have his
testicles removed without anesthesia. The proven technique for
sedating a large boar was to inject the anesthetic into one of the
testicles. As the boar began to absorb the drug and proceeded to
fall asleep, the injected testicle would be removed first, and there
would be ample time to remove the remaining testicle before
the pig woke up. That all sounded quite reasonable. I asked Mr.
Winston if he was ready, and he said, "Let's do it."

I calculated the anesthetic dosage and prepared the syringe.
I then grabbed ahold of one of the enormous testicles, and at
the very moment he felt the initial touch of the needle, he let
out an ear-splitting, bellowing squeal that could have been heard
in the next county. He jerked his powerful, muscular neck with
tremendous force and instantly dismantled the hay manger. Once
free from restraint, he then started running around the enclosure
with a large wooden plank from the dismantled cow manger,
dangling from his neck. This whole affair was rapidly turning into
a real fiasco. The huge boar wouldn't let us get close enough to
even untie the rope, and who could blame him? He kept running
and squealing until finally he got his big head stuck into the
opening of a large metal farrowing crate that was situated in one
of the corners of the barn. That farrowing crate (a structure that
protected the piglets from being rolled upon when the sow was
farrowing/giving birth) was heavy, but the boar easily lifted that
crate onto his shoulders. He continued his evasive maneuvers,
and now he was not only dragging a large wooden plank, but he
was toting a farrowing crate on his back as well. Suddenly, as if
by an act of providence, the crate got wedged into a corner. The
moment of opportunity had presented itself, and I quickly took
advantage of it. I raced in there and performed the castration so

fast that he didn't really feel or know what was happening. Done! Eventually the pig managed to back out of the farrowing crate, and the squealing stopped.

Whew! Mission accomplished, and best of all, no one got hurt. That whole incident was a very valuable lesson for me. In the future, I would make every possible effort to *never* again *assume* anything.

MIKEY

There once was a television commercial that featured a cute little boy who liked to eat just about anything, and his name was Mikey. The tag line of the commercial was "Mikey likes it." Those three simple words epitomized one of my closest friends.

Joyce Beauchet was a different sort of person. She was a single, self-proclaimed successful businesswoman from Southern California who moved to the Pacific Northwest to seek anonymity and isolation. She chose not to have a telephone and was emphatic about keeping her personal matters totally private. Ms. Beauchet simply did not want anyone to know who or where she was. In addition, she chose to conduct all business transactions by cash only, thereby leaving no trail of financial activity. One might say that she was a person who raised many eyebrows, and who was, without a doubt, a very eccentric individual who better not be double-crossed.

It was one of those high-intensity days at the veterinary clinic, and time management was a priority. I had just finished an appointment, when Janice, our receptionist interjected, "Doc, there's a lady on the phone who is very unhappy. She says that someone dropped off a cat at her place, and she doesn't want it. She'll have someone shoot it if you don't take it."

I couldn't let that happen, so I told Janice, "Just tell her to drop the cat off with us, and we'll find it a good home." I thought to myself, *not another one!* About an hour later, Joyce Beauchet made her grand entrance and unabashedly plopped a young cat, around sixteen weeks old, on the front counter, then sternly said, "Here, it's yours!" She turned around, without even a thank-you, and abruptly departed.

Left behind and sitting calmly on the counter was perhaps one of the most beautiful cats I'd ever seen. He was a red classic tabby. The color pattern of a classic tabby is quite unique because of the bull's-eye marking pattern symmetrically located on the sides of its body. This young cat was very striking to look at and instantly made himself at home in his new surroundings. Actually, he seemed relieved, and who could blame him? As I picked him up, an infectious purr motor automatically erupted and continued as he gently nestled into my arms. I was smitten with the little guy and knew, right then and there, that he'd found a new home— with me. I'd always wanted a red cat, and knew that someday, if I ever found the right one, I'd name him Mikey. Well, that someday had come; I'd found him, thanks to Ms. Beauchet, and this little guy's name would, most definitely, be Mikey.

It didn't take Mikey very long at all to settle in as the resident mascot of the clinic. He'd conveniently situated himself on the counter, becoming the clinic's official greeter and PR (personal relations) cat. He was good at it too, and it wasn't long before he had his very own fan club. Adults and kids would often come into the clinic just to get their "Mikey fix." He really grooved on all the petting and attention, and truthfully, he'd come to expect it. He didn't discriminate either; in fact, he'd didn't care if a person liked or disliked cats; he'd still befriend them. We'd often hear some anti-cat people say, "I usually don't like cats, but this one is different. I like this one! What's his name again?" I'd say, "Mikey or Mike, whichever you prefer. You know why he's different? He doesn't think he's just a cat, he thinks he's a purr-son." That statement probably wasn't too far from the truth.

Mikey had a unique ability to sense a person's loss and would suddenly appear and offer his consoling presence to them in their time of need. Over the years, he provided needed comfort to many. He truly was very special and one of a kind. On other occasions, whenever anyone talked to him, he'd vocalize to them in varied tones and inflections as if having a friendly, meaningful conversation. It was amazing to see. Mikey was a blessing to me in many ways, and he was by my side through thick and thin. He lived a long and happy life and will be fondly remembered by all who knew and loved him. I will forever be grateful to Ms. Beauchet for complaining about that dumped-off cat because she provided me with a devoted friend and confidant who greatly enriched my life.

ONCE IN A LIFETIME

Almost everyone is familiar with the publication *Ripley's Believe It or Not*, and knows that it focuses on the bizarre and unusual. It can be quite fascinating and interesting to read some of that stuff. So it shouldn't come as much of a surprise to us when we encounter something very unusual and rare, because certain things in life really are stranger than fiction.

Mr. George Cravits called the clinic that beautiful Spring morning with the startling news that his cow had just given birth to a two-headed calf, and it was still alive! I'd studied about and seen pictures of cases like that in vet school, but I'd never seen an actual, *live*, two-headed calf up close and personal before. I was really looking forward to seeing this one. So I grabbed my medical bags and equipment and was on the road in a flash.

A two-headed calf is an extremely rare occurrence. Most are delivered dead, or if born alive, they don't survive very long. It's also very unusual for a cow to deliver a two-headed calf without veterinary assistance because the head size is often too large to pass through the birth canal. In that case, a caesarean section or an episiotomy would usually be necessary to deliver such a deformed calf. However, in Mr. Cravits's cow's case, she delivered the deformed calf without any complications, and that in itself was totally amazing.

I arrived at the Cravits's ranch within minutes and quickly made my way to the calf. I found Mr. Cravits kneeling next to the recumbent Hereford calf, supporting the calf's head in his hands. "Have you ever seen anything like this before, Doc?" he asked.

"No, never have, not even in vet school. I'd only seen photos, but never the real thing," I responded.

The calf was definitely alive and breathing. One of the two centrally located eyes slowly blinked. The calf had two distinct muzzles, two lateral eyes, two central eyes, two ears, and the heads were fused, or joined, in the middle. The calf attempted to move his head (heads) but was unable to raise them because of the increased weight. The little guy opened his left muzzle slightly and made a feeble attempt to bellow, but there was no sound. The ultimate outcome was glaringly obvious—this calf wasn't going to survive.

I thought to myself, *The vet school should really have a chance to see this calf before it dies.* So I told Mr. Cravits, "This calf needs to be transported to the Washington State University Veterinary School right away. It's about ninety miles from here. The vet school would be very appreciative and could learn a lot from this little guy."

Mr. Cravits generously complied, and I immediately loaded the calf into my truck, and down the road we went. The little calf, as expected, lived only two days. He wasn't able to stand, nor could he eat. He was humanely put down, but he provided the veterinary school and students with a wealth of valuable information, so he didn't die in vain.

Two-headed calves are a very rare birth and, in most instances, make widespread, if not global, news. This little guy was no exception. There was extensive local and regional television and newspaper coverage, and he was written about in various veterinary journals as well.

I'd found the saying to be true. Some things in life really are stranger than fiction. I know. I was there, and it was a once-in-a-lifetime experience.

A MATCH MADE IN HEAVEN

Golden retrievers have the reputation of being gentle, fun-loving dogs who seem to just go with the flow and have that, c'est la vie, attitude about life. That's probably why they are such a popular breed.

I first met Delicia, a two-year-old spayed female golden retriever, when her owner, Steve Thorten, brought her to the clinic because he was concerned about some recent changes in her behavior and activity. She used to play fetch with the ball and liked to go for walks, but she'd lost her enthusiasm for all that, and now just moped around. Mr. Thorten went on to say that due to his busy work schedule and not being home very much, he was afraid that she'd just lay around and get fat.

"Mr. Thorten," I asked, "how long has Delicia been acting this way?" He replied, "Quite a while." When I asked Mr. Thorten if there had been any recent changes in the household, he thought for a moment and then said, "Yeah, I guess. The cat used to keep her pretty busy, and they played together almost constantly, but the cat got hit by a car and died."

Bingo! I told Mr. Thorton, "I think Delicia has been grieving because she's lost her little friend. What we need to do is try to find her another companion, preferably a cat. Maybe that would solve the problem."

Several days had passed, and as I was pulling into my driveway after a busy day at the clinic, a little red-orange colored tabby kitten came trotting over to the car. It held its tail up high in the air and seemed quite friendly. I looked down at that scrawny little kitten and said, "Hi there, little buddy, what's your name?" Just then, my neighbor, Bill, came walking around the corner of his house. "Hey Bill, I said, "what's your new cat's name?"

"Oh, that thing isn't mine. It's been hangin' around here the last couple days. Somebody must've dumped him off," Bill responded.

All the while this little ragamuffin was prancing around with its tail in the air, and he kept rubbing up against my pant legs, marking me as his new possession. He looked up at me as if to say, "Hey you, don't you know I'm yours? Boy, are *you* lucky or what!"

As I picked up the scrawny little stray, I immediately saw fleas scurrying and weaving through his hair like downhill skiers traversing a slalom course. The little guy's ears were also filled with dry crusty debris, suggestive of ear mites. He had a nasal discharge, weepy eyes, and then on top of it all, he sneezed directly into my face. Yet as bad as he looked, he kept purring and kneading away with his paws. This kitten was a mess, but a happy mess, and he needed a lot of help. So I placed this little vagabond into a carrying crate, and off to the clinic we went for an extreme makeover.

He got a bath, had his ears cleaned and medicated, was treated for fleas, vaccinated, wormed, and had his eyes cleaned too. He'd gotten the full monty and didn't complain at all. He was one little happy camper, now that he'd been all cleaned up. Life was good, or at least a heck of a lot better. Now he needed a name. The most striking feature about this kitten was his red-orange colored hair coat. We decided to name him "Rudy" because one of the meanings of the word *rudy* is red hair or skin. It seemed to be a good fit for him.

The next task at hand was to find Rudy a good home. Delicia came to mind almost immediately, but the question was, would they get along? I called Mr. Thorten and told him that we might have a little friend for Delicia, and he was receptive to the idea. He knew how much Delicia missed the other cat and was hoping this kitten might get her out of the doldrums. Mr. Thorten picked up Rudy within the hour, and now, time would tell if it was the right move.

Several days later, I received a phone call from a very ecstatic Steve Thorten. He said, "Doc, you won't believe this, but those two hit it off the moment I let the cat out of the crate! They acted like long lost buddies, and they're even sleeping together. Delicia has been licking and grooming him so much that he's covered with slobber and is wet most of the time, but he doesn't seem to mind. Thanks, Doc!"

I told Steve, "It seems like a match made in heaven, doesn't it?"

He wholeheartedly agreed.

Delicia and Rudy—what a wonderful success story. Delicia regained her zest for life, and Rudy found a loving home. It couldn't get much better than that! Those two became devoted companions to each other and remained inseparable for many, many years.

THE UNSINKABLE MOLLY

Margaret Tobin was a survivor of the ill-fated passenger ship, Titanic. It was reputed that she rowed lifeboat #6 for seven and one half hours and delivered herself and her fellow passengers to safety. She was the only woman to do such a thing, and that act of courage, will, and stamina earned her the nickname "the Unsinkable Molly Brown."

I once had a patient whose name was Molly, and she too displayed tremendous courage, a strong will, and unequaled stamina in overcoming a potentially devastating injury. She was a three-year-old Brittany spaniel with true grit and was, without a doubt, the canine version of the famous Unsinkable Molly Brown. Molly was a very gentle, affectionate, thirty-pound Brittany spaniel, who had boundless energy and loved to hunt. She was a pleasure to have as a patient because she was easy to work with and always seemed eager to please. I really liked that little girl.

It was late September when Roger Carney, Molly's owner, called the clinic to set up a time to have her leg checked. As Molly entered through the front door of the clinic, it was glaringly obvious that she'd sustained a major injury to her right front leg. She was holding up the leg, and when she attempted to place the paw, it knuckled over at the carpus (wrist). The leg was unable to support any body weight whatsoever. Molly was ushered into the exam room, and I began an assessment of her condition. Her leg was severely swollen, edematous, the dorsum (top) of the paw and foreleg were badly scraped and bloody, and there was no response to pain stimulation of the paw. In addition, the righting reflex (paw placement) was absent. I couldn't detect any broken bones on palpation, and x-rays confirmed that fact. It didn't look very promising. At that point, all findings indicated a radial nerve paralysis, and that type of injury could be either transient (temporary) or permanent, depending upon the degree of damage to the nerve. If permanent, she'd never be able to use that leg again.

I asked Mr. Carney if he knew what happened and when the injury occurred. He looked down toward the floor, paused momentarily, and with a tone of regret in his voice, he said, "I accidentally hit her with the pickup a couple weeks ago, but I thought she might snap out of it."

The scrapes on the paw and foreleg appeared to be the result of a more recent injury, so I asked him if he knew what may have caused those injuries. He said that he'd taken her out hunting, and the scrapes were from her dragging the leg through the weeds and underbrush. That was unbelievable! Molly still had the will to hunt using three legs and dragging the paralyzed one. I told Mr. Carney, "I'm sorry, but her leg doesn't look good at all, and with the nerve paralysis, I'd recommend that the leg be amputated for her welfare. If we don't, she'll continue to drag that paw, it will then become severely infected, and it could eventually be life threatening. Mr. Carney said that he'd think about it, but for now, he only wanted to treat her with antibiotics and ointment for the scrapes. He'd erroneously convinced himself that if the leg were amputated, then she wouldn't be able to hunt. I assured him that Molly would still be a better hunter on three legs than most dogs are on all four, but he still declined. My hands were tied, and I honestly felt sorry for Molly.

Two weeks had passed, and Mr. Carney brought Molly back to the clinic. Her leg was now severely infected, and she had become septic. Molly was gravely ill, and her life was definitely in peril. There was no other option at this point—amputate the leg or put her down. Finally Mr. Carney realized the gravity of the situation and signed the consent form to amputate the leg. We were good to go! I patted Molly on the head and said to her, "Molly, hang in there with me. We're going to get you through this, and then you'll be able to hunt again, okay?"

We got Molly all hooked up to the IV fluids and prepped for surgery. It was a lengthy procedure. I amputated the leg high, at shoulder level, and reconstructed a protective cushion of muscle over the remaining portion of bone. The leg, along with all the devitalized necrotic tissue, was successfully amputated. Antibiotics and pain meds were administered, and it wasn't long before she started to wake up. Molly was a great patient! What a trooper! When she was discharged the next morning, she was raring to go and already appeared to be feeling much, much better! Everybody got excited as we watched Molly come hop-running down the hallway. Even Mr. Carney smiled, now with some signs of hope and optimism in his eyes.

A week had passed, and it was time to recheck Molly. I saw Mr. Carney pull up with his pickup in front of the clinic. When he opened the door, Molly jumped out and took off running down the street. She ran faster on three legs than most dogs could on four. When Mr. Carney finally caught her, he was the one who was winded. Molly looked and acted great! Everything was healing well, and in another couple weeks, she could once again be out there hunting. Needless to say, Mr. Carney was very pleased and thankful. Molly had overcome extreme adversity with courage and a very strong will. She continued to be an outstanding hunting dog and proved to everyone that she was indeed the *unsinkable* Molly!

THE THREE AMIGOS

Good intentions are what they are—plans put into action with hopes of positive outcomes. As we all know, our good intentions don't always result in the manifestation of what we purposed. It has even been said that the road to hell is paved with good intentions. So if that be true, it becomes very apparent that many good intentions go unfulfilled. The question then is, how do we respond?

Sandy's grandmother, Kate, lived in a nice retirement center that had a small aviary placed in the center of the main lobby. When we visited her, we'd pass by the large birdcage that housed around twenty small birds of varying colors, ranging from gray and white with red on their heads to simply brown and white. They all appeared quieter than most birds, and their soft chirping was very soothing to the soul. That pleasurable sound seemed to have a calming and almost hypnotic effect to it. I told Sandy, "What do you think about getting a bird like that and placing it in our waiting room? I think the clients would like that, don't you?" Sandy agreed, and I guess you could say that our intentions were good.

We went to a pet store and described to the clerk the type of bird that we wanted to buy. She told us that the bird we were looking for was called a zebra finch, but she had just recently sold the last one. She did, however, know of a bird breeder and wholesaler who had lots of them. So off we went in hot pursuit.

When we found the place and entered the building, the loud incessant noise created by all the squawking, chirping, and whistling was enough to drive a sane person mad. I wondered how in the world could anyone work in such a noisy place like this. It wasn't long before the owner noticed our presence, waved acknowledgement, and approached us. I noticed that he moved his hands up to his ears and was fiddling with something. He was adjusting his hearing aids! This guy was either nearly deaf or very hard of hearing, and that explains why all the racket didn't bother him—he tuned it out! Smart! He then ushered us into the main room, which was much quieter, and asked us what kind of bird we were looking for. I told him that we wanted to buy a zebra finch. He asked, "Just one?" He then went on to say, "You shouldn't have just one. You'll need two or more so that the birds don't get lonely." I reluctantly went along with his recommendation, but specified only two males because I wasn't interested in the hassle of raising birds. He then told me that having just two males wasn't a good idea either because one of them is usually more dominant and would likely pick on the other one and then there'd be problems. He recommended that we purchase three. Wow, how could such a simple idea get so complicated? I finally gave in, and the guy caught up three nicely colored male finches. In the end, we walked out of there with three male zebra finches, a large birdcage, two designer perches, and a big bag of special finch food. My initial intent was to get one little soft-chirping bird at minimal cost, but here I was, walking out of the place with a mini aviary and a major investment.

Once the birds were all set up in the waiting room, it didn't take long to realize that dogs and cats rushing up to the birdcage wasn't a good idea. So all the paraphernalia was moved into my office, and the three birds seemed to like that much better. Mikey, the clinic cat, would get right up next to and on top of the birdcage, but they didn't seem to be bothered by him, in fact, they sort of liked him. Initially the birds got along together pretty well, so we called them, the Three Amigos. Well, all that was about to change too.

One of the birds was becoming more dominant and started harassing and pecking on the other two. Not good! I ended up purchasing another birdcage just for him. That rowdy little mouthy guy was becoming a pain! I started calling him "PITA" because he had become a real pain in the, you know what. The other two also needed names, so we named them "Shazbot" and "Tookus". Those two were good boys, and both made those soothing chirps that we'd hoped to hear, but Pita remained his obnoxious self and continued to disturb the other two guys. I had no other choice but to get Pita out of there, which meant eventually taking him home.

It took a while, but Sandy and I became pretty fond of ole Pita. We placed his cage in a room where he could see all the outside bird action, and that really made his day! Any sharp sound in the house or on the radio or television would set him off. He'd start his mouthy chattering. When I would go up to his cage and ask him how he was doing, he'd charge right up to me, ruffle up his feathers, and chew me out. This cheeky little bird definitely did not fit the zebra finch mold, but he was a lot of fun.

He was a great escape artist too. Many times I had to play "catch the flying finch midair." On one occasion, Sandy forgot to secure the cage door, and when she didn't hear Pita sounding off as usual, she went in to check. The cage was empty, and no Pita in sight. Sandy looked down, and sitting quietly right beside her desk was Bob, our bobtailed cat, and there were finch tail feathers sticking out of his mouth. Sandy gently grabbed hold of the tail feathers and sternly commanded, "Bob, open your mouth!" He slowly opened his mouth, and Sandy pulled out a *live* but wet Pita, totally unharmed. Sandy quickly put him into his cage. He sat for a moment, shook his feathers back into place, then proceeded to chew everybody out again. What a schmuck! We loved him anyway. The average lifespan of a zebra finch is said to be around five years. Pita lived to be fifteen years old, and that was truly amazing. He was exceptional in so many ways, and lived life to the fullest, for a zebra finch. Pita was a real kick in the pants, and although he was a cheeky little fella, he'll always be fondly remembered as a good amigo.

CODE BLUE

Color codes are designated to various emergency situations encountered in medical facilities. Code red indicates a fire emergency, code orange refers to a hazardous material spill, but a code blue signals a medical emergency. When code blue is announced, all medical personnel immediately spring into action and work together as a team in an attempt to save a life.

Ray Shaw was a conscientious man of high moral character who dearly loved his dog, Shilo. Shilo was a thirty-five pound, slightly overweight beagle, who had a gentle spirit and was a pleasure to have as a patient. Shilo was the ideal companion for Mr. Shaw because the dog's laid-back demeanor and complete trust provided him with stress relief. The last thing Mr. Shaw needed in his life was more stress, especially with having a heart condition, and those two were really good for each other.

It was midsummer when Mr. Shaw called the clinic. He was short of breath, and there was a sense of panic and dread in his voice. "My neighbor just shot my dog in the head, and he's bleeding all over the place. I'm bringing him in right now."

Sandy hung up the phone and verbally sounded the alarm, "Code blue! We've got an emergency on the way!" She quickly relayed the nature of the emergency, and all staff members stepped it up a notch and began preparations for the medical crisis to arrive. Within minutes, Mr. Shaw burst through the clinic door, clutching Shilo in his bloody arms. His face was an ashen-gray color—not good considering his heart condition—and his white T-shirt appeared red because it was saturated with Shilo's blood. He was taken from Mr. Shaw and rushed to the surgery room while Sandy, a nurse by profession, assisted Mr. Shaw and his immediate needs. Instead of being faced with one code blue, we were confronted with two—Shilo fighting for his life and Mr. Shaw with a heart condition. It was imperative that cool heads prevailed, and everyone stayed focused!

Shilo's most urgent needs to be addressed were to stop the hemorrhaging and initiate treatment for shock. Once that was achieved and Shilo was stabilized, then the other issues, such as bone fractures and tissue trauma, were assessed. The .22 caliber bullet had entered the left side of Shilo's face, fractured the left mandible (lower jaw bone) and exited the right side of the muzzle, totally obliterating the right mandibular canine tooth and the right mandibular first premolar tooth. There was also extensive soft tissue trauma that would require reconstruction. It was a mess! X-rays revealed that the mandibular fracture was a good candidate for alignment and stabilization with stainless steel wires. The teeth, however, were history. Gone!

The critical phase of the emergency had passed. Shilo's condition had stabilized, he was no longer in a state of shock, and the hemorrhaging was under control. Mr. Shaw had calmed down and was less stressed, knowing that his beloved Shilo would survive, but he was still very angry at his neighbor for doing such a heartless thing, and who could blame him?

Due to the compromised bone fractures, Shilo was referred to a veterinary orthopedic surgery specialist, and the surgery went well. The jaw bone fragments were successfully aligned, reunited, and stabilized with surgical stainless steel wire, and the soft tissue reconstruction came together nicely. I felt confident that Shilo would make a complete recovery, minus a couple teeth, and he did.

Looking back, a code blue always demands that a team effort be put forth, and our staff handled this one very well, and the outcome was good too. Thanks, everybody.

SWEET SUCCESS

Veterinary journals and publications provide current and pertinent information pertaining to the diagnosis and treatment of various diseases and maladies. Over the years, I saved and categorized many articles for potential future reference. Several articles were especially intriguing because they featured the use of honey for the treatment of certain wounds and thermal skin injuries. The results were dramatic and very impressive. It seemed strange that in today's world of advanced and high-tech medical procedures and treatments, an age-old remedy dating back to the ancient Egyptians, would be revisited. I recalled what Mother used to say, "The proof is in the pudding," and "New is not always better." Those words of wisdom made sense. I was fascinated with the holistic and unconventional treatment method and hoped that someday I'd have an opportunity to see for myself if treating certain wounds topically with honey really did promote healing.

Perhaps one of the most emotionally gut-wrenching situations for a veterinarian is being confronted with a seriously injured animal and the owner being financially strapped with extremely limited monetary resources. We did have a small compassion fund that was used for hardship cases, but unfortunately, some emergency conditions could have easily depleted that fund. We, as well as all other medical providers, were limited as to how much donated, gratuitous, "free" medical services we could provide. So tough, often unpleasant decisions had to be made. Such was the situation encountered with Whitney Mosher and her three-year-old neutered pit bull named Tippy.

When I entered the exam room, Tippy was laying on the exam table with his weeping owner standing by his side. His left hind leg had been severely traumatized as the result of being bitten by another dog. The skin was badly torn, exposing the underlying muscles and tendons, in two distinct areas between the knee and hip. The four-inch long gaping wounds were separated by a mere one inch band of skin.

As I was explaining what needed to be done and the surgical reconstruction process, Ms. Mosher tearfully interrupted and said, "Just put him to sleep. I don't have any money, and I can't afford to have anything done for him." I hated the thought of putting Tippy down. There just had to be another way to deal with this problem. Then it hit me: *try the honey*! I told Ms. Mosher, "I've got an idea. I can't promise anything, and it might be considered off the wall by some people, but I think Tippy would be an excellent candidate for the honey treatment." Ms. Mosher looked puzzled until I showed her the veterinary articles and pictures of how honey was used to treat wounds and severe burns on dogs. Her interest instantly peaked when she saw those pictures. I went on to explain that honey was used in ancient times by the Egyptians and the Greeks to treat and heal wounds and honey is also being successfully used today in human medicine for certain skin conditions. Ms. Mosher asked how it worked, and I told her that honey is bactericidal, meaning that bacteria can't live in it, and that's a good thing. I also explained to her that the honey promoted healing by stimulating granulation (the process of filling in with scar tissue). She was now starting to really get excited! I cautioned her that she'd have to be very conscientious about applying the honey twice daily, and that it would be a sticky, messy job, but it could possibly work if she were willing to put forth the effort.

Ms. Mosher smiled and said, "I'm okay with that! No problem! I'm not working, so I can be with him all day long if I have to. I'd be more than willing to do that for my Tippy." Great! Ms. Mosher was given some final instructions, Tippy was placed on oral antibiotics, and now the work began.

Tippy was rechecked weekly for the first three weeks, then every two weeks thereafter. Ms. Mosher was very diligent with Tippy's honey treatments, and the results were evidence of her commitment. The healing that had taken place after three weeks of treatment was simply astounding! After seven weeks, the wounds were completely healed and barely visible. It was remarkable, almost unbelievable! Before and after photos, with dates, were taken, and served as proof of the dramatic healing that had taken place by simply using honey! Tippy was now happy and active again, and Ms. Mosher was elated. The honey treatment was a resounding triumph, and I was looking forward to using it again in the future, which I did, and it worked again. Heck, the honey treatment was, without question, a sweet success!

TRIFECTA PLUS ONE

Although the word *trifecta* is associated primarily with the sport of horse racing, it can also mean three grand events. Cinder may not have been a racehorse, nor were her events all that grand, but they were nonetheless notable because they all occurred within the first year and a half of her life.

Cinder was a very active red Siberian husky who loved the freedom and excitement of living in the country. She was, however, a little on the klutzy side, with a persona not unlike that of Inspector Clouseau. Essentially, she was a disaster waiting to happen, and it did.

It all started one summer day when Cinder was in hot pursuit of a rabbit. With reckless disregard for her own safety, she quickly dove under a lowboy trailer in an attempt to catch the prey. Her forehead forcefully struck the metal frame of the trailer, resulting in the tearing back of a large portion of her scalp from her skull. Her owner, Amy Easton, was shocked by what she saw and immediately rushed Cinder to the clinic. The clinic door swung open, and in romped Cinder, with her dislodged scalp waving in the air like a loose toupee tossed in the wind. Cinder didn't display any signs of pain though, in fact, she simply ran directly into the exam room and stood in front of the goody drawer, waiting for a treat. I grabbed the leash and said to her, "Sorry, Cinder my dear, but we've got to take you to surgery, put you back together, and make you pretty again, okay?" So down the hall we went, on our way to a major makeover.

The surgical reconstruction of the failure to duck debacle was, to say the least, very challenging. The point of impact was directly above her eyes. The scalp was peeled backward from that point, going between the ears, and extending to the back of her skull, where it still remained attached. There was only a thin membranous covering left on the skull to serve as an attachment base for the scalp sutures. Reattaching and stabilizing the scalp would prove to be an intricate task.

Numerous sutures were delicately placed from back to front, and the end result looked good. Cinder healed very nicely, all tissue survived, adhesion was good, and in two weeks post-op, she looked great.

Two months later, Amy called the clinic and, with a voice filled with panic and dread, said, "Cinder got her foot caught in a trap or something, and I think she's going to lose her foot. It really looks bad! I'll be in there in a few minutes."

We got all prepared for Cinder, and when she did arrive, she was transported directly into the surgery. Amy was right. It did look bad! The medial (inner) side of her left front paw was severely crushed and mangled and could not be salvaged. She did lose three digits plus the corresponding metacarpal bones. I was, however, able to save the fourth and fifth digits. She'd still have a paw, albeit half a paw. Cinder was placed on antibiotics and pain medications and eventually made a successful recovery. I will never cease to be amazed at how rapidly most animals recover and adapt to a major surgical procedure. Cinder acted as if having only half a paw was no big deal. Her indomitable spirit wasn't quenched, and she still retained her zest for life. Cinder was truly an inspiration to all who witnessed her courage, adaptability, determination, and perseverance.

The trifecta was to be completed several months later. Cinder's paw had totally healed, and since she didn't favor the leg at all, it appeared as if nothing had happened. However, Cinder was back to her ole klutzy self. The old saying, "The road to hell is paved with good intentions," was very apropos in this instance. A hole had been dug to serve as a receptacle for remnants of cut metal, shards of glass, and pieces of conduit and rebar that had accumulated around the ranch. The intent was to safely bury these items and prevent any potential injury to man or beast. The hole, with all its contents, hadn't yet been covered over with dirt. So when Cinder went running by, she of course fell in, and was instantly impaled and cut on her right side by the sharp metal and shards of glass. Amy immediately called the clinic and said that Cinder had, once again, gotten herself in trouble, and needed help. No kidding!

As usual, Cinder came bounding through the clinic door and made a beeline for the goody drawer. She was all happy and playful, seemingly oblivious to her massive wounds. Her right side looked like a jigsaw puzzle of lacerations and punctures, with hair, dirt, debris, and blood mixed within the traumatized tissue. I held her head in my hands and asked her, "Cinder, what in the world did you do this time?" She just looked back at me with those big innocent eyes and continued her incessant tail wagging. That was par for the course with Cinder. So off to surgery we went—again. It took three of us, myself and two assistants, over half an hour to irrigate, clean, disinfect, and complete the debridement of nonviable tissue, plus another hour of surgical reconstruction and placement of Penrose drains. Our primary concern was embedded contaminants and tissue necrosis (dying and decaying) due to compromised blood supply to certain areas.

When discharging Cinder the next day, I said, "Look, Cinder, I really like you, but we've got to stop meeting this way." That bit of advice basically went in one ear and out the other. She wouldn't leave the clinic until given another treat. The thought then occurred to me, "Who's being trained here? Me or Cinder?" It appeared to be moi! The Penrose drains were removed the following week, and the surgical site was examined. Miraculously, all the tissue was viable, healing was progressing nicely, and Cinder had once again dodged a bullet. This was now the third major incident for Cinder over the span of a few months, thus completing the trifecta. It's been said that things tend to happen in threes. Well, if that's true, then she shouldn't have much to worry about for a while.

No more than a month had passed before Cinder was in serious trouble again. Amy called and said, "I think Cinder has really done it this time. She can't stand, can't hold her head up, kind of rolls her eyes like she can't focus, and just lays there. I think she might have broken her neck." When Amy arrived at the clinic, we used a stretcher to transport Cinder from the car to the exam room. Cinder was lying very still and made a few feeble attempts to raise her head. I tried to get a history from Amy and discussed the possibility of poisonings and the need for blood analysis and x-rays. My initial examination revealed no significant abnormalities. Her respirations, mucous membrane color, temperature, pulse, heart rate, and blood analysis results were all essentially within the normal ranges. She didn't exhibit any signs of pain, but she did have delayed muscle reflexes, and her eyes were slow tracking. I was just about to take some x-rays of her neck and spinal column when suddenly she belched. The smell was foul and strongly resembled the odor of something undergoing fermentation. I asked Amy if Cinder could have possibly eaten some fermenting grain or fruit.

She thought for a moment and then said, "Well, Cinder will eat just about anything, and come to think of it, she's been eating a lot of mule poop lately. My neighbor rides his mules by here just about every day, and Cinder goes after that mule poop like it was candy or something. It's gross and disgusting! Could eating that stuff cause a problem?"

I told Amy that just about anything was possible with Cinder, but if the mules had been eating a sweet feed that contained grains and molasses—well, I couldn't totally eliminate that as a possibility. I decided to hospitalize Cinder for observation and told Amy that I'd give her a report in the morning. As I placed Cinder in the recovery cage for monitoring, she looked up at me, rolled her eyes, and once again made an uncoordinated, feeble attempt to raise her head, then loudly burped. Whew! It really did smell like something fermented.

As I entered the clinic the next morning, Cinder was right there, standing up, happy as usual, barking for food and attention and ready to go. No signs of illness or paralysis. Her coordination appeared to be normal, and her eyes were tracking normally as well. Her breath didn't seem to have that fermentation smell either. Could she have tied one on? I couldn't prove it, but all signs were sure pointing in that direction. When Cinder was sent home, I told Amy to keep Cinder away from the mule poop, even if it meant picking it all up, because that poop may have been the culprit. Cinder was kept away from the mule biscuits, and no more problems!

Cinder and her owners moved to Western Washington later that summer, and I lost contact with them. I'd often wondered how klutzy Cinder made it through life. Twenty years had passed, and by some act of providence, I met one of Amy's relatives. I asked the lady about Cinder, and she laughed as she recalled Cinder's accident-prone early years. She told me that Cinder lived to be almost sixteen years of age and, amazingly, never experienced another accident or serious injury after the move to the coast. That was great because the Trifecta plus one was enough to last a lifetime.

MURPHY

There are many reasons why dogs have been referred to as man's best friend. They are often loyal, devoted, faithful friends and trusted companions who grace us with unconditional love. They become part of us, and when they're no longer here, we can fondly recall those cherished memories that are forever etched in our hearts. Murphy was an unusual six-year-old Rottweiler. He was a lover, not a fighter, and he behaved more like a reincarnated lap dog. Instead of having the typical bulky, muscular physique that is usually associated with the Rottweiler breed, Murphy had a long, lean body, with super long legs that actually made him look more like a mini racehorse. He was a good boy who wasted no time zoning in on the treat drawer the moment he walked into the clinic. Murphy won me over, and I thoroughly enjoyed having him as a patient.

It was time for Murphy's annual physical exam and vaccinations, and when he walked into the exam room, I noticed him slightly favoring one of his front legs. He looked good physically—his coat was sleek and shiny, he had normal heart and lung sounds, and his ears, eyes, nose, and throat appeared normal as well. Jeff, Murphy's owner, had been feeding him top quality food because as Jeff put it, "He's my buddy, and he's worth it!" Jeff was a good and conscientious owner.

I asked Jeff if he'd noticed Murphy limping on his left front leg. Jeff said, "Yeah, he must've sprained it or something." He'd noticed Murphy limping off and on for the last couple of weeks but didn't think it was that big of a deal. He'd given Murphy an aspirin several times, and that seemed to help. He asked, "What do you think is going on, Doc?"

I told Jeff that there were a myriad of things that cause a dog to limp. As I began my examination of the leg, I detected a slight swelling on the distal (lower) end of Murphy's radius bone. The swelling was firm and mildly painful when palpated. I had a bad feeling about that swelling because osteosarcomas (bone cancer) often appear at that location on the long bones, especially with big dogs. I told Jeff that we needed to do an x-ray of Murphy's leg to see what was going on.

Jeff's facial expressions went from cordial to very concerned and serious as he asked, "You don't think its cancer do you, Doc?"

I told him that I couldn't tell for sure without taking an x-ray. I knew, however, that there was a 98 percent plus chance of it being an osteosarcoma because all the evidence, so far, was pointing in that direction. The x-rays showed an enlargement of the bone on the distal (lower) end of the radius with interruption of the cortex (outer layer) of the bone and secondary bone lysis (disintegration) along with areas of bone deposition. All these findings confirmed my suspicions that Murphy did indeed have bone cancer, and the prognosis was not favorable.

I reviewed the x-rays with Jeff, as Murphy was happily indulging in the treats he was getting from our vet assistant. I explained all the options available for treatment including chemotherapy, radiation treatments, pain management, amputation, and anti-inflammatory medications. Jeff was numb with shock and disbelief because sitting next to him was a dog that actually didn't appear sick.

He asked, "How much time does Murphy have?"

I told Jeff, "Murphy has about six to nine months, and even with amputation and chemotherapy, the best scenario wouldn't give him more than one to one and a half years." Jeff definitely needed some time to process the catastrophic situation he was now facing.

Several days later, Jeff told me that after a lot of soul searching, he'd come to a decision regarding Murphy. He'd elected to keep Murphy on pain medications only, allowing his buddy to live free of pain for as long as possible. Murphy was examined monthly for the next several months. The bone cancer had rapidly grown to the size of a small cantaloupe since first diagnosed six months earlier. Murphy was now unable to use the leg, his appetite had markedly decreased, he'd lost a tremendous amount of weight, and he had become very weak. Without question, his quality of life had drastically deteriorated. Murphy had fought the good fight, but the time had come to compassionately relieve him of all the discomfort and suffering. Jeff requested that Murphy be allowed to cross over at home, and I agreed because transporting Murphy twenty-five miles would be too stressful for him. Murphy had always liked coming to the vet clinic because he got treats from the cookie man, me.

As I entered Murphy's home, I could see him lying there on the sofa, completely stretched out from one end to the other. When he recognized me, his eyes lit up, and with a strong, determined will, he lifted his weak and frail body off the sofa and shuffled across the room on three legs to meet me, then collapsed. He'd given all he had to come see his ole friend, cookie man doc. I gave him a cookie that he had come to expect from me, but he only had the strength to take a couple bites. I told him that he'd been such a courageous boy and that I'd come to help him go to a place where he'd be free from all the pain and where he'd be all healthy again and could run and play all day. I gave him a big hug, and he licked my hand as I told him how much I would miss him.

I then gently and lovingly helped my friend, Murphy, cross over that rainbow bridge.

Perhaps the most difficult task for me to perform as a veterinarian was to put a patient down. I always knew, deep down inside, that I was relieving the pain and suffering and that it was, more than anything else, an act of compassion, but there was always an ache in my heart. God gave us these special friends and faithful four-footed companions for a reason—to help us more fully understand the meaning of unconditional love. They have, without a doubt, enriched our lives and will live in our hearts forever.

MOHAIR MANIA

Angora goats are a special breed of domestic goats that were introduced to the United States around 1850. The breed originated in Ankana (Angora), Turkey, and this particular breed of goat is renowned for its lustrous, soft hair fiber that's called mohair. They tend to be gentle, delicate animals and, as such, are often vulnerable to predators.

Janice, a previous employee, met and married a young dentist, and went on to assist her new husband in his profession. Although not directly involved with veterinary medicine anymore, she still retained her love of animals, all kinds of animals, including her angora goat named Reddi-Locks.

I'll never forget the day when Janice called the clinic and said that her goat had just been attacked by a dog and that the little goat's leg was severely injured. When Janice arrived at the clinic, Reddi-Locks was transported straightaway to the surgery room. The little thirty-pound goat was in a state of shock, and that life-threatening condition had to be immediately addressed before proceeding any further. Dog bite wounds can be very traumatic, but Reddi-Locks's injuries were the worst example of tissue trauma that I'd ever seen! A mangled mess! The injuries extended from the hoof to a level above her elbow and went completely around the leg. The skin was shredded, the muscles of the foreleg had been savagely torn to beyond recognition, and there was a high probability of blood vessel and nerve damage. The possibility of saving Reddi-Locks's leg appeared to be extremely remote, and the chance of her ever regaining use of the leg seemed very unlikely. Amputation looked to be the only viable option. Janice understood the gravity of the situation, but nevertheless pleadingly requested that I attempt to salvage the limb in spite of the unfavorable odds. I surveyed the mutilated appendage, knowing full well that Janice wouldn't change her mind, so I told her, "Janice, I'll give it my best shot. It doesn't look very promising, and a lot of things can go wrong, but maybe we'll get lucky."

Local anesthetics were administered to relieve the pain and discomfort because a general anesthetic would have been too risky, considering Reddi-Locks's compromised condition. Next began the arduous and time-consuming task of cleaning all the ground in dirt and embedded hair from the wound. Once that was accomplished, reconstruction was started. The muscles had been ripped, torn across, and mangled to such an extent that their identification was nearly impossible. My only recourse was to recall the normal anatomical structures and systematically approximate the muscle pieces according to their size and relative position. Basically, it was an educated guess! Sutures were used to reattach and stabilize the torn sections of muscle, and I did my best to identify and make the proper reconnections. The extent of nerve damage and impairment was difficult to assess. If there were to be any paralysis, it could be either temporary or permanent, depending upon the degree of damage, but only tincture of time would tell. Reconstruction of the macerated skin was the next challenge I faced. Some sections of skin were totally missing, gone, and some portions had to be removed because they were severely mangled and their viability was questionable.

Many sutures were needed to rebuild the skin, but eventually that too was completed, and Reddi-Locks looked like she had a leg again, or something that resembled a leg. Lastly, I bandaged the leg and fabricated a stabilizing splint for her leg and hoof. I modified the bottom of the splint in such a way as to place the hoof in a walking position, hoping to restrict movement while the tissue was healing and allow scar tissue to stabilize the carpal joint of the hoof. I cautioned Janice that due to potential nerve and muscle damage, Reddi-Locks would most likely never have tactile sensation to the leg, and she'd probably knuckle over at the carpus for the rest of her life. That would not be good, and if it reached that point, the leg would most definitely have to be amputated. I also told her that I was concerned about having adequate blood circulation to the reconstructed muscles and skin. Poor blood circulation would result in deterioration of the tissue, and that would necessitate removing the leg. There were a lot of variables, but we'd just have to wait and see, cross one bridge at a time.

Reddi-Locks had her bandages changed every few days for the next several weeks, and it was amazing how well the tissue was healing. The pink color of the skin was a good sign, and hair was even beginning to grow. Reddi-Locks was feeling much better overall too; in fact, her appetite was good, and she was even placing weight on the leg. There was also the incessant tapping of her splint on the floor that strangely sounded like a peg-legged pirate roaming about on the premises.

Four weeks had passed, and it was time to remove the splint. The big questions now were, would there be any paralysis from nerve damage, would she be able to normally place her hoof, or would she need a splint for the rest of her life? When the splint was removed, Reddi-Locks licked her hoof a couple times, and then promptly took off walking down the hallway of the clinic. She was placing her hoof normally, and there was only a slight limp. Wow!

Reddi-Locks steadily improved over the next few months. As her muscles regained their strength, she returned to her usual antics of running all around and jumping up on things. Reddi-Locks had defied the odds. I was totally amazed and thankful for her astounding recovery. So was Janice.

PROPHETIC WORDS

Fred Macumber was a Pearl Harbor survivor who had devoted his life to the service of his country. This proud man stood six feet, four inches tall and towered over his delicately petite wife, Lois, who was barely five feet and probably didn't weigh more than ninety pounds. Fred was always cheerful, spoke with a soft Texas drawl, and doted on his eight-year-old Shih-Tzu buddy named Ming.

It was always a pleasure visiting with Fred and Lois when they brought Ming to the clinic for exams and vaccinations. Seeing that tall, slim, happy-go-lucky Texan toting a spoiled little dog in his arms with a quiet, diminutive wife by his side would make almost anyone smile. It was quite the sight. Fred did all the talking, but Lois controlled the purse strings, and she knew it too. She was all business, and it didn't take long to figure out who governed that household. Lois may have been small, but inside that little frame was a dynamo.

Ming had been a healthy little guy, so the only time I'd see the Macumbers was when Ming was due for his annual routine checkup. Several years had passed, and the next time Fred brought Ming to the clinic, Lois was conspicuously absent. Fred was more subdued than usual, didn't smile as much as before, and Ming appeared more unkempt. I sensed that something wasn't right, and just as I started to examine Ming, Fred said, "You know, I lost my Lois." "Oh Fred" I replied, "I'm so very sorry to hear that. I know how much Lois meant to you."

Tears welled up in his eyes as he said, "It's really been hard. I miss her so much." He apologized for Ming looking so shabby, but I told him that it wasn't a big deal and that I understood. Losing a spouse can be very devastating, especially after spending so many years together. Fred had lost a soul mate and was overwhelmed with sadness and grief. It definitely showed. Ming had now become Fred's sole companion, and I was very concerned for both of them.

Six months had passed. It was on a Thursday when Fred called the clinic and told our receptionist that his little dog hadn't been eating for a while, was drinking a lot, vomiting, and now was just laying around, doing nothing. Ming was put on the daily schedule, and it wasn't long before Fred walked into the clinic, clutching Ming tightly in his arms. I was glad to see that he was accompanied by his eldest son, Mike. Ming appeared listless, depressed, dehydrated, and there was a very strong uremic odor to his breath. Ming's history and symptoms were very suggestive of kidney failure, and the outcome didn't look good for him. I needed to confirm my suspicions, so I drew some blood for analysis. The tests showed elevations of the BUN (blood urea nitrogen), potassium, and phosphorus levels, and he was also anemic. Those results were definite indicators that Ming was in the advanced stages of kidney failure. The prognosis was grave. I explained the results of the tests to Fred and his son, stressed the extreme severity of Ming's condition, and told them that Ming needed to be placed on IV fluids and other appropriate medications immediately.

Fred then said with fear and desperation in his voice, "Doc, don't let him die because if he does, I'll die too." I was stunned by what Fred had just said because I knew that Ming was in serious trouble and would very likely die regardless of all the treatments. I told Fred and Mike that I'd do my best to save Ming, but he was in the advanced stages of kidney shutdown, and his chances of survival weren't very good.

Ming died the next day, which was a Friday. Four days later, on Tuesday, as I was reading the morning newspaper, I glanced at the obituary column, and there it was. Fred Macumber, a Pearl Harbor survivor, had passed away. I was shocked! Fred's prophetic words came flooding over me. He told me he'd die, and he did! He had lost both of his soul mates, the two who had made his life meaningful, the two who had given him a reason to live. I truly believe that this gentle man had indeed died of a broken heart.

I asked myself many, many times if there was something more that I could have done, but there wasn't. I'd come to the realization that I couldn't save them all, no matter how hard I tried. One thing is certain, we should be deeply thankful for our soul mates and companions while they're still with us, and once they're gone, we need to hold them gently in our hearts, honor their memory, and love them forever.

LILY

Compassion is defined as concern for the sufferings and misfortunes of others. Not only should compassion be directed toward our fellow man but also toward our four-footed companions. Stray, abandoned, and neglected animals also deserve compassionate care. This humane need prompted us to establish a compassion fund that would help provide veterinary care for some of the unfortunate ones.

Lily was a two-year-old calico farm cat who, according to the owner, hadn't been using her right front leg for three weeks. He wanted her checked out but made it perfectly clear that he couldn't afford to spend any money on an ole barn cat. He said that he had a lot of cats around the place, but they'd usually disappear, either wander off or get eaten by the coyotes.

Lily was a beautiful calico cat and quietly purred as I stroked her head. Her right paw was flexed (curled backward) due to muscle contractions and lack of use of the leg. As I palpated the leg, movement and swelling could be detected at the midpoint of the humerus bone (upper forelimb bone). I told the owner that the cat's leg was broken, and x-rays needed to be taken to assess the extent of damage. The owner replied, "Forget that! I'll just take her home, and she'll have to learn to get around on three legs."

I told the owner that she'd be prime coyote bait, but he didn't seem that concerned. I didn't want to see the nice little cat end up that way, so I suggested the possibility of him relinquishing ownership of the cat to me. I'd then do the surgical repair of the leg and find her a good home where she'd be safe. The man mulled the idea over in his head for a few moments, then quickly signed the transfer of ownership papers and left. Lily was now legally mine, and when all fixed up, she'd at least have a chance to live a normal life.

The pre-surgical x-rays revealed a midshaft comminuted (many pieces) fracture of the humerus bone, and there were signs indicating that the body was attempting to heal the fractures but wasn't doing a very good job of it, because there was instability of the bone fragments. Lily was taken to surgery where I had to remove many of the unhealthy (nonviable) pieces of bone, freshen the ends of the remaining sections of bone, and reunite the bone fragments using stainless steel IM (intramedulary) pins and stainless steel circlage wires. It was a lengthy, detailed, often frustrating surgery, but in the end, I was satisfied with the outcome. Lily's leg would be permanently shorter, but she had moxie. She was a boldly determined little girl, and I was confident that she'd do just fine. Lily recovered from the surgery very nicely and was a pampered patient throughout her eight-week recovery period. When the IM pin was removed, she started walking on that leg almost immediately. We'd all become fond of her and knew that Lily had definitely found a good home—here with us as our PR clinic cat.

It wasn't long before Lily would hop up on the front counter and act as our unofficial greeter. She loved people and especially loved ladies leather purses. She'd dive right into a handbag and help herself to whatever struck her fancy. It was a riot watching her pull stuff out. Thankfully no one was offended. No doubt about it, she was a real charmer who even licked and groomed some of her most favorite people, especially Candace, our animal behavior consultant. Lily was amazing—a determined, often headstrong little girl, who learned how to compensate for her shorter front leg—and actually walked without a limp and jumped like a mini gazelle. Lily really was the little ray of sunshine that brightened our days and was a spoiled member of our staff for many years.

JOHN DEER

When I took the Veterinarian's Oath, I solemnly swore to use my scientific knowledge and skill to relieve animal suffering. The oath, in my opinion, lacked specifics and was therefore open to interpretation. The State Fish and Wildlife Department had, for whatever reason, authorized only a select few veterinarians to provide veterinary care for wildlife.

Unfortunately, I was not on their list. When presented with a severely injured fawn that the State authorities would have likely put down rather than treat, I found myself smack-dab in an ethical quandary. I asked myself, do I honor my veterinary oath, or do I go along with political correctness protocol? To me, life takes precedence over political correctness, so my decision was easy to make. I was willing to go against the rigid bureaucrats, take a risk, and save a life.

A lady entered the clinic, toting a medium-sized dog crate that contained a tiny twenty-pound fawn. It appeared amazingly calm, perhaps due to a combination of being overwhelmed with fear and the instinctive behavior of lying perfectly still when injured so as to avoid detection. The fawn had been found entangled in some thick brush near the lady's home. The young deer was most likely running through the brushy forested area and got its left front leg wedged in the V-shaped section of two diverging branches. When the front knee (carpus) got caught, the momentum of the fawn's body kept going forward, resulting in the knee being almost completely pulled apart. A small band of tendon was the only remaining structure of the knee joint. It was a no-brainer. The leg had to be amputated.

I anesthetized the fawn, amputated the leg at the level of the knee, and constructed a cushion of soft tissue over the remaining bones. The leg was then bandaged, and the little guy was done. I'd saved a life and had given the little deer a fighting chance. I felt good about that. The only thing left to do was to give the little guy a name. I started calling him John—you know, John Deere, like the tractors.

The next big question was, what do we do with him? Where could we place him so that he could recover safely and secretly? One of our veterinary assistants had relatives who lived in a wooded area about eighty miles north. They had a small barn and corral that wasn't being used, and I thought to myself, *that place would work perfectly*. Now, all we needed to do was to get their permission and cooperation. Contacts were made, and within a couple days, John was on the way to his new home.

As the months passed by, John healed and easily adapted to his new surroundings. He ran, jumped, and played like any other deer, only minus half of a front leg. We were told that he'd occasionally jump out of the corral, go frolic with the other wild deer in the area, then return home and jump back into his corral. John was thoroughly enjoying life again, and his case was a true "feel good" success story.

Today, whenever I see a green John Deere tractor or combine, I don't just see a farm implement, I think of John, the other John Deer, and visualize him running happy and free.

MERCEDES

Random acts of kindness and concern can restore one's faith in humanity and, in some instances, can even save a life. Such was the case of Mercedes.

Perhaps the last thing on a person's mind when pulling into a truck stop for gas is to become a hero of sorts. As fate would have it, while gassing up her car, this businesswoman saw a young calico cat drop out from the engine compartment of a Mercedes delivery truck that had just pulled up to an adjacent gas pump. The cat appeared dazed, and its face was covered with blood. Forsaking her own time schedule, this good Samaritan took the initiative to seek medical attention for the injured cat. She inquired at the checkout stand for the location of the nearest veterinarian, who just so happened to be me, and it wasn't long before she burst through the clinic door with the injured cat in hand. As the young cat was being rushed into the exam room, the benevolent stranger made a generous donation to help cover some of the treatment costs and promptly went on her way, never to be seen again.

The cat was unfortunately another fan belt victim. The entire end of her nose had been torn away, and was barely hanging on by a small strip of skin. She didn't respond to sounds, the pupils of her eyes were dilated, and her body movements were uncoordinated. She had experienced a major blow to the head and sustained a concussion as well. Instead of referring to her as simply "cat," we decided to give her an appropriate identity. So we named her after the make of the delivery truck, Mercedes. "Mercedes" was treated for shock and stabilized before attempting to repair her nose. Veterinary school prepares a person to handle many different medical conditions, but I never thought that I'd be called upon to reattach a nose. These were uncharted waters that I was entering, but I was more than willing to give it a go. I used very tiny sutures to reconstruct the nose, and when completed, it looked pretty good. The question now was, would the tissue survive, and would Mercedes' hearing and eyesight improve? Time would tell.

As the days and weeks passed, Mercedes' nose healed remarkably well, and it looked great, almost as if nothing had ever happened. Her coordination had improved, but her eyesight and hearing problems remained unchanged. My hope was that with tincture of time, there'd be some positive developments. Sandy and the rest of the staff would carry Mercedes with them throughout the clinic as much as possible, but we all realized that Mercedes needed a permanent home. It was decided to place Mercedes on Craig's List as a lovable special needs cat. A certain individual involved with a dog rescue program saw the listing and told us of her friend who operated a special needs cat rescue in the city of Ellensberg, about 170 miles away. It was essentially a cat ranch for disabled felines. That was the perfect place for Mercedes! We contacted the cat ranch and discussed Mercedes' case with the ranch director, and she agreed to accept her into their facility. They already had several deaf and blind cats at the ranch, so they were familiar with handling cats with those types of disabilities. Arrangements were made, and Mercedes was transported to her new home.

The owner of the special needs cat ranch was wonderful. She sent us periodic pictures of Mercedes and updates on her condition. As time passed, her hearing and eyesight did improve, and she was once again enjoying life. She fit in nicely, got along well with all the other cats, and eventually Mercedes became the queen of the household. We couldn't have been happier for Mercedes. It is definitely true—random acts of kindness can indeed save lives and bring joy.

SAMMY

Animals can teach us many things about life in general, but we must be observant and perceptive. Adaptability, resilience, and perseverance are several attributes that come to mind when I recall a little cat named Samantha ("Sammy"). Her indomitable spirit enabled her to rise above her disability to live a relatively normal, happy life.

Sammy was presented to the veterinary clinic with a horrendous ear mite infestation involving both ears. Ear mites can be very irritating to the patient because the little guys burrow down into the ear canal tissue and produce intense itching. The patients will respond by doing the obvious—they instinctively scratch and rub at their ears almost nonstop. This response further complicates the situation by introducing bacteria to the already irritated and inflamed tissue. In some advanced cases, the ear mites and infection can penetrate deeply into the middle and inner ear. Not a good situation, because the inner ear houses the cochlea and semicircular canals which act somewhat like a gyroscope to help regulate equilibrium and influence balance. When or if those structures are damaged, the effects are often irreversible. Unfortunately, such was the case with Sammy.

The owner had been battling the ear mite problem for quite a while, periodically using OTC (over the counter) ear mite preparations from discount stores. She hadn't seen much, if any, improvement. Her main concern at this point was the tremor-like head bobbing and equilibrium issues that the cat was experiencing. I explained the complexity of the situation and the distinct possibility that the inner ear could be permanently affected. That didn't go over very well with the owner! She emphatically said, "I've had enough! I'm not going to spend any more money on that cat, and I just want you to put the cat down." I told her, "I won't do that, but if the ownership of the cat was signed over to me, I would treat the cat and find it a good home." The lady signed the transfer of ownership papers without hesitation and was gone. I looked down at the sweet little bobble-headed cat, and said to her, "Sammy, you're mine now, so let's see what I can do for you, okay?"

The next day Sammy was placed under general anesthesia so that her ears could be painlessly cleaned and treated. Her ear mite infestation and ear infection resolved, but as expected, her equilibrium issues persisted. Sammy was destined to have balance challenges for the rest of her life, but I knew she'd make it because she impressed me as being a survivor, a real overcomer. The amazing thing about Sammy was that her disability bothered other animals more than it bothered her. She was essentially a normal cat who unfortunately possessed some major locomotion issues. When she would get excited or tried to chase and play with other animals, her head-wobbling and leg-flailing really intensified. Sometimes she'd actually lose her balance and fall over on her side, but she handled it like a pro. She'd collect herself and get right back up. Heck, she acted like it wasn't such a big deal, only a minor inconvenience. That resilient little charmer had a lot of chutzpah.

Sammy liked everybody, and she assumed that everybody liked her too and wanted to play. So it wasn't unusual to see her take off in her wild and unorthodox gallop toward some unsuspecting dog or cat. Her head would shake like some bobble-head doll, and her legs would gyrate in all directions. She may have thought that she was in control, but nobody else did. Most of the animals just froze, startled and bewildered at the sight of this whirling dervish coming kind of straight at them. Many couldn't process the weird sight and took off running in the opposite direction, but a few seemed amused by her unorthodox movements and let her approach, and some even played with her. You know, like the saying goes, "different strokes for different folks"!

It wasn't long before a client told his son and daughter-in-law about the sweet special needs cat at the vet clinic that needed to find a loving home. The young couple stopped by the clinic to take a look at Sammy and were instantly smitten with her. It was a perfect match in many ways. Sammy had found the home that she really needed and deserved.

Sammy is a real success story of a cat with a disability, who when given a chance, showed how she could adapt to and overcome her handicap. She continues to improve and now can even jump up on furniture and scold the birds outside the window. Sammy has brought love and joy to her new home, and she continues to be an inspiration to all who are fortunate enough to meet her.

ALTERNATIVES

The ancient healing art of acupressure and its use in veterinary medicine had been a subject of interest to me for many years. When the opportunity presented itself, I enrolled at an acupressure institute in Colorado to receive formal training. After completing the course, it didn't take long before I was presented with a case where I could apply my newly acquired skills.

A lady entered the clinic with a young black kitten cradled in her arms. She'd found the kitten lying in the middle of a secondary county road, unable to use its left hind leg. It was her compassion for animals that prompted her to rescue the little guy and get him to a veterinarian for medical treatment. She told Megan, our receptionist, that she was on her way to work and wasn't able to keep the cat but was willing to make a donation to our compassion fund. She then thanked us and went on her way.

Sitting there nonchalantly on the exam table was a black four-month-old kitten with big gold eyes, seemingly *under*whelmed by all that was taking place around him and showing absolutely no signs of pain or discomfort. The initial exam showed no evidence of any wounds, scrapes, bruises, or broken bones. The left hind leg, unfortunately, appeared to be paralyzed. The leg muscles were flaccid (limp) and unresponsive to the toe pinch-reflex test. The leg was non-weight bearing, the righting-reflex of the paw was absent, but the blood circulation to the leg appeared to be normal. X-rays confirmed that there were no vertebral or pelvic abnormalities. All the findings were pointing toward a major nerve injury, specifically the sciatic nerve and its branches. Such nerve injuries usually do not improve, and the affected limb remains permanently paralyzed and nonfunctional. The conventional treatment protocol for such injuries was amputation. I paused for a moment and was considering my limited treatment options, when Sandy, our office manager, interjected with a pivotal question, "Would that acupressure point therapy help in a case like this?"

I said, "Good question. Let's take a look." I quickly checked my references for any acupressure points that could benefit hind leg paralysis cases. Voila! There they were! I made diagrams of the specific point locations and proceeded to teach the vet assistants how to stimulate the designated points. I explained that this alternative therapy regime was definitely a long shot, and I needed to have everyone actively involved. The entire staff came on board, and we were now good to go.

The kitten, who we named Panther, was scheduled for acupressure point stimulation twice daily. Pinch-reflex test responses and righting-reflex responses were to be monitored and recorded daily as well. In addition, I placed Panther on a holistic oral supplement that stimulated the release of his own stem cells into his circulatory system to aid tissue repair. Panther thoroughly enjoyed his treatment sessions and all the attention. He thought the sessions were just a special time to play scratch and tickle. Two weeks of dedicated treatments had been completed without seeing any response whatsoever. Even though our efforts hadn't produced any positive results, we still remained committed to completing an entire month of treatments before reassessing the case.

When the pinch-reflex test was performed during the third week of treatment, Panther's toes moved ever so slightly, and his paw retracted a tiny bit. The spontaneous hoots and hollers of joy that erupted from the staff actually startled poor little Panther. He wasn't frightened for long because he was quickly smothered with petting and praises. Over the next two weeks, his responses to the pinch-reflex test continued to improve and get stronger, and by the seventh week, Panther was able to successfully place his paw and support weight. A week later, he was walking on the leg, and the following week, Panther astonished us all by running down the hallway, albeit with a limp. From that point on, it was "Katie bar the door." Panther's newfound confidence transformed him from a laid-back little guy into a thrill seeker who had to be up and on anything and everything. That was the not-so-subtle clue that Panther needed to find a permanent home. Since many people had been watching Panther's progress and were enamored with his "little engine that could" personality, it was an easy task to place him. In fact, within days, he'd found a loving home just six blocks from the clinic.

Panther was my first acupressure therapy patient, and I was very pleased with the outcome. I'd found that alternative therapies can afford viable options of treatment in veterinary medicine, and Panther was a prime example.

LITTLE WILLOW

The road of life can have many ups, downs, twists, and turns. Getting lost or sidetracked along the way can pose some very difficult challenges. Such was the case with a small Scottish Fold cat.

It was impossible to know where the cat's journey began. What is known is that the original owner named the cat "Heath" but couldn't care for it. She gave the cat to a young lady named Crystal, who lived in a small apartment and was financially strapped herself. Being unemployed, Crystal had to move back home to live with her parents. During the move, the cat somehow got away and disappeared. Crystal went back to the apartment several times and looked for Heath but couldn't find him. Three weeks later, a neighbor found the cat huddled in a stairwell. He had lost a lot of weight, was very frightened, and refused to eat. Crystal knew something was wrong and that Heath needed some medical help right away, so she called the clinic.

Crystal placed the thin, anorexic, and scared grey colored tabby cat on the examination table. The two-year-old cat was rather small, only about five pounds. As I raised its tail to insert the thermometer, I noticed that the plumbing was that of a female,

213

not a male. I said to Crystal, "Did you know that you have a female here?"

Crystal replied, "Really! We didn't ever see him come into heat, so we thought that he was a male. No wonder." She laughed sheepishly, and said, "Wow, that's weird." I told Crystal that we needed to give *her* a more feminine name, so we came up with "Willow".

Willow possessed the typical folded-over ears that are characteristic of the Scottish Fold breed. Her legs were shorter than most cats, and her joints were visibly swollen, deformed, and not very flexible when manipulated. Willow, unfortunately, had osteochondrodysplasia, a hereditary disease that is unique to Scottish Folds. The condition produces a severe crippling lameness early in life and, in time, progresses to a full-blown, painfully debilitating arthritis. Willow's life was destined to be an agonizing struggle.

Willow had many issues going on. I told Crystal that first of all, blood tests would be needed to assess the health state of Willow's internal organs, and testing for feline leukemia and feline immunodeficiency disease were also very important. Willow was severely dehydrated and would need to be placed on IV fluids, plus she'd need nutritional supplementation and pain medications for her arthritic joints. X-rays were also recommended to evaluate the heart, lungs, and internal organs for any abnormalities and tumors indicative of cancer. Poor Crystal was overwhelmed by what she'd heard. She told me that she liked the cat but was financially unable to do anything for Willow.

Then Crystal asked, "What should I do? Should I put her out of her misery? I don't want to see her suffer this way."

I told Crystal that Willow was an exceptional little girl with a sweet spirit, but regrettably she possessed a fragile little body. "Crystal," I said, "what do you think about the clinic becoming Willow's new permanent home? We would do all the testing and treatments, and if the test results were negative and if she responded to the treatments, then she could stay here. She'd live in a safe place, get lots of attention, get her daily treatments, and have all her needs met."

You could almost see the heavy burden of concern lift from Crystal's shoulders. Crystal smiled and said, "Yes. That would be good. Let's do that."

Willow was a good patient. She successfully made it through the initial testing and therapy and then became one of our clinic cats. She had her own quiet place, a soft therapeutic bed, and specially formulated food for arthritic conditions. She also received an array of medications, injections, and nutraceutical supplements to ease her arthritic pain. Willow responded really well! She gained weight, and there were times when she even felt good enough to play. She was finally enjoying life, and everyone loved her.

Two years had passed, and Willow had been living a sheltered life. Then she began to slowly lose weight, her appetite decreased, and she become less active. Her trips to the water bowl had also increased. Those patterns of behavior raised a red flag and prompted us to run some blood tests and take x-rays of her abdomen. Her BUN (blood urea nitrogen) and creatinine (a breakdown product formed in protein metabolism) levels were abnormally high, and the x-rays showed that her kidneys were enlarged. Not a good sign. An ultrasound was scheduled and performed, and it showed that her kidneys had many fluid-filled cysts—polycystic kidney disease was confirmed. It was a problem frequently encountered with the Scottish Fold breed. How can kidneys function this way? The answer, —- they can't!

The handwriting was on the wall, and it was just a matter of time. All efforts were used to make Willow as comfortable as possible throughout her final days, but the eventual outcome was inevitable. We had given little Willow as good a life as could have been expected, considering the circumstances. The courage and gentleness that she showed throughout her short life would forever be a source of inspiration to all who knew and loved her.

BARTERING

Bartering is an age-old process involving the exchange of goods and services without the use of money. It is an arbitrary transaction, and the items bartered can range from the ridiculous to the sublime. Our intent was to essentially hold the bartered item as collateral until the incurred veterinary bill was paid in full. Most of the items were returned to the owners, but there were occasions where the bartered items were never reclaimed. The scenario that usually existed involved an animal that needed veterinary care and an owner with very limited or no finances.

Over the years, we held radios of all makes and sizes, and occasionally a nice boom box was bartered. Most of the items were of excellent quality and worked well. We also received an assortment of power tools, wrenches, and socket sets—very useful things—but as expected, they were always reclaimed. One of the most unusual items bartered was an old saddle. It didn't look like much, but it was a prized possession to the owner. I thought that I'd be stuck with an old, dirty, smelly saddle, but the guy paid off his veterinary bill within two months and took off with his treasure—thank goodness.

It was always interesting to see what people offered as collateral to cover their bills. There were rings, wrist watches, and even car titles. One particular client, who just so happened to be an artist, asked me if I'd be willing to trade veterinary services for an oil painting of Mikey, our clinic cat. I told her, "Sure!" I'd known Mrs. Collins for many years, had seen her work, and it was very good. Several weeks had passed, and then one day, Mrs. Collins came walking into the clinic with a fourteen-by-sixteen-inch framed oil painting of Mikey in hand. Her face beamed with pride as I hung the painting on the hallway wall. She stepped back, cocked her head to one side, and suddenly her smile turned into a frown as she said, "There's something wrong with that painting. It just doesn't look right."

I took a closer look and said to Mrs. Collins, "Mikey doesn't have a nose."

"You're right!" she said. "I forgot to finish his nose. Heck, we can't have that. I'll just have to take him back home with me and give him a proper nose. How did I ever miss that?" Well, it wasn't long before she returned with the finished product. Mikey now had a nose. The painting looked complete and adorned the clinic hallway wall for many years to come.

· · · · · · · ·

We've all heard the old saying, "You can't judge a book by its cover." That adage perfectly applied to Ms. Tremble. Ms. Tremble was a new client who had two cats that needed to be checked over, wormed, vaccinated, and treated for fleas. She was a very imposing woman, tall, broad shouldered, ruddy weathered complexion, and wore a man's red and black plaid long-sleeved shirt. As she placed the cats on the exam table, she asked, "Would you be willing to trade services? I don't have much money." If there was ever such a thing as a female Paul Bunyan, she was it!

I didn't want to tick off this person, so I said, "Uh, sure. What do you have?"

"Canned goods and preserves," she replied. I told her that would be great, but honestly, I had some major reservations. She asked me how much I needed, and I told her that she could bring in as much as she thought was fair. She nodded approval and said that she'd bring the goods by the next day. I then continued to work on her cats and asked myself, *what have you gotten yourself into now?*

The following day, Ms. Tremble entered the clinic toting two huge cardboard boxes. She placed them on the exam table and said, "I hope this is enough." As she gently removed the contents of the boxes and placed them on the table, my eyes almost popped out of my head. There before me were jars and jars of the most beautiful and perfectly prepared fruits, vegetables, and preserves that I'd ever seen. Each container could have easily won top honors at any state fair in the country! The colors, the clarity, and the arrangement of the contents looked absolutely flawless! I was astounded! I complemented Ms. Tremble on her work and told her that these weren't just canned goods, they were works of art. She smiled and her rosy cheeks blushed a little. She was proud of her work and pleased that someone appreciated all her devoted and painstaking efforts. I'd learned a valuable lesson that day—never prejudge people and their abilities.

• • • • • • • •

The bartering process had proven to be fun, interesting, and profitable. It turned out to be a win-win situation for everyone involved, but most importantly, the animals received the medical care they needed.

CEDAR

The rising morning sun heralded the beginning of a new day of challenges and opportunities. A person had to be mentally and emotionally prepared for what lay ahead because the ensuing day could to be a roller coaster of events filled with triumphs and tragedies, but such is the life of a veterinarian.

Allergic reactions to certain foods and plants had been a lifelong battle for me. I'd experienced periodic episodes of severe skin irritation, inflammation, rashes, and itching. Dietary restrictions, oral medications, and nutritional supplements helped to moderate the problem, but acupuncture therapy was very helpful in providing relief. I'd made an appointment for an acupuncture treatment, and while sitting in the waiting room, I heard the muffled lonesome whines of a dog in the adjacent room. I got up from the chair and went to investigate what kind of dog was making those forlorn sounds. As I peered over the door gate, there he sat—a big, handsome, well-groomed golden retriever.

I looked down at him and said, "Hey, buddy, what's your name?"

At that very moment, the acupuncturist, Ms. Jessup, opened the door to the waiting room and walked over to the dog and said, "Cedar, you know better than that. Stop your whining."

I asked, "Is he your dog?"

Ms. Jessup responded, "Yes, he is, and he knows that he's supposed to be quiet. He's a very good boy most of the time, but once in a while, he gets a little lonesome."

Cedar was now standing up, wagging his tail, and had that happy-go-lucky smile look on his face. You could tell by the looks exchanged between Ms. Jessup and Cedar that there was a very strong bond between those two. I usually carried dog treats in my car, so I asked Ms. Jessup if I could give Cedar a few treats. She gave the okay. I ran to the car, grabbed a couple treats, and rushed back to a patiently waiting, enthusiastic Cedar. He chowed down the goodies, and now we were bosom buddies for life. He quickly became my shadow, accompanied me to the therapy room, and patiently sat by my side throughout the acupuncture session. That scenario was to be repeated many times over the next several months of treatments, and during that time, Cedar and I forged a strong friendship.

It was a warm Wednesday afternoon in June that I'd scheduled an appointment with Ms. Jessup for another acupuncture treatment. Cedar, of course, had to get his treat and be there with me during my session. Ms. Jessup had just finished inserting the acupuncture needles all over my body, and then she told me that Cedar needed to go for a short walk and that they'd only be gone a few minutes. She asked me if I'd mind being by myself. I told her, "Heck, I don't mind." Then off they went. I was just lying there, listening to the soothing music, when suddenly I heard the sharp screeching of tires, then a dull thud. I will never forget that sound! It wasn't the characteristic metallic sound one would expect from two cars colliding. It was more muffled. My immediate thoughts were that perhaps a pedestrian or someone on a bike got hit— or maybe a dog. Then I remembered that Cedar had gone on a walk—I hoped that it wasn't him—but I had that sick feeling in the pit of my stomach.

Suddenly Ms. Jessup came bolting into the treatment room. Her face was pale and she was visibly shaking. She started frantically pulling the acupuncture needles from my body, and with a trembling voice, she said, "Cedar just got hit by a car. He slipped out of his collar and ran out into the street. It happened so fast! I gotta go!" Then off she ran.

I immediately jumped off the table, tossed on my white T-shirt, and jetted out of the building, barefoot, and in my running shorts. There in the middle of a very busy four-lane street lay Cedar. The traffic had come to a standstill, and many of the onlookers appeared stunned and deeply concerned. I ran to Cedar, oblivious to the cars and moving traffic, got down on my knees next to Cedars's motionless body, and immediately started giving him CPR, and even attempted mouth-to-mouth resuscitation. He didn't look good. He was slipping away. I kept telling him to stay with me, but all my efforts were in vain. He wasn't breathing on his own, and I watched the pupils of his eyes slowly dilate and become fixed. As the pink color of his gums slowly turned ashen pale, I knew he was gone. It happened so fast! I tried, did the best I could, but wasn't able to save my buddy. I closed his eyes, stroked his head, and told him that I was so very sorry that I couldn't help him. I then lifted his lifeless body into my arms and carried him from that surreal scene. My T-shirt, hands, and face were covered with Cedar's blood, and I felt a numbing sense of loss. It all seemed like a cruel nightmare, and I just wanted to wake up and it would all be gone—but it wasn't. The day had started out so good, but it ended up being truly heart-wrenching.

Throughout the years, whenever I'd see a golden retriever, I'd be reminded of my very special friend, Cedar. We sure enjoyed each other's company, and one thing was certain, I was there with him at the end, and I even carried him home.

REGGIE

The anatomy classes in veterinary school demanded many hours of intense study and memorization. All that hard work and effort paid off, especially when confronted with cases involving severe traumatic wounds that left structures so terribly damaged that they were almost unrecognizable.

The man on the phone simply said that his dog had been shot in the leg, and he thought it needed to be checked out. When the Rottweiller-cross canine walked into the clinic, he was holding up his right hind leg. His owner appeared to be disgusted and inconvenienced with the whole situation and really didn't seem all that concerned. He actually thought that the wound would heal by itself, but his girlfriend convinced him to at least have it checked out. There was a large amount of dried blood on the leg, causing heavy matting of the medium length hair, obscuring the true extent of the injury. I told the owner, "Reggie needs to be placed under a general anesthetic so that the wound can be thoroughly cleaned, and treated without inflicting any more pain." The owner grudgingly consented.

Once the hair and the matted debris was shaved and removed, it was plain to see that Reggie had been shot most likely with a smaller caliber hollow-point bullet. There was a small point of entry hole on the back of his leg, midway between his knee and hip. It was obvious that Reggie had been somewhere where he shouldn't have been and was shot as he was running away. X-rays revealed no broken bones, the bulk of the bullet had exited, but there were remnants of the projectile dispersed throughout the muscle tissue. The bullet had miraculously missed the major arteries, veins, nerves, and the femur bone as well, but there was massive muscle damage as the bullet exited out the front of his thigh. Hollow-point bullets tend to mushroom out, tumble, and deviate upon entry. Such projectiles grab and rip tissue and produce huge exit wounds. Reggie had large hunks of disfigured quadriceps muscle protruding from the six-inch-wide hole in front of his leg. The quadriceps muscle is made up of four subdivision muscles, which control the extension of the knee (stifle). The torn, mangled, and severed muscles had to be identified and reattached to their corresponding members in order for Reggie to have any hope of walking or even running normally again. It was a long and tedious surgery, but when finished, I was confident that all the muscles had been correctly reunited. Reggie now had a very good chance of making a complete recovery, and he did just that.

It had all worked out well for Reggie. There was, however, one major fly in the ointment. We did not get paid for our services, not a red cent. Nothing. Zippo! The owner walked out on his bill. Flew the coop. Bailed out. Left the area. I would never see Reggie again, but I knew, deep down inside, that I'd done my best to help that dog, and my efforts had allowed him to once again walk and run free. I could live with that!

A MOVIE MADE THE
DIFFERENCE

I can't remember the name of the movie, but there was one particularly graphic scene that stuck in my mind. The movie was set in medieval England, around the 1400s, during the reign of King Arthur. There was a pregnant young maiden who'd been in labor for a very long time and, due to complications of childbirth, was nearing death. An old peasant midwife was summoned, but she arrived at the castle a moment too late. The young maiden had just drawn her last breath and died. The old woman entered the room, saw the dead maiden, and immediately yelled, "We must save the child!" Then, without a moment's hesitation, she grabbed a large knife and proceeded to perform the fastest and most crude caesarian section that I'd ever seen. She'd rescued a live infant from a lifeless mother. That was a shocking and very troubling scene to view, and one which I'd never forget. I often wondered how I would have responded if placed in a similar situation.

The owners of a very pregnant dachshund named Tilly had left on vacation and asked their neighbor, Karen, to care for and supervise Tilly in their absence. Karen called the clinic that fateful day and, with a voice filled with concern and trepidation, said, "I'm caring for my neighbor's pregnant dog, and she started pushing to have puppies a couple days ago, and now nothing is happening, she's just laying there, barely breathing, and I think she's dying." Kathleen, our receptionist, told Karen to get Tilly to the clinic as fast as possible because the dog was in serious trouble.

Karen arrived within a few minutes, entered the clinic carrying a lifeless, pregnant dachshund, and was speedily ushered to the surgery room. Tilly's pupils were fully dilated and fixed, there was no heartbeat, but her body was still warm. She had just died! At that very moment, I recalled the morbid movie scene from years past. I quickly grabbed a scalpel, made a swift incision down her swollen abdomen, exposed and elevated the enlarged uterus, made another incision, and proceeded to remove three seemingly lifeless puppies. I quickly handed the lifeless puppies one by one to the vet assistants, and within seconds the puppies were being resuscitated. Believe me, there is no sweeter sound than the first cries of a newborn.

Soon Sandy chimed out, "This one's starting to breathe!" Then the puppy cried. That really got everyone excited! It didn't take long before the puppy Vicky was working on started breathing too. The third puppy, however, didn't respond.

The two surviving puppies had to be hand-raised, but eventually they grew up to be very healthy, spoiled, little wiener dogs. It was truly rewarding to see them escape the grip of death and grow up to enjoy life. I'd often think about those puppies, how their lives were in such extreme peril, and that they were literally within seconds of dying. I needed to make a quick decision at a very critical moment, and oddly enough, the disturbing movie scene that was etched in my mind made the difference! Basically, each of us is the summation of our experiences, and those experiences can, and do, influence our behavior and actions, actions that someday might make the difference between life and death.

A WILD EXPERIENCE

The time had come for the vinyl flooring in the waiting room to be replaced. We'd looked at many samples and finally selected a nice commercial grade linoleum that promised to meet our needs. We didn't, however, anticipate that the new flooring would be so thoroughly tested the day after installation.

Mrs. Schaeffer had arrived a few minutes early for her 9:00 a.m. appointment, and was patiently sitting in the waiting room with her recently groomed little Pomeranian named Lady. Mrs. Schaeffer was an older German woman who was always punctual and fastidious about her home, her appearance, and her dog. The clinic door suddenly swung open wildly, and a 130-pound Nubian goat standing about thirty inches tall at the withers, came charging into the waiting room with its owner, Betty Jones, in tow on the end of the lead rope. She hadn't made an appointment and assumed that she could just walk in the front door with her goat. Mrs. Jones blurted out, "Can you take a look at my goat's bag? I think she has mastitis or something else going on down there. It feels warm."

Just as Donna, our receptionist, was telling Mrs. Jones that we couldn't examine a farm animal in the waiting room, but we could out back, the goat cut loose! It raised its tail, semi-squatted, and peed a lake! Urine flew all over the place, and then the goat pooped! After *totally* relieving itself, the goat started swinging around the waiting room on its lead, stepping in and kicking poop pellets soaked in urine everywhere.

Poor Mrs. Schaeffer. She sat there with goat pee and poop all over her ankles and shoes, a disgusted expression on her face, and a protective grip on little Lady. As Betty Jones and her goat were being ushered out the door and to the back of the clinic, Betty casually said, "I'll help clean up this place." I examined the goat out back of the clinic while some of the staff members attended to cleaning up the waiting room and Mrs. Schaeffer. As I was finishing up with the goat, Mrs. Jones nonchalantly said, "Oh, I left home so fast that I forgot my purse. Just send me a bill." She then loaded the goat into her pickup and took off. She'd left us with a waiting room full of goat feces and urine and a client who was almost in a state of shock after enduring the horrendous "voiding goat" experience.

Our new floor had been baptized, not by fire but by goat poop and pee. Thankfully, the weather was warm, because all doors and windows had to remain open for the remainder of the day, just to air out the clinic. We did manage to eventually get the waiting room clean, and the new flooring had withstood the test with flying colors.

NEVER A DULL MOMENT

Some jobs and professions can be dull, boring, and unfulfilling, but not veterinary medicine. If variety is supposed to be the spice of life, then veterinary medicine is a well-seasoned profession. Unusual cases, unexpected events and situations made life very interesting and challenging. There was never a dull moment because no two days were ever the same, and that was the new normal.

THE TAIL

The color of paint chosen for the clinic waiting room was called Navajo white. It was a pleasant off-white neutral color that went well with the wooden paneling and burnt orange–colored chairs. Sandy and I did the painting after hours on the weekend, and there was still a faint new-paint smell when we opened the clinic for business the following Monday.

A young lady called and scheduled an appointment to have her Russian wolfhound's tail checked. She said that the end of the dog's tail had gotten slammed in the door, and she'd managed to apply a bandage to stop the bleeding. Now, Russian wolfhounds are large dogs that possess long, skinny tails, and it was understandable how something like this could happen. As the lady entered the clinic, she proceeded to praise the dog for being such a good boy, and he responded by wildly wagging his long, thin tail. The centrifugal force generated from the vigorous tail wagging caused the bandage to immediately fly off, exposing the bloody tail, which instantly started to actively bleed again. The dog was, by nature, a happy, excitable guy, and the more the owner consoled him, the more he wagged his tail, and the more it bled. Blood was soon being flung everywhere throughout the room—on the floor, up the walls, and even across the ceiling. Our newly painted waiting room now looked like a macabre work of modern art.

The dog was quickly restrained, and the tail was examined. The tip of the tail had been extensively crushed and damaged. The only viable option of treatment in this case was amputation of the end of the tail. The surgical procedure took approximately thirty minutes to complete, but it took three people more than two hours to clean the blood-spattered waiting room. Thankfully, we used a paint that was capable of being washed.

THE LUCKY PUP

Angela, our receptionist, hung up the phone and promptly announced, "There's a guy coming in with his puppy that's just been attacked by an eagle." I'd never heard of anything like that happening in this area before, so maybe the owner was mistaken. Anyway, we'd find out shortly.

It wasn't long before the owner arrived at the clinic and was ushered into the exam room with a frightened twelve-week-old, sixteen-pound black Labrador retriever puppy cradled in his arms. I asked the owner if he was sure that it was an eagle that attacked his pup, and the owner responded, "Heck, yes, I'm sure! I saw it happen! The eagle tried to grab both pups, but as he tried to take off with a pup in each claw, the weight must have been too much for him, so he dropped this pup and flew off with the other one." As I examined the puppy, the talon marks were glaringly obvious on the puppy's sides. There was no doubt about it! Only a huge bird, like an eagle, could make puncture wounds like that.

The puppy was anesthetized, and his wounds were cleaned, treated, and sutured. Thankfully the talons had not penetrated the thoracic or abdominal cavities. The little guy was fortunate to be alive. He healed nicely, made a total recovery, and always kept a wary eye looking upward, ever vigilant for any danger that might be looming overhead.

A REAL SURVIVOR

A strong will to live is a powerful force that can literally determine whether an individual lives or dies. This phenomenon can be seen with animals as well as people, and witnessing its impact can be an amazing and often inspiring experience.

A little white eight-month-old miniature poodle named Alice had been sick for two days. According to the owners, Alice was vomiting, had bloody diarrhea, wasn't eating, and appeared weak. When the owners arrived at the clinic, they carried a prone, motionless Alice on a piece of plywood board into the first exam room. At first glance, she appeared totally lifeless, but then she made a feeble gasp. Alice was extremely weak. There was blood-tinged vomit stuck to the hair around her mouth. She was severely dehydrated, and watery foul-smelling bloody diarrhea was oozing from her rectum. She was in tough shape, and this definitely looked like a parvo virus case. She appeared to be on her way out, and in instances like this, euthanasia would have been considered an act of kindness. I was just about to recommend that option to the owners, but first I leaned over, patted her on the head and told her, "Alice, you gotta help me get you through this. Okay?"

As weak and sick as this dog was, she struggled to raise her little head and looked me straight in the eyes. That's all I needed to see! She may have been very close to death, but there was that undeniable "will to live" glint in her eyes. I told the staff, "Let's go for it. This little lady has a chance. She wants to live!" Everyone jumped into action. It was a real team effort. Blood was drawn for tests, IVs were placed, and life-saving fluids flowed into her veins. Antibiotics and gastrointestinal sedatives and protectants were also given while other staff members cleaned up Alice's soiled little body. The tests confirmed that Alice did indeed have parvo, a severe hemorrhagic enteritis condition where the parvo virus attacks and destroys the mucosal lining of the intestinal tract. It is a very serious disease, which often results in death.

Alice's response to the treatment was utterly amazing! Within hours, she was sitting up and wagging her little stump of a tail. She continued to receive IV fluid therapy for the next twenty-four hours, and the following day, she was discharged with specific medications and instructions. Alice's complete recovery was a testament to her strong will to live, and she proved that little miniature poodles can be pretty tough customers. Alice was, without a doubt, a real survivor.

A COMMON BOND

A good Samaritan brought two recently orphaned white shorthair kittens to the clinic, hoping that we could find them good homes. The mother cat had been hit by a car and died, leaving the kittens to fend for themselves. Since that time, they had sought refuge under the lady's deck. These two bright-eyed, frightened little orphans needed some help, and I reassured the lady that we'd take the kittens and do our best to place them in loving homes. She smiled, thanked us, and went on her way.

The first order of business was to give these eight-week-old kittens a thorough physical exam, then deworm and vaccinate them. These little tykes appeared well fed, thanks to the concerned lady, and they were also free of ear mites and fleas. So far, so good. Their eyes were clear, their temperatures were within normal limits, and they had normal lung sounds, but the tiny female had a very distinct heart murmur. It was congenital, and most likely a mitral valve or septal defect. There was an outside chance for some improvement with tincture of time, but that possibility was highly unlikely. The bottom line was that this little girl would need special care, including a heart healthy diet, heart medications, and supervised activity. She could, however, live an essentially normal life, but in all likelihood, her lifespan would be shortened. It would certainly be a challenge to find a suitable home for a kitten that was clearly behind the eight ball. It didn't take long for the staff to come up with names for the duo. The little boy was named "Marshmellow", and the tiny girl was given the fitting name "Cotton". We monitored the kittens' health for two weeks before attempting to find them homes. When we put them up for adoption, Marshmellow found a home at the drop of a hat, but poor, sweet, little Cotton—no one seemed to want a defective kitten.

I actually forget who came up with the Craig's List idea, but it was decided to place Cotton on Craig's List, clearly stating, so as to eliminate any misunderstandings, that the kitten had a congenital heart condition and needed special care. Within thirty minutes after making the posting, a lady called and asked if Cotton was still available for adoption. Sandy told the caller that Cotton hadn't yet been adopted. The caller went on to say, "Oh good! My sixteen-year-old daughter, Sara, saw Cotton's posting and immediately wanted her. You see, our daughter, Sara, also has a congenital heart defect. When she read the posting, her eyes lit up, and she told me that she felt a common bond with Cotton—kind of a special, shared identity with the kitten. We'd sure like to adopt Cotton."

Sandy asked the caller a few more questions and then told her, "Sounds like Cotton has found herself the perfect home."

Sara and her mother were at the clinic bright and early the next day. It was truly heartwarming to see Sara embrace little Cotton. They really were kindred spirits. I couldn't have imagined a better outcome for Cotton, and I was also happy for Sara. As the ole saying goes, "Ain't it great when a plan comes together."

OVERSEXED CAT?

Seeing an animal for a second opinion was always an interesting and often delicate situation. The owners and their animals were clients and patients at other veterinary clinics or hospitals, and for whatever reason, the patient wasn't improving as expected. The owners had become increasingly frustrated at the lack of progress being made, and either questioned the original diagnosis or simply needed reassurance that the diagnosis was correct and to stay on the course of treatment as prescribed.

Irma Walters, an eighty-year-old widow from a nearby town, had made an appointment to get a second opinion concerning a problem that her two-year-old cat, Susie, was experiencing. Irma was on time for her appointment, and this very spry, white-haired, diminutive senior plopped the overweight gray tabby domestic shorthair cat on the exam table.

"Hi there, Susie. What seems to be your problem?" I asked.

Irma abruptly chimed in, "She's oversexed! That's what the other vet said, just oversexed!"

That statement caught me a little off guard. I'd never heard that one before, and I spontaneously blurted out, "Oversexed?"

"Yup, that's what he said," Irma retorted.

I immediately looked at Susie's medical records, and it stated right there in black and white that she was spayed.

So I asked Irma, "It says on her records that she was spayed at six months of age. Is that right?"

Irma replied, "Yes, but she still comes into heat, cries out with a strange sound, rolls all over the place, and raises her hind end up in the air. I took her back to the vet and asked him if he took everything out. He said that he did, but when I asked him why was she still coming back into heat, he just said that the cat was oversexed! So that's why I'm here, to get a second opinion, because that just didn't sound right to me."

That didn't sound right to me either. "Mrs. Walters," I said, "sometimes, if a tiny bit of ovary were missed or retained during the surgical procedure, then that very small piece of ovary would be sufficient reproductive tissue to generate enough estrogen hormone to cause the cat to come into heat. If that is the case with Susie, then it could be very difficult to find that minuscule piece of tissue in her abdomen, especially now that she has put on some extra pounds and has a lot of fat on the inside."

Irma responded, "Well, we've got to do something for the poor girl. She can't go on like this. It's hard on her, and me too."

I told Irma that I would schedule Susie for an exploratory surgery, and hopefully I'd find some retained ovarian tissue, remove it, and then the problem would be resolved.

The day for Susie's surgery had arrived, and she was anesthetized, shaved, and prepped for the exploratory laparotomy surgical procedure. Susie was a pudgy little girl, and I knew that finding a remnant of ovarian tissue hiding in all that abdominal fat would be like finding a needle in a haystack. I made a longer incision in order to gain more exposure for the ensuing "treasure hunt." Wow! She had more than her share of fat in the abdominal cavity. The good thing was that her fat was whiter in color, which is usually the case with younger individuals. The whiter color would allow more contrast of any retained tissue. Nothing was found on the left side. However, on the right side, deep in the abdominal cavity, nestled within the white abdominal fat in the vicinity of where a normal ovary would be found, there was a small pink piece of tissue, about the size of the head of a stick pin, about 1 mm in diameter. That's what I was looking for! I excised the tissue and felt confident that I'd found and removed the culprit. I then put Susie back together, and she recovered beautifully. The specimen was sent to the histology lab for microscopic identification, and several days later the lab report confirmed that it was indeed ovarian tissue, and that it had been completely excised.

I called Irma and when I told her the results of the lab report, she said, "That's good news! I knew there had to be something causing the problem and that there was more to it than just being oversexed."

Susie was Irma's lap cat, who remained portly, and never went into heat again. Oh yeah, the neighborhood tom cats stopped visiting her too. It was a real success story and truly a big relief for both Irma and Susie.

EXTREME FACIAL MAKEOVER

Andrea Kramer was a consummate librarian at a large high school in a nearby city. This highly intelligent lady had a deep passion for cats and took it upon herself to help any homeless cat that ventured her way. Andrea lived in an area of town that had more than its share of traffic, so it wasn't a surprise when she called about a cat that had just been hit by a car. But at midnight!

It had been a busy, but productive day at the veterinary clinic. What I really needed now was a nice quiet evening at home and a good night's sleep. It was about eleven thirty that night when the phone rang and roused me from my deep sleep. My first thought was, *Oh no. An emergency! Maybe it's a wrong number. I sure hope so.* I answered the phone with, "Dr. Roloff here." That's as far as I got before the caller interjected, "I'm sorry for calling you at home at this time of night. Thank you for picking up. This is Andrea. Gretel just got hit by a car! She looks bad! I don't think she'll make it till morning. Can I bring her in…now?"

I told Andrea to get Gretel in the car, and I'd meet them at the clinic. I got up, dressed, grabbed a quick cup of coffee, and drove to the clinic with the car windows down to help clear the cobwebs. It was about midnight when Andrea pulled up and walked through the clinic door with a severely injured cat, Gretel, held gently in her arms.

Gretel, a petite, black domestic shorthair, one of Andrea's personal favorites, looked to be in pretty tough shape and barely hanging on to life. Gretel had to be given IV medications immediately to counteract shock, and once stabilized, she could then be evaluated more thoroughly. Poor little Gretel's head was all messed up! She was struggling to breathe, and her face was physically distorted. Her right eye was protruding from the eye socket, and the pupil of her left eye was pinpoint, very constricted, suggesting a concussion. Gretel's lower jaw was misaligned and unstable, likely fractured, and her hard palate (roof of the mouth) was split wide open, approximately 1 cm, providing a clear view directly inside her nasal cavity.

Andrea asked, "Can you save her? Please say yes! She's such a good girl."

"It doesn't look good!" I told Andrea. "For starters, Gretel has a concussion, and she'll be blind in her right eye because the optic nerve was damaged beyond repair when the eye was prolapsed (displaced from the socket). I'll try to replace the eye into the socket for esthetic purposes, but I can't guarantee anything. Her lower jaw is fractured at its midpoint, needs to be repositioned and stabilized with stainless steel surgical wire, and the gaping split of her hard palate needs to be sutured closed." I went on to tell Andrea I was quite concerned about Gretel having inhaled blood from the traumatized hard palate, and there was a distinct possibility of her developing pneumonia. Not a good thing!

Gretel was a surgical risk, but I had no recourse. Reconstructing the separated palate would be challenging, but I thought I could successfully pull it off. Gretel was anesthetized, blood was suctioned from her mouth and throat, and she was then intubated. Positioning her head at the correct angle was critical in providing the best exposure to that tiny space. There wasn't a lot of room available to work, but in time, the delicate procedure was completed, and the split roof of her mouth was closed and reunited. Next, Gretel's head was x-rayed to check for bone fractures, and her lower jaw (mandible) was the only fracture seen. The symphysis (the center union point of the right and left sides of the lower jaw bone) was broken and very unstable. Stainless steel surgical wire was used to realign and stabilize the jaw bone. Now she'd be able to eat. The final procedure involved replacing her protruding (prolapsed) right eye to its normal position. A canthotomy (incision at the outer corner of the eyelids) was made to create more space for ease of reducing (replacing) the prolapsed eye. The procedure was successful, but the eye would be blind because of the damage to the optic nerve. The only thing left to do was to clean and treat the superficial scrapes and minor cuts. I was done! Gretel was now back together, and she looked a whole lot better! Gretel was a good patient and fortunate too, because Andrea gave her excellent home care following all that reconstructive surgery. The roof of her mouth and jaw healed nicely, and the right eye, although blind, looked essentially normal.

Gretel had an unconquerable spirit and was a very lucky little girl. She was blessed to have a loving owner like Andrea who was willing to do what was necessary to save her. Gretel had learned a valuable lesson about busy streets, was graced out, and went on to live a long and pampered life. You couldn't hope for anything better than that!

ABOUT - FACE

Preconceived notions can deprive an individual from experiencing some very enriching relationships. Such was the case with Fred Limpkin, a retired Air Force veteran. For some unknown reason, Fred disliked cats, but he loved his dogs and doted over his twenty-four-year-old Pekinese named Ming until she passed on. Now, for the first time in many years, Fred was without an animal companion.

Fred's son, Mark, had recently graduated from college and accepted a job on the East Coast. The cross-country move was a great career opportunity for Mark, but he couldn't take his big ebony-colored cat, "Blackjack", along with him right away. So Mark reluctantly asked his dad to care for Blackjack for a few months, knowing full well that Fred hated cats. Fred wasn't too keen about the idea but eventually gave in. He did, however, set down some ground rules that included the cat staying out of his way! Blackjack quickly settled into his new digs and seemed to take a particular liking to Fred. He started following Fred around the house like some groupie idolizing a rock star. Wherever Fred would go, Blackjack was close behind. When Fred sat down in his favorite chair, the cat tried to join him, only to be quickly and sternly rebuffed. Those two were the epitome of the odd couple, yet Blackjack's fondness for Fred never faltered. Gradually, Fred became more tolerant of the cat's incessant need for contact and eventually conceded and began gently stroking the big black cat that had finally made it onto his lap. Blackjack knew what he wanted and sensed that in time, persistence would pay off—and it did.

A bond between those two gradually developed and strengthened over the next few months. Fred had come to enjoy Blackjack's company and even accompanied him to the vet clinic for exams and vaccinations. On one particular visit, Fred told me, "Ya know, Doc, here I am, almost seventy years old, and this is my first cat. I never knew what good friends they could be. But this guy is really somthin' special." He gently patted the big ebony cat several times, smiled contentedly, thoroughly smitten with the cat. He went on to say, with a certain tone of regret in his voice, "And to think that I used to hate cats. I sure missed out on a lot for all those years."

I reassured Fred, "Hey, better late than never."

It was a bit of a tense situation when Mark came back to visit and retrieve his black cat. Fred had become quite attached to Blackjack and wasn't about to relinquish his buddy. Mark saw the tight bond that'd been forged between those two and wisely chose not to rock the boat, and let them remain together. It was truly uplifting to witness the joy that Fred and Blackjack brought to each other.

As the years passed, both aged gracefully, but then Fred, unfortunately, was diagnosed with having terminal cancer. During those ensuing months of illness, Blackjack never left Fred's side and was a constant source of comfort and companionship through the hard times. Then one day, Mrs. Limpkin phoned the clinic and said that Blackjack, now sixteen years old, was vomiting and not eating. An appointment was scheduled, and when the time had arrived, a pale, feeble, very sick old man came shuffling through the front door of the clinic, with a black cat gently cradled in his arms. Fred, as ill as he was, was not about to abandon his buddy in time of need. One quick glance at this man, and it was glaringly apparent that he didn't have much time left on this earth! Blackjack was thin, weak, listless, dehydrated, vomiting, anorexic, and had that strong, foul, ketone odor on his breath— all signs associated with kidney failure! Blood tests were needed for confirmation, and the results left no doubt whatsoever— Blackjack indeed was in the final stages of kidney failure, and he wasn't going to live much longer. I spoke to Mrs. Limpkin in another room and delivered the bad news. She asked, "Can you keep him going a week or two? I don't want him to die before Fred does. He really needs that cat." I assured Mrs. Limpkin that I'd do my best to keep Blackjack alive and comfortable for as long as possible, and I did. Blackjack was placed on IV fluids initially, given subcutaneous fluids and special nutritional supplementation daily, and also received medications to calm the nausea and vomiting. His condition stabilized, he was relatively comfortable and wasn't suffering. We'd achieved our goal.

Fred died the following week with Blackjack by his side, and Blackjack departed to be with Fred just a few days later. That ebony-colored cat had changed Fred's attitude about cats from downright distain to absolute affection. He'd undergone an amazing about-face. Blackjack enabled Fred to experience the joy, comfort, and companionship of a loving cat, and those two remained faithful friends and buddies to the very end.

A TRIPLE WHAMMY

We've all heard the expression "Things happen in threes," and most of us have experienced this uncanny phenomenon. Is it just a coincidence, or is it some kind of self-fulfilling prophecy? We'll never know, but one thing is sure: it does happen.

Mandy Ann was one of the happiest dogs I'd ever seen. Nothing seemed to ever bother this ten-year-old Springer Spaniel. She was unflappable and had that Alfred E. Newman philosophy of life, "What? Me worry?" She loved to come to the vet clinic because she knew she'd get goodies from the "treat man," me. I'll admit that maybe I'd give her a few extra treats during her clinic visits, but hey, we were having fun, and I enjoyed spoiling her, just a little bit.

Mandy Ann's owner, Karen Jones, had become concerned about a bulge that was growing on the inside of Mandy Ann's lower right eyelid, and she wanted it checked out. When Mandy Ann arrived at the clinic, she ran straight into the exam room and promptly sat directly in front of *her* treat drawer. She wasn't bothered by the fact that another dog was on the table, and I was in the middle of an examination. Karen sternly yelled out from the waiting room, "Mandy Ann, you come back here right now!

It isn't your turn yet." Mandy Ann reluctantly obeyed her owner's command and left the room.

Finally, it was Mandy Ann's turn, and she jumped onto the lift table, anticipating the ride upward to my eye level. Her problem was staring me right in the face—a large growth on the inside of her lower right eyelid, causing the eyelid to evert. The growth was firm, non-pigmented, and had been growing pretty fast, according to the owner. Not good, because cancerous growths usually grow quite rapidly. I told Karen my concerns and scheduled Mandy Ann for surgery ASAP.

The surgery went well, and when Mandy Ann awoke from the anesthesia, she pranced out the clinic door as if nothing had happened. What a trooper! I sent the tumor to the histopathology lab for analysis and was not surprised by the report. It was diagnosed as an amelanotic melanoma of the conjunctiva of the eyelid. The prognosis was considered guarded, but the one bit of good news was that the tumor had been completely excised and hopefully hadn't yet metastasized to the lymph nodes. Time would tell. Mandy Ann healed well, and there were no complications.

About six months later, Karen called the clinic and said, "Mandy Ann has been having some trouble eating, and moves her tongue around in a funny way. I opened her mouth, and it looks like there is something growing under her tongue." Once again, Mandy Ann came bounding into the clinic as if she didn't have a care in the world. Upon opening her mouth, I could see a tumor about the size of a large egg growing on the right side of her tongue, and it was pushing her tongue to the left. The tumor definitely had to be removed, but that also meant removing part of her tongue in the process. The tongue is a very vascular structure, and controlling the hemorrhage during surgery would undoubtedly be a challenge. Mandy Ann was scheduled for surgery, and once again, she was an ideal patient. The surgical procedure went well. The amount of blood loss was marginal, but about one quarter of her tongue had to be removed. The histology report stated that the tumor was a squamous cell carcinoma, a potentially aggressive cancer that tends to invade the lymphatics and metastasizes to the lymph nodes. But the good news was that I'd had gotten it all out, even though the margins were small. Mandy Ann had once again dodged a bullet. That was her second major cancer surgery, and hopefully the last.

A year had passed, Mandy Ann's tongue had healed nicely and was functioning well, even with a good sized divot on the right side, and her lower right eyelid looked as good as new with no regrowth of the tumor. However, *now*, Mandy Ann's *left* upper eyelid was swollen. At first, Karen thought it was a mosquito bite and surmised that she'd just wait for it to go away, but it never did. When I examined the swelling, it felt hard and appeared to be growing *within* the eyelid itself. This was Mandy Ann's *third* tumor within a relatively short period of time. The tumorous growth could not be easily accessed from the underside of the eyelid, only from the top, outer surface. The problem with removing the tumor from the outer surface of the eyelid was the potential for cutting or damaging critical nerves to the eyelid itself. If that were to happen, she could end up with a permanently drooping upper eyelid. I consulted with eye and surgical specialists, and they weren't very encouraging. I told Karen the bad news, and she asked, "Would you do the surgery? That's okay if she has a droopy eyelid. I just don't want to do nothing and watch her suffer."

I took a deep breath and said, "All right. I'll do the surgery, but please understand that the outcome might be less than desired."

Karen responded, "Oh, Doc, I understand. I'm just glad that you're willing to do it."

The surgery day for Mandy Ann had arrived. She was anesthetized, prepped, and positioned. It was a long, tedious, and delicate surgery. The tumor was firmly embedded within the tissue of the upper eyelid and had to be painstakingly dissected free. Once removed, it was a tricky procedure to reconstruct the eyelid and close the empty cavity created by the tumor's absence, but eventually I got it done. When Mandy Ann awoke, she was her old happy self, but with a swollen, bruised, and droopy eyelid. The histology report confirmed my suspicions. It was another amelanotic melanoma, and it had been completely excised. That was really good news!

Mandy Ann made a successful recovery, and in time, as the swelling subsided, the eyelid still drooped, but much less than expected. In fact, she held the eyelid three quarters of the way open most of the time, kind of a modified wink. Karen was pleased. Mandy Ann went on to live many happy, tumor-free years. She'd beaten three malignant tumor episodes within a relatively short period of time and had none thereafter. So there just might be something to that ole saying that, "Things happen in threes" or perhaps it could be said that "the third time's the charm."

GETTING STONED!

Bob Dylan's songs and lyrics about getting stoned referred to laying back, chilling out, getting high, and having a good time. To my patients, getting stones or stoned meant that they couldn't pee, and it wasn't fun! It was a painful and potentially life-threatening experience for them.

Bladder stones, also referred to as uroliths or calculi, are solid masses or concretions of minerals—usually calcium, magnesium, or urates. They tend to form in the urinary bladder following a bacterial infection in the urinary tract. The bladder stones can vary in size, shape, and color, depending upon their mineral content, and the number of stones present can also range from just a single stone to many of different sizes. Smaller ones, about the size of a BB or smaller, often pass easily, especially with females, because they have larger plumbing. The bigger stones, however, usually restrict or totally obstruct urine flow, and that could lead to a life-threatening situation. In most cases, surgical intervention with the removal of the bladder stones is the only viable solution to the problem.

" COCO "

Melanie, our receptionist, answered the phone, talked briefly to the caller, then turned to me and said, "You need to talk to this lady, Doc. She wants you to give antibiotics for her dog's bladder infection but doesn't want the dog examined. We've never seen animals for this person. She's new to the area."

I took the phone, introduced myself, and asked, "What seems to be the problem with your dog?"

The caller, Ms. Myrna Krume, sternly replied, "My dog has a bladder or urine infection and is leaking urine all the time! I've seen this before because I've raised a lot of dogs. All she needs is some antibiotics."

I told Ms. Krume, "Your dog really needs to be examined because there are other conditions, in addition to bacterial infections that can cause your dog to leak urine. She could have bladder stones, tumors, or even a hormone imbalance problem. I can't just hand out antibiotics indiscriminately."

Ms. Krume was not particularly happy and told me that her other vet would have given her the antibiotics. I responded by telling Ms. Krume that I was *not* her other vet and that I wouldn't compromise! Ms. Krume mumbled a few unintelligible words but then reluctantly made an appointment for the dog to be seen.

Ms. Krume was on time for the appointment and plopped the miniature poodle, named Coco, on the exam table. Coco was a sweet, but timid, chocolate-colored little girl. As I palpated (felt) her urinary bladder, I detected a large, solid structure that seemed to occupy the entire bladder. I told Ms. Krume that I suspected a large urolith was causing the problem, and I needed to take an x-ray for confirmation and also check for any smaller stones. Ms. Krume looked at me with a skeptical expression, told me that she'd never heard of such a thing in dogs, but eventually gave her consent—grudgingly. Coco was a good patient and lay quietly while the x-ray was taken. The developed x-ray revealed a *huge*, solitary bladder stone about the size of an extra, extra large egg.

It literally took up all the interior space of the urinary bladder, leaving absolutely no room for the urine to accumulate. The urine essentially flowed around the gigantic stone, and leaked out. No wonder Coco was leaking urine almost constantly. It couldn't be held in the bladder—no room! I showed the x-ray to Ms. Krume, who wasn't overly impressed and told her that Coco needed to have the urolith surgically removed immediately. Ms. Krume once again mumbled a few words under her breath but finally conceded that the surgery was necessary.

The surgery went well. An abdominal incision was made, the urinary bladder was then incised, and the humongous bladder stone was successfully removed. Coco was put back together, recovered nicely, and was maintained on IV fluids and antibiotics for the next twenty-four hours. All systems were working as they should, and amazingly, Coco wasn't dribbling urine anymore! Wow! Go figure! I showed the huge bladder stone, which incidentally had conformed to the exact shape of the bladder, to Ms. Krume, but she was *under*whelmed and didn't say a word.

That would be the first and the last time I'd ever see Ms. Krume and Coco. For whatever reason, Ms. Krume never returned. One thing to feel good about was the fact that I'd relieved the pain and suffering of a sweet and very forgiving little dog, made her much more comfortable, and essentially saved her life.

" ABBY "

Christmas Eve is a special time for getting together with family and friends, attending church services, and phoning loved ones with season's greetings. It was 7:30 p.m. on one particular Christmas Eve when the telephone rang. Sandy quickly grabbed the phone, anticipating a call from our son. It wasn't him. I was Jerry Pratter.

"I'm sorry for calling you on Christmas Eve, but I don't know what else to do. It's "Abby", She's very sick and really weak. I don't think she's going to make it. Could you please take a look at her?"

Sandy handed me the phone and said, "We've got an emergency!" My heart sunk. All my plans for the evening went right out the window. A patient and her owner desperately needed help, and that took precedence! I dropped what I was doing and told Jerry to bring Abby to the clinic right away.

Sandy and I rushed to the vet clinic and began preparing for the emergency. A few minutes later, Mr. Pratter entered the clinic clutching a limp, seemingly lifeless little white dog in his arms. Jerry and his wife, Dawn, again apologized for interrupting our Christmas Eve and graciously thanked us for being there to help. Abby, a young Bichon Frise, was extremely weak, had pale mucous membranes, diminished reflexes, and her heart rate and respirations were alarmingly slow. Her abdomen was tender, and her urinary bladder was grossly distended. A quick x-ray showed a small bladder stone lodged in the urethrae, preventing any urine from exiting the bladder. I inserted a long needle through the skin and into the bladder, removed 40 cc of urine, which temporarily decreased the distention and eased some of the pain. Abby's condition was rapidly deteriorating. She was on her way out, and she'd surely die if that bladder stone wasn't removed immediately! We didn't have much time! It was definitely a life-or-death situation. I explained Abby's critical condition to the Pratters and the possibility of her not making it through the surgery. They understood the surgical risks and were willing to take the chance.

The surgical procedure was very challenging, to say the least! The urinary bladder was incised, and a small forceps was inserted in the bladder, then through the neck of the bladder, and finally into the urethrae. A small, bean-shaped, tightly wedged bladder stone was then grasped with the tip of the forceps, gently maneuvered free, and removed. Urine started flowing immediately like gangbusters! Problem solved! Abby made it through the surgery, although there were several moments where things got pretty touch and go, but that tough little gal hung in there! She did good!

Jerry and Dawn were overjoyed and understandably very thankful that Abby had pulled through. Believe me, that was one Christmas Eve they'll never forget, and neither will I!

" BRUCE "

"Bruce" wasn't your typical farm dog. He was a pudgy, well-groomed, purebred miniature Schnauzer who loved pickups and country life. He was his owner's little sidekick. Wayne Steppe, Bruce's owner, had become concerned about his little buddy's recent behavior.

Mr. Steppe said, "Bruce acts like he's trying to go, and nothing comes out except a few drops. He just stands there with his legs spread and back hunched up, but nothing happens. He acts like something's plugged up."

I told Wayne that it sure sounded that way, and a couple x-rays should give us some answers. The x-rays showed that Bruce wasn't constipated, and there weren't any blockages in the urinary bladder, *but* there was a small bladder stone that had moved from the bladder, down through the urethrae, and was now lodged directly behind the os penis (a bony structure in the male dog's penis through which the urethrae passes). That bony structure doesn't allow the urethrae to expand, so a small stone lodged behind the os penis would definitely stop the flow of urine. Bruce was in major trouble: he couldn't pee, and he needed help *pronto*!

The small urolith (calculi), a little larger than a BB, could not be pushed retrograde (backward) into the urinary bladder, nor could it move forward through the os penis. My only option was to surgically remove the calculi through a ventral (underside) incision through the skin, subcutaneous tissue, and then through the extremely thin urethrae. After removing the small stone, I reconstructed a new, larger and permanent underneath opening for Bruce.

The surgery was a very delicate procedure, but a complete success, and Bruce didn't have to strain to void anymore. It did look a little unusual though because whenever Bruce felt the urge, he'd hike his leg to pee, and urine passed out the new porthole on the underside of his penis. It may have looked a little weird, but he didn't seem to mind.

FOREIGN BODIES

Life can get awfully complicated when things are out of order or in places they shouldn't be. That scenario was often seen when animals ingested objects other than food, and when that happened, those foreign bodies usually created some very big problems.

" DOMINO "

Domino, a two-year-old black-and-white domestic shorthair cat with a voracious appetite, had recently refused to eat his food. That concerned his owner, Sally Ahern. She told Heather, our veterinary technician, "Domino is usually a very lively and playful cat, but now he just sits in the corner, all hunched up in the middle, and doesn't want to move." Mrs. Ahern didn't want something bad to happen to her young daughter's special friend, so she made an appointment to have Domino checked over.

Domino was a very docile cat who didn't object to being examined. His temperature was normal; he was moderately dehydrated. But when I felt his abdomen, he flinched and pulled away. *Bingo!* I told Mrs. Ahern that Domino felt severe pain in the upper abdominal area, and x-rays might show us why. The x-rays revealed a dense, oddly shaped foreign object seemingly trapped in his stomach, and it didn't belong there! The handwriting was on the wall—surgery!

Domino was quickly prepped for surgery, and in we went. A gastrotomy (incising the stomach) procedure can be tricky, and extra caution is required to avoid spilling contaminated stomach contents into the abdominal cavity. The surgery on Domino went flawlessly. The stomach was incised, nothing spilled. The mysterious invader was isolated, grasped with a forceps, removed, and placed in a tray for further examining. I told him, "Hey, Domino, little buddy, you should be a lot more comfortable now with that thing outta there." I closed him up and placed him in the recovery cage. We were done.

The mysterious object turned out to be a small wooden rubber stamp with an image of a cartoon character on it. When I showed Mrs. Ahern the object that was removed, she exclaimed, "Oh my gosh! That's one of my daughter's favorite toys. She plays with them all the time. I've seen Domino batting those little stamps around the house, and he likes carrying them in his mouth too. I never thought that he'd actually eat or swallow one of them." I advised Mrs. Ahern to go home and pick up all the small toys and tiny objects so that Domino wouldn't be tempted and become a repeat offender. Domino went on to make a complete recovery, and all those little wooden stamps amazingly disappeared from her daughter's toy box.

" BOBBY "

Phil Stangley called the clinic and told our receptionist that he was worried about his ten-week-old Springer Spaniel named "Bobby", and then he said, "The last couple days, when he tries to poop, he squats, strains a little, then cries. Then he turns around and licks his butt."

Bobby was a cute little guy, especially with those long brown ears. He didn't look sick; in fact, he acted like a normal puppy when first placed on the exam table, but he cried when he sat down. As I raised his tail to examine the rectal area, Bobby whimpered again. I noticed a tenting of skin just slightly to the left of the rectum as if something was embedded and poking from under the skin. When palpated, it felt hard and pointed. X-rays were taken, and I was amazed at what appeared on the films. It was a two-inch long sewing needle! I placed a local anesthetic at the tenting site, made a very small, one-quarter inch incision, and like magic, the pointed tip of the needle popped into view. Using a small forceps, I grasped the needle and applied slow, gentle, and steady retraction. The needle was easily withdrawn, but I was surprised to see that there was at least twelve inches of heavyweight thread still attached to the needle. The surgical site was then medicated, and only one suture (stitch) was needed to close the small incision. Bobby healed very nicely and without any complications. The odds were extremely small for a swallowed needle and thread to successfully pass down the esophagus, into and through the stomach, then on through the tortuous small and large intestines, and almost make it out the rectum. The needle could have punctured or penetrated the viscera, and the thread could have become entangled, both of which might have been life threatening to little Bobby. It was nothing short of a miracle for everything to almost pass completely through like it did.

I kept the needle and thread in a special formalin specimen bottle as a teaching aid. Clients could see, firsthand, what needs to be kept away from inquisitive puppies. Phil also made sure that his wife was more careful with her sewing stuff.

" JERRY "

Jerry was a three-year-old German Shepherd who was having digestive problems for several weeks. His owner, Mary Farmer, tried to help Jerry by offering him a bland diet consisting of boiled hamburger and rice. She also gave him a kaopectate tablet twice a day in an attempt to firm up his soft, unformed stools. Jerry's condition hadn't improved, so Mrs. Farmer made an appointment to have him examined, treated, and put back to normal, at minimal expense.

When I examined Jerry, he appeared to be underweight, almost malnourished. His coat was dry and dull, and he lacked energy and enthusiasm. He was pretty blah. His rectal temperature was normal, but he winced and pulled away in discomfort when I palpated his abdomen. There was a section of the small intestine that felt larger than normal, somewhat thickened, and that concerned me.

"Mrs. Farmer," I said. "I think Jerry might have an intestinal obstruction."

Mrs. Farmer couldn't understand how that could happen. She went on to say, "Jerry is always with me, and I watch what he eats, so I don't see how he could have eaten anything to cause this. I don't give him bones or anything that's hard to digest."

I went on to explain about other conditions such as intussusceptions (telescoping) of the intestines and malabsorption conditions that could exhibit similar signs. I told Mrs. Farmer that a stool analysis, blood tests, and x-rays were highly recommended and needed in order to get to the bottom of Jerry's problem. Mrs. Farmer declined the tests and x-rays, and was essentially looking for an "easy fix." I thought I'd ask just one more question. "Mrs. Farmer, could Jerry have ingested any of his toys or some child's toy?"

She emphatically replied, "No! He doesn't eat his toys, and he hasn't been around any kids either." So, getting nowhere, I placed Jerry on gastrointestinal sedatives, GI protectants, and a special diet specific for diarrheas and malabsorption conditions. I firmly told Mrs. Farmer that if Jerry didn't improve in one week, then x-rays *must* be taken. Mrs. Farmer nodded her head in agreement.

A week passed, and Jerry hadn't improved, in fact, his condition had worsened. Mrs. Farmer finally conceded that x-rays were necessary. The x-ray films revealed a strange semitransparent object wedged in the small intestine, and surgical removal was the only recourse. Jerry was prepped, and into surgery we went. I made an abdominal incision, and the swollen, inflamed, and discolored section of small intestine wasn't difficult to isolate. The small intestine was carefully incised open (enterotomy), and the offending object was gently removed with the aid of a forceps. As I dropped the object into the tray held by my surgical assistant, I said, "Here, have a baby bottle nipple!" Jerry was put back together, transferred to the recovery room, and was maintained on IV fluids for the next twenty-four hours.

I showed the rubber baby bottle nipple, which also had the end chewed off, to Mrs. Farmer. She was surprised, and said, "Oh, I forgot. Jerry had been over to my daughter's house, and he must have gotten hold of her baby's bottle." Finally the pieces of the puzzle had come together, and the mystery was solved! Jerry made a dramatically successful recovery. He started eating again, gained weight, had normal stools, and developed a nice shiny hair coat. He looked like any other healthy German Shepherd now—minus the baby bottle nipple that was wedged in his gut!

MAC

Some dogs are fiercely independent and hate to be shackled by a collar, no matter what it looks like. Mac, a pit bull cross, was one of those dogs. He'd destroyed his share of collars, but when his owner, Paul Verdel, found a super heavy-duty, double-reinforced, one-inch-wide collar, he thought, "There's no way Mac will get this thing off." It wasn't but a few days, and the collar was off. Mac had shown Paul who was boss. The only problem, Paul couldn't find the collar! Oh sure, he found a few pieces, but the bulk of the collar was missing. Paul thought that Mac might have buried it somewhere around the yard, but he couldn't find any evidence.

It wasn't but a few days later that a listless Mac started vomiting, and Paul entertained the notion that Mac could have actually eaten the dang thing. Paul brought his sick buddy to the clinic, told me the history, and asked if there was anything that could be done for Mac. I told Paul, "First, I start with x-rays to check for any possible abnormalities in the digestive tract." The x-ray films showed several areas where the intestines appeared to be bunched up together. Not a good sign! Paul asked, "If the collar is in there, can you get it out? I'd sure hate to lose ole Mac."

I told Paul that I'd do the best I could to help Mac, but sometimes with obstructions, there can be irreparable damage to the intestinal tissue—some can be saved, some can't. Mac's surgery was a long and painstaking procedure. He had indeed eaten the collar. There where seven separate sections of the chewed-up collar, connected by several strands of nylon fiber, and those sections were dispersed throughout Mac's intestines. So, seven separate enterotomies (incisions into the intestine) were needed to completely remove the collar. One enterotomy operation is bad enough, but to do seven on the same patient was unbelievable. It was touch and go for Mac, but he made it through the surgery. Now, time would tell if the tissue was viable, and if the intestinal sutures held. Any leakage of intestinal contents into the abdominal cavity would have been disastrous. Mac was kept on intravenous fluids for two days, plus antibiotics and a soft bland diet for ten days. He was a pretty sore boy for a while, but he made a slow and steady recovery back to his normal self. Mac was fortunate to have survived the ordeal. Paul also learned a valuable lesson, and from that time on, he still let Mac run free, but without a collar.

OTHER CASES

Over the years, I surgically removed many different kinds of foreign bodies from both cats and dogs. In addition to those already mentioned, the "Hall of the De-Famed" included hazelnuts, rocks, glass fragments, a cigarette lighter with lighter fluid still inside, balls, fishing lures, socks, and small toys. Fortunately, all my surgical patients survived their ordeal and hopefully learned from their experience.

IT WAS MEANT TO BE

Some of the most endearing creatures on the face of the earth are healthy puppies and kittens. These cute little bundles of energy bring joy to our lives and shower us with unconditional love. Their playful antics make us laugh and give us momentary stress relief from the hectic events we deal with every day. These precious little ones are truly gifts from God.

Tiger, an eight-week-old brown classic tabby, was a very special kitten. His owner, Penny Tatem, carried him under her light jacket into the exam room for his first vaccinations. When Penny handed Tiger to me, he immediately positioned himself under my chin and then began to purr. He sought security in close, intimate contact. This gentle and affectionate kitten was a real charmer.

It had been over a year since I'd last seen Tiger. In most cases, no news is good news, but not in this instance. Penny called the clinic, and with a voice filled with anxiety, she told our receptionist, "I'm a little concerned about Tiger. He just hasn't been himself lately. He doesn't act especially painful, but something's definitely not right, and I think he needs be seen by the doctor."

When Tiger arrived at the clinic, I was a little surprised to see how big and handsome he'd become. He sat nonchalantly on the exam table, almost oblivious to all the activity going on around him. He was stoically preoccupied with discomfort of some nature, and now it was up to me to find the source of the problem. As I palpated his abdomen, an enlarged section of his intestines could easily be felt. He was, without question, uncomfortable, and x-rays would be needed to help clarify what was going on inside his little body. Penny's finances were limited, and she expressed that she couldn't afford, nor was she interested, in treating Tiger. She bluntly said with an obvious lack of emotion, "Just put him down!"

I was caught off guard, to say the least. As I looked into Tiger's big amber-colored eyes, I recalled the gentle little kitten that once cuddled under my chin. I wanted to help him, not "deep six" him. So I asked Penny if she'd consider relinquishing ownership of Tiger to me, I'd do the workups and surgery, if needed, and that way he might have a chance to live. Without a moment's hesitation, Penny signed the transfer of ownership papers, and now Tiger was legally mine. Saving his life was priority number one.

X-rays were quickly taken of Tiger's abdomen, and the developed films revealed a huge problem. There appeared to be a six-inch section of Tiger's small intestine that was obstructed with something that couldn't be easily identified. It really didn't matter at that point; because whatever it was, it had to be removed *immediately*. Tiger was anesthetized and prepped, an IV catheter placed, and within minutes, I made the initial abdominal incision. The problem section of the small intestine was quickly and easily identified because of its increased size and discoloration. I carefully isolated and packed off the surgical site to avoid any contamination of intestinal contents into the abdominal cavity, and then proceeded to perform an enterotomy (incising open the intestines). There it was! A large, long wad of twisted, entangled dried decorator plant material that Tiger had obviously eaten. I delicately removed the offending obstruction, then surgically closed the intestinal and abdominal incisions. Tiger was administered antibiotics, and while still hooked up to IV fluids, he was placed in a nice warm recovery cage. I'd done all that I could do, and it was now up to Tiger. When he awoke from the anesthesia, he stood up, stretched, and started meowing for food and attention. It was truly astounding! He acted as if nothing had happened!

Sandy had received a greeting card with a beautiful charcoal sketch of a big cat reclining in a wicker basket on the front of the card. It was entitled, "Henry's Basket." Amazingly, that cat looked almost exactly like Tiger! Now that Tiger belonged to us, and he'd gotten a new lease on life, Sandy thought he also deserved a new name. So we named him Henry!

Henry has been part of our family for twelve years. He is one of the most gentle, affectionate, and intuitive cats that I have ever seen. Henry has been my constant companion who loves to be with me, and yes, that svelte fifteen-pound cat still cuddles real close, with his head under my chin. Henry's a good boy. It's funny how life works, how we found each other. It often seems like we were destined to be together. I guess it was simply,—meant to be.

CASANOVA LOUIE

The television action series *MacGyver* ran from 1985 to 1992 and was a huge hit with the viewing public. The main character, named MacGyver, found himself in unusual dilemmas where he had to use his imagination to solve a problem. He was a very resourceful individual, whose ingenuity allowed him to create unorthodox solutions to the challenges he encountered. Essentially, he had to use his head and what was immediately available to make something work. Thus, the term *MacGyvering* was coined, referring to the process of taking what was available and successfully making it work. Over the years, there were occasions when I was confronted with a tough case that required some surgical MacGyvering, and Louie was one of those cases.

Hazel Roemer was a respected and successful dog breeder of miniature French poodles. She had shown the dogs competitively, and her kennels had garnered many champions over the years. As time passed, her days of showing dogs was but a memory; however, this strong-willed, seventy-eight-year-old woman still operated a breeding kennels in spite of her issues of being very arthritic and experiencing dwindling eyesight.

Hazel presented "King Louis of Avalon", a seven-year-old silver male French poodle, one of her remaining breeding males, to the clinic because of a licking problem. Hazel told me, "Louie is constantly licking himself. I've looked, and I can't really see anything, but I can smell it, and it smells like he's got an infection." She went on to say, "It's getting harder for me to keep up with those dogs. I just can't get around like I used to, and I have trouble seeing these days."

While Hazel was still talking, Louie got himself into a comfortable sitting position and started licking at his genital area. I moved his head to the side so that I could get a better look, and saw the reason for his incessant licking—and the foul smell. Half of his penis was black as coal—necrotic, rotten, — essentially gangrenous.

"Hazel, here's why Louie's been licking so much and smells so bad," I said. "His penis is rotting off." Hazel bent over and got close enough to see for herself.

She then asked, "How could this have happened?" I told her that it was hard to tell, but something had clearly interfered with the circulation of blood to the area because there was such a well-defined line of distinction between the healthy tissue and the necrotic tissue. I could tell by Hazel's facial expressions and demeanor that she really cared for little Louie and was very concerned about him.

She soberly asked, "Can anything be done for my poor Louie?"

I told her that Louie couldn't live this way and there was no other choice but to amputate his penis, reconstruct a new opening for him to pee through, and also neuter him at the same time. Hazel was more than willing to have the surgical procedure done for her favorite little poodle, especially if it meant possibly saving his life.

Louie was anesthetized and prepped, and it was now time to do some major surgical MacGyvering. I amputated the necrotic penis, removed the os penis (bony structure), and performed a urethrostomy. A urethrostomy is a procedure that creates a new permanent opening of the urethra to the exterior, and this new opening allows for the passing of urine. After that was successfully completed, I then neutered him. He had gotten the "Full Monty". Louie had gone from the main breeder in Hazel's kennel to a little guy who literally didn't have any equipment remaining. His breeding days were definitely over, but he was alive and could live a good life, and that's what really mattered. Following the surgery, I dissected the amputated penis, looking for a possible cause for the problem. I found a cordlike band of twisted hair that had somehow gotten up inside the sheath of the penis and wrapped itself around the base of the penis, effectively strangulating the feeder vessels, and that ultimately resulted in the death of the tissue (necrosis). The mystery was solved!

Louie made a rapid recovery, his new pee-port was working as it should; he stopped licking at his genitals, and once again, he acted like a normal dog. Hazel was quite pleased, but two weeks later, she called the clinic and had a question for me.

"Doctor Roloff, Louie is doing very well, but I thought you said that you neutered him. He sure doesn't act like he's been neutered. He's out there mounting all the females that are coming into heat, and he acts like the Romeo he'd always been."

I assured Hazel that all his male parts were gone. They were history. I was glad to hear that Louie was back to his ole self and told her, "It's like the saying goes, 'Old habits die hard,' and Casanova Louie is livin' in the past, except now he's just shootin' blanks."

ANIMAL CRACKERS

We've all had experiences that have left indelible images etched in our minds. Some of those images are pleasant, some aren't, and no matter how hard we try, we just can't erase them from our psyche. The "Frankie incident" was one of those unpleasant experiences that created a repulsive mental picture, and it has remained in my mind for years.

Frankie was a five-year-old dachshund who was the canine version of Dennis the Menace. He was a mischievous little guy who kept his owner on her toes, so it came as no surprise when he helped himself to a large bag of frosted animal crackers. Frankie definitely had too much of a good thing and was now reaping the consequences. His swollen abdomen and lack of energy prompted his owner, Sue Milton, to rush him to the clinic for help.

When Frankie arrived at the clinic, he was really hurting. His abdomen was grossly distended, and that boy was really uncomfortable. He just stood there on the exam table with his legs slightly splayed and his neck extended forward in an attempt to ease some of the abdominal pain. It was imperative to get all that stuff out of his stomach, and that meant making him vomit. I immediately went to the emergency crash cart, grabbed the apomorphine, placed a small amount into the conjunctival space of his left eye, and within thirty seconds, Frankie pitched it! He lost his cookies, literally! I let him retch and vomit several more times to ensure complete emptying of the stomach contents before rinsing out his eye with saline solution, in an attempt to remove any residual apomorphine and stop the induced vomiting.

Once the purging episode was over, Frankie just stood there, much relieved and definitely more comfortable! His abdomen had returned to its normal size, and he looked around as if to say, "What the heck just happened?" I can tell you what just happened. There on the exam table was a large foul-smelling pool of vomit—consisting of mushed-up, partially digested animal crackers, with swirls of pink and white frosting everywhere. There were also hundreds of those tiny round blue and white candy sprinkles floating throughout the whole stinking mess. It was gross and disgusting, but Frankie felt better, and that's what counted.

Frankie left the clinic acting as if nothing had happened. He bounded out the door, bright-eyed and bushy-tailed, looking for his next misadventure. I cautioned his owner to be very watchful and keep all cookies out of Frankie's reach, but we both knew that would be a major challenge. Frankie was a lovable little guy who was, and remained to be, an accident waiting to happen. To say that Frankie had a profound effect on me would be a complete and total understatement. To this very day, I cannot look at an animal cracker, especially those pink and white frosted ones, without recalling little Frankie and visualizing the vomit scene on the exam table. That mental image is permanently etched in my memory bank and has forever curbed my appetite for animal crackers.

ROAD WARRIOR

It's never a pretty scene when cars and animals cross paths. Some animals miraculously escape the carnage, while others may survive, but they pay a high price with broken bodies and permanent scars. Then there are those who never get a second chance. It's always sad to see a deceased animal lying on the road, and there have been times when I've stopped and moved an animal's remains to the side of the road in an attempt to prevent any further desecration.

That one particular day started out pretty uneventfully, but then the clinic door abruptly swung open, and a lady stuck her head inside the door and blurted out, "I don't know who to tell, but there's a cat laying in the middle of the street just a block from here, and I think it's dead. Somebody needs to pick it up and get it off the road so cars won't run over it." Although I was in the back of the clinic, I could definitely hear the lady, so I quickly went to the waiting room and assured her that I'd go immediately and take care of the situation. I grabbed a cadaver bag and latex gloves in preparation for the gruesome task, then jumped into the car and was at the scene in very short order. She was right! Lying there all stretched out and motionless, smack-dab in the middle of the street, was a young black-and-white cat. I approached the cat, didn't see any blood, then checked its eyes and saw that the pupils were not yet fully dilated—that was a hopeful sign. The cat, however, didn't appear to be breathing, but when I listened to the chest with my stethoscope, I heard a faint, slow heartbeat.

I muttered to myself, "This cat is alive, but barely!" Without delay, right there in the middle of the street, I started administering heart and chest compressions. That went on for about a minute or so when suddenly the cat's chest heaved, and it took a deep breath. Yahoo! I continued the cardiac massage and chest compressions for a little while longer and then took another listen to the chest. The heartbeat sounded stronger and more regular, and the lung sounds were slightly raspy, but at least the cat was now breathing on its own. This cat had a good chance of making it, barring any major internal injuries or broken bones. I placed the recumbent cat *on* the bag, instead of in it, and then rushed the patient back to the clinic.

I entered the clinic through the back door with the injured cat securely held in my arms and called out to the staff, "We've got a live one here! I need some help! Get the oxygen and IVs ready!"

Everyone immediately swung into emergency mode. The cat was quickly hooked up to the oxygen. IV catheters were placed. Fluids started flowing into its veins, and drugs to counter shock and tissue swelling were injected into the IV line. It was amazing and encouraging to see how fast the cat responded to the treatments.

Once the cat was stabilized, we then started checking it over for other injuries, and in the process, we found it to be a young male, about five months old with a blue collar, suggesting that he probably belonged to someone. He had multiple scrapes, abrasions, and minor cuts—typical "road rash" stuff. The injury of most concern, however, was the instability and grinding that was detected on the right side of his pelvis. X-rays were taken and showed that the little guy had a fracture at the midpoint of the body of the right ilium bone of the pelvis. It was a major break that resulted from the impact of the car. The repair options for fractures of that nature included surgical plating, wiring the pieces into place, or placement of an intramedullary (within the bone marrow) stainless steel rod (pin), either by open or closed reduction. But there was a fly in the ointment: the owner's signed authorization was needed before any surgery could be done, and no one had come forward to claim the cat.

The cat was hospitalized and medicated over the next few days while the staff searched for the owner. They canvassed the neighborhood, put up posters, and placed notices in the local newspaper. All was done to no avail. It was beginning to look like the little guy was purposely dropped off and abandoned by someone. Four days quickly passed and still no owner, the surgery needed to be performed, and a decision had to be made. I couldn't wait any longer, so I decided to take full responsibility for the cat and do the required surgery. The little guy needed a real name though, instead of just being referred to as, "the cat." I'd been calling him "Crash". It seemed very fitting because that's what he'd been through. Everybody agreed, so Crash became his official name.

Crash was scheduled for surgery the next day, and I'd elected to perform a closed reduction intramedullary pinning of the fractured pelvis. The procedure entailed making a small skin incision along the brim of the pelvis, then passing a stainless steel rod, or pin, down through the medullary (marrow) cavity of the bone, aligning the fractured pieces by feel and finally seating (screwing) the pin into the harder cortical layer of the bone. Knowing the anatomy and mentally visualizing the procedure as it's taking place is critical for success, and a little luck doesn't hurt either. I felt good about the surgery, and the postsurgical x-rays confirmed that the pin was perfectly placed, and that the fractured portions of the pelvis were in excellent alignment.

Crash's road-rash injuries were then treated, antibiotics were given, and he was done.

Crash was an ideal patient, and he healed rapidly, as most young patients do. He was happy and playful, in spite of having a stainless steel rod holding his pelvis together, and it wasn't a surprise that he'd become a favorite of clients and staff. At eight weeks post-op, x-rays were taken and showed that the fracture had completely healed, and it was now time to remove the rod and find Crash a permanent home. It didn't take very long before that charismatic little guy found a loving family, and he accompanied them to sunny California.

All in all, Crash's remarkable recovery was a testament to his incredible will to survive. He was a true road warrior, in every sense of the word, and was an inspiration to all who met him and heard his story. I'm truly thankful that a concerned stranger stopped by the clinic that day and told us about him lying on the road. Her actions helped save Crash's life, and he remains one of my most rewarding cases.

TITANIUM FLASH

Perhaps one of the most imposing villains of the cinema was Jaws in the James Bond movie, *The Spy Who Loved Me*. Jaws had a menacing set of titanium teeth, and he sure knew how to use those things. He definitely was one individual that you wouldn't want to meet in a dark alley. On the other hand, titanium teeth aren't so bad when used for a good reason, and such was the case with an endearing black Labrador retriever named Caly.

Jerod Phillips was an avid outdoorsman who thoroughly enjoyed his hunting and fishing. He loved his dogs too, especially Labrador retrievers and spent many hours patiently training them for retrieving downed waterfowl. Caly was one of his favorites, and she basically lived to hunt and be with Jerod. She wasn't an overly big Lab either, actually more medium-sized, but she was a real dynamo when it came to getting those birds.

Jerod, along with his sidekick, Caly, occasionally dropped by the clinic for an impromptu visit, just to say hello. Caly knew exactly where the cookie drawer was located, and it didn't matter to her if I was in the exam room with a patient or not. She figured that she was a good girl, deserved some treats, and was determined to stand in front of that drawer and wait patiently until I opened it and delivered the goods. It was rewarding to see clients and patients feel comfortable and enjoy coming to a vet clinic for a change. That was one of my goals. I must admit though, at times, I tended to spoil my patients—just a tad—but hey, it was fun! I had a genuine fondness for my patients.

Jerod stopped by the clinic one day and told me that Caly had recently been showing some reluctance to grab onto the downed ducks, and he also noticed that she was refusing to pick up her practice dummy. Jerod went on to say, "Caly has been eating and drinking slower, and that's just not her. She acts like somethin's hurtin'."

I told Jerod that I needed to examine Caly because all kinds of things like dental issues, sores, abscesses, tumors, foreign bodies, nerve problems, and even fractures could account for her acting the way she was acting. We needed to find out specifically what was going on in her mouth.

Caly arrived at the clinic, happy and energetic as usual, acting as if nothing was wrong—except she didn't go to the treat drawer. I began to examine her mouth. There were no sores, foreign bodies or tumors, and her teeth appeared to be in relatively good condition, but Caly flinched and pulled her head back when I put pressure on her upper canine teeth. "Aha! I said. "I think I've found her problem. Caly could very likely have an abscessed tooth, and that abscess is causing inflammation and swelling, which in turn is putting pressure on the nerve and surrounding bone. That's what's causing her pain, and that's why she won't hold onto the practice dummy or the ducks. It hurts! It's too painful for her."

Jerod asked, "What do we have to do, Doc? She wants to hunt and retrieve, but she can't do it this way. Do we need to pull her teeth? I'd sure hate to do that because then she sure as heck couldn't hunt." I replied, "Jerod, root canals would most likely be the only option available for saving Caly's abscessed teeth, —but they are pretty pricey procedures."

"Doc," Jerod said, "nothin's too pricey for my Caly. I don't care what it costs! If she needs it, I'll do it for her. When can you do it,

Doc?" I responded, "Jerod, I don't have the necessary instruments and equipment to perform the type of root canals that Caly would need, but I could refer you to a veterinary dental specialist in Seattle. It would mean a 350 mile trip, but Doctor Bishop is an excellent canine dental specialist."

In the blink of an eye, Jerod said, "Great! Set me up an appointment." I promptly called Doctor Bishop's office and set up an appointment for Caly.

· · · · · · · ·

Three weeks had passed, when Jerod called and scheduled a recheck for Caly as per the dental specialist's recommendations. Caly came bounding into the clinic, her usual happy self, looking for treats this time. Jerod quickly grabbed Caly, flipped up her gums, and proudly said, "Take a look at those babies, Doc! She's got 'em on the uppers and lowers. They're titanium, —- titanium caps! Pretty weird lookin', huh, but she sure feels a lot better, and now she's grabbing stuff again. No problems, no pain. Thanks, Doc."

Caly's shiny new titanium caps instantly reminded me of Jaws, the huge villain in that James Bond movie. But Caly was no villain, just a real happy camper. The dental specialist had performed root canals on the two upper (maxillary) canine teeth, then capped them as well as the lower (mandibular) canine teeth. Caly looked tough, but as we all know, looks can be deceiving.

Caly was an outstanding hunting dog for many years, but when Jerod unfortunately succumbed to a very untimely and tragic accident, Caly suddenly lost her soul mate and hunting companion. That bond between those two had been broken, and her will to hunt was never the same. Caly lived a few more months, but then she left to be with Jerod. Sometimes, in my mind's eye, I can see the two of them together again, out there somewhere, enjoying each others company, and Caly's titanium teeth flashing in the sun.

HARRY HOUDINI

Something just wasn't right! Lilly and Mikey, our clinic cats, weren't acting quite themselves. They appeared more apprehensive and hesitant about going upstairs to their main living quarters in the clinic. What also seemed strange were their increased appetites. Their food dish was polished clean, and they usually didn't do that. Something mysterious was going on.

As Sandy, our business manager, was going upstairs to check some archived records, she caught a glimpse of two eyes peering out from under the steps of the stairwell. She was startled momentarily, but then cautiously bent down to take a closer look. The mature face of a gray tabby cat with light green eyes serenely looked back.

Sandy asked the cat, "Who are you, and how'd you get in here?"

It responded with a soft muffled meow and slowly emerged from its secure refuge and moved toward her, as if seeking reassurance. The cat was a potent male, about a year and a half old, and actually quite tame. Based on his demeanor, he must have belonged to someone, but why and how did he get into the clinic? That was the big question. Until we had some answers, the cat stayed at the clinic in a comfortable cage—that was escape-proof. The search was on to find any possible point of entry. He surely didn't walk through the front door, and there was no way that he could have gotten in through the ventilation system. We kept looking, and eventually found a small triangle-shaped opening about 4"×3"×3" in an upper corner of the outside exercise enclosure that we'd built for the clinic cats. At first glance, that opening seemed awfully small for a ten pounder to squeeze through. It would take some determined effort or a little bit of magic to accomplish that feat, but this cat did it! Some of his gray hair got caught on the fencing, and that was the evidence we were looking for. I guess the old saying is true, "Where there's a will, there's a way." Once he'd made it into the exercise enclosure, it was no big deal for him to enter the clinic through the cat door. You'd think that a cat wouldn't want to break *into* a veterinary clinic, but this guy magically found a way inside. So we named him Harry, as in Harry Houdini, the renowned escape artist, but our Harry was a reverse Houdini. He escaped *in*!

Before we could find Harry Houdini a permanent home, we needed to test him for feline AIDS and feline leukemia. He was negative to both of those devastating diseases, and that was a huge relief to all of us. The next steps in Harry's "magical makeover" included a bath, getting neutered, vaccinated, dewormed, and microchipped. Harry was now a very handsome cat with a new identity. It wasn't a surprise to any of us that Harry Houdini soon found a good home, but it took a bit of magic to accomplish that trick.

YELLOW JACKETS

Summer is a great time of the year because there are so many fun and exciting things to do. Going to the lake has always been a popular activity enjoyed by people and their dogs. The dogs get to go swimming, fetch things thrown in the water, and even go for boat rides. Everyone's having fun—until something goes wrong.

There were five lakes within a six mile radius of the veterinary clinic, and I saw my share of summertime emergencies. Everything, from fishing hooks and lures embedded in lips and mouths to swallowed triple hooks, cut foot pads, blunt force traumas, eating too much of a good thing, and insect bite reactions. The worst kind of insect bite or sting came from the very aggressive yellow jacket wasp. The after effects of such a sting often produced severe reactions, and some of those reactions were even life threatening. There were two dramatic cases that I shall never forget.

A family had come to one of the nearby lakes to do some fishing, and they brought along their two-year-old buff-colored Cocker Spaniel, "Trudy". She loved to go out in the boat with the rest of the family. The boat was stocked with all kinds of goodies and refreshments for a day on the water, including a variety of soft drinks, cookies, and sliced watermelon. Unfortunately, all those things were sweet, and they attracted the yellow jacket wasps like crazy. It didn't take long before the pesky yellow jackets were homing in on the boat and the cache of goodies. Trudy did what most dogs would do—she got annoyed at the marauding insects and bit at them repeatedly. Suddenly she yelped and instantly collapsed in the boat, —- unconscious! The family was horror-stricken and knew that Trudy was in serious trouble, so they quickly raced to shore, got directions to the nearest veterinarian, which was me, and sped into town.

The door of the clinic swung wide open, and a man dressed in shorts and a blue tank top charged in with a seemingly lifeless cocker spaniel dangling in his arms. He frantically hollered, "My dog's been stung by a yellow jacket, and she's not breathing! I dropped what I was presently doing and immediately went to help the dog. Trudy was in a state of anaphylaxis (an acute allergic reaction to an antigen, which was from the sting). She was unconscious, not breathing, and the membranes in her mouth were turning blue from lack of oxygen. She was on the verge of dying! I quickly applied a tourniquet to her left front leg and attempted to raise a vein, a very difficult thing to do when the blood pressure is extremely low, as hers was. The vein didn't raise much, barely enough to be seen. I quickly injected dexamethasone and epinephrine intravenously. Those two medications are used to counteract the vascular collapse associated with severe allergic reactions and shock. The distraught family was standing there in the room as I gave the injections. I told them, "Say a prayer and cross your fingers that this works. I hope we got to her in time." It was really touch and go!

It didn't take but a few seconds, and her gums (the membranes in her mouth) started to turn pink again. Trudy then took a breath and began showing more signs of life. As her respirations continued to increase and as she started moving her legs and blinking her eyes, her owners began shedding tears of joy and relief. They kept telling me, "Thank you, thank you, thank you."

I hospitalized Trudy for several hours and monitored her recovery. Once she was acting like a normal dog again, I sent her home. I told her family that when Trudy bit at the yellow jacket, it stung her directly into a vein located under the tongue. Trudy had essentially been mainlined with the venom of the yellow jacket, and it could have killed her. I also cautioned her owners about the habits of yellow jackets, what attracts them, and what to avoid. Trudy was a very lucky girl to have survived such an ordeal, and hopefully she wouldn't snap at yellow jackets anymore.

· · · · · · · · ·

Another yellow jacket stinging incident occurred with a seven-year-old female Bassett Hound named Bailey. According to her owner, Janet Artson, Bailey was busily eating her hard food when suddenly she yelped, pulled away from her bowl, and shook her head. Then she started becoming a little wobbly and had what Janet described as a small seizure. Janet went on to say that Bailey's ear quickly swelled up like a balloon, especially the bottom half, and it didn't take long before the skin started looking discolored. This really concerned Janet, so she wanted to have Bailey checked out ASAP.

When Bailey arrived at the clinic, it was easy to see why she got stung in the ear. Her long pendulous ears were most likely hanging in and around her food bowl while she was eating, and the yellow jacket wasps were trying to get in on the action at the same time. Both wanted the food, and neither wanted to share. The aggressive wasps must have been aggravated by the floppy ears getting in their way, so they instinctively stung whatever moved and it just so happened to be Bailey's ungainly ears. The bottom half of Bailey's left ear didn't look good at all. It was swollen, discolored, and painful to her. There was also a distinct line of demarcation between the healthy and damaged portion of her ear. The wasp venom had caused such a severe allergic reaction within the ear tissue that it eventually resulted in irreparable tissue death. The bottom half of Bailey's ear had to be amputated; there was no other feasible option.

The amputation was successfully completed, and Bailey made a smooth recovery. She was a very good patient with a high pain threshold, and following the surgery, she acted like she hadn't missed a beat. Her head looked a little lopsided though, especially with the bottom half of her left ear missing, but she didn't seem to care. There was, however, one benefit from this incident. In the future, Bailey only had to be concerned about one ear dangling into her food bowl instead of two.

NOT A BB!

A lady and her Australian cattle dog, Tilly, had recently moved from Texas to the Pacific Northwest. The lady had a soft southern accent and was very knowledgeable about her dog and that particular breed. One day she noticed a small lump with a tiny opening on the dog's side and assumed that Tilly had somehow been shot with a BB gun. Her concern was that the site might become infected, and she wanted it treated before that happened.

Tilly was a very enjoyable patient. She was well behaved, friendly, and nicely groomed. There was definitely an emotional connection between that lady and her dog. Her gentle reassuring touches to Tilly, and the way Tilly gazed back at the lady, it was obvious that love went both ways between those two. I think that's the way the good Lord intended it to be.

I trimmed some of Tilly's hair so that I could get a closer look at the problem area. There it was, —- a quarter-sized, raised swelling of the skin with a perfectly round, tiny hole, approximately 3 mm in diameter, located smack-dab in the center of the lesion. Most of the dogs that I'd seen who'd been recently shot with a BB or pellet gun showed smaller points of entry, and there usually wasn't that much swelling involved. In this instance, the raised

JIM ROLOFF

swelling with a small spherical central opening suggested one very likely culprit—a botfly or blow fly larvae.

Botfly cases are usually seen in warmer regions of the country. They cause skin problems in cows, horses, and occasionally in people. I'd seen several cows with embedded botfly larvae, often referred to as warbles, but I'd never witnessed a dog with that condition. The swelling with the small hole on Tilly's side sure looked like a botfly case. There was one sure way to find out and confirm my diagnosis—make it wiggle. I deposited several drops of hydrogen peroxide directly into the opening, which was the larvae or grub's air hole. The hydrogen peroxide instantly started to foam and bubble up, and it also irritated the embedded larvae, causing it to wiggle and writhe under the skin. The owner and several staff members just couldn't resist taking a closer look at the "larval dance," and the comments ranged from "Oh gross!" to "Oh wow" to "How interesting." It really did look a little sick and weird. There was absolutely no doubt about it. It wasn't a BB. It was a botfly or blow fly larvae (grub), and that guy needed to be removed *pronto*! Embedded grubs or larvae of the botfly must be carefully removed from the skin. If the larvae were torn or ruptured during the extraction process, toxins from the grub or larvae could potentially be released and enter the patient's bloodstream. That could result in severe allergic reactions and even anaphylactic shock, a serious life-threatening condition.

I administered a sedative to Tilly and used a local anesthetic around the swelling, then proceeded to surgically excise the entire swelling containing the grub. The larvae was removed completely and undamaged. It was three-quarters of an inch long and three-eighths of an inch wide—pretty ugly looking too. The owner asked, "How could this have happened?"

I told her, "A puncture, bruise, or any trauma could have compromised the skin tissue, and that resulted in the ideal place for a botfly to lay its eggs. When the eggs hatch, the larvae feed on the damaged tissue, and the larvae grows. In time, the larvae emerges, drops to the ground, and a young botfly comes out. Tilly most likely had some sort of initial injury that set the whole scenario into motion."

Tilly was my first and last dog–botfly larvae case. I kept the grub/larvae in a small formalin-filled specimen jar and frequently used it as a teaching aid for both clients and students. Believe me, it was effective!

SONG RELIEF

It's been said that certain strains of music can calm the restless spirits and soothe the troubled minds of humans as well as animals. I'd found that to be true, not only for myself, but for a couple of my patients too.

The Alverez family loved their two bassett hounds, and those lucky dogs lacked for nothing. Their names were Heckel and Jeckel, and in all honesty, they were quite spoiled, but nice dogs nonetheless. There was one big problem though, and that was their incessant baying when they visited the clinic. They were happy and excited but unfortunately let everyone within a half mile know it too. Their baying was loud, distracting, ear-piercing, and unsettling to all the other animals on the premises. To any pedestrian outside the clinic, it must have sounded like a full-fledged fox hunt going on inside, with Heckel and Jeckel in hot pursuit of their quarry.

The odd thing about the whole baying issue was the tonal pitch of the howl. It may sound weird, but the sound frequency of their baying made my ears itch. There I was, attempting to examine these two happy, excitable bassett hounds, and all the while they were loudly howling next to my head. My ears started itching like crazy, and in order to maintain my sanity, I started singing and humming, —- anything! Heck, if I didn't know the words, I just made up new ones—kind of musical improvisation. An amazing thing happened when I started singing, — the baying stopped, and my ears miraculously stopped itching too. I'd sing stuff like, "Over the river and through the woods, Heckel and Jeckel did go. They went to the little vet'nary clinic through ice and drifted snoooo-oh." The dogs looked at me like I'd just lost my mind—I was getting pretty close—but it worked! They were quiet, or at least quieter, and I was able to continue the exams without having my ears assaulted.

Over the next several years, whenever Heckel and Jeckkel visited the clinic, I had to sing to them in order to keep the decibels at a manageable level, and it worked every time! My ears didn't itch, and the Alverez family appreciated the noise relief too.

The day came when the Alverez family, along with Heckel and Jeckel, were to be relocated to the Seattle area. Mr. Alverez had gotten a job promotion, and although they liked the Medical Lake area, the opportunity was too good to pass up. Mrs. Alverez was concerned about how the move would affect their dogs, so she came to the clinic and solemnly inquired, "Do you know of, or could you recommend any singing veterinarians in the Seattle area?"

I smiled and said, "No. I think I'm the only one who sings to his patients."

Mrs. Alverez responded, "Oh, I wish there was one, because they were so good for you when you sang to them." I nodded my head in agreement and thought to myself, *Sometimes you gotta do what works.*

BUILT ON FRIDAY

Sometimes a car that turns out to be a real lemon is referred to as a car that was built on Friday—meaning, those responsible for assembling the car were more concerned about the weekend than building a car. That "Friday focus lapse" often resulted in a car that was haphazardly put together and had problems. Unfortunately, assembly foibles can also occur with humans and animals.

The owner, with tears in her eyes, gently and lovingly placed the kitten on the exam table and asked, "Should I have her put to sleep? Is it cruel for me to keep her alive?" I told the lady that I'd check the kitten over first, and then give her my honest opinion. There before me was a cute little white kitten, about eight weeks old, and it was plain to see that she had some major physical birth defects. Snowflake was the kitten's name, and she moved around on the exam table in a manner suggesting complete unawareness of any physical challenges. She had a totally white hair coat and big blue eyes, a genetic combination that is often associated with deafness in cats. When I tested Snowflake's hearing by having a veterinary assistant blow on a whistle, Snowflake didn't respond, and it was glaringly obvious that her hearing was impaired. Her meow was also rather loud and harsh—another finding with deaf cats. Not only was little Snowflake hard of hearing, but she also had a severely deformed right front leg that was abnormally short, withered, and shaped in the form of a hook. There wasn't much of a paw either, just a small rudimentary foot pad with only two small nubs masquerading as toes. Her left front leg was much shorter than normal too, but not as drastically deformed as the right front leg. Snowflake was able to stand and support her weight on her left front leg, but not her right. On top of all that, her hind legs were longer than normal, and together with the short front legs, Snowflake looked as if she was perpetually hopping downhill. She didn't seem to mind though. To her, that was "the normal". Snowflake simply had that unflappable "no big deal" attitude.

I told the owner that Snowflake had some genetic and congenital defects, and although she looked like she was "built on a Friday," she had nonetheless adjusted and adapted extremely well to her physical challenges. Snowflake didn't walk like a normal cat either. Instead, she hopped like a rabbit and played with her toys by hooking and grasping them with her deformed right front leg. She was enjoying life, and I told her owner that in my opinion, Snowflake wasn't suffering at all, and she should be allowed to live out her life—her way.

Snowflake had adapted amazingly well to her physical disabilities and challenges and did in fact live a good life. That happy-go-lucky, affectionate cat, with a can-do attitude was a true inspiration, not only to us, but to everyone who had the pleasure of seeing and meeting her.

ON THE ROAD AGAIN

Mary Chorde was driving down the I-90 freeway with only ten miles to go before arriving at home. It had been a long day for Mary, and the last thing she expected to see that summer afternoon was a scared little dog running alongside the road. But there it was, and Mary came to its rescue because of her genuine passion for dogs. She quickly pulled to the side of the road, put on the emergency flashers, got out of the car, and started calling out to the scampering little canine. It took a little doing, but Mary eventually managed to befriend the frightened dog, and held the trembling little guy in her reassuring arms. The little dog was obviously lost, and Mary, knowing that she couldn't just leave the dog alone way out there in nowhere, decided to take the little guy home with her and try to find its owner later on.

A week had passed, and in spite of Mary's most ardent efforts, no owner was found. It was beginning to look as if the little dog had found a new home—with Mary. So she brought her new acquisition to the veterinary clinic for a checkup and vaccinations. I asked Mary if the dog had a name, and she told me that she'd decided to name the dog "Freeway" because that's where she'd found him. He was a fairly young, bright-eyed, lean, and energetic little dog that looked a lot like a purebred Silky Terrier. He also appeared to be well groomed and in good physical health overall. The big question was, "How did a purebred Silky Terrier get so lost and end up running alongside the interstate highway miles from any city or town?" It just so happened that there was a freeway rest area about two miles from the location where Mary found the dog. His previous owners had most likely stopped at the rest stop, and let Freeway stretch his legs—and stretch 'em he did! He ran. Silky Terriers like to run —- anywhere! He was a defiant, very independent little cuss, and when his owners let him take a little run, well, he kept running and running and running! I'm sure they looked for him, but he was long gone, and they must have been heartbroken. As time waned and their dog couldn't be found, his owners reluctantly had to leave him behind. Freeway was on his own and had to fend for himself. Fortunately, Mary came along, and her love for animals essentially saved his life.

Mary lived two blocks down the street from my house, and I'll never forget the day when a little gray-black-tan-colored dog came streaking down the street, his head up high with fine hair flowing in the breeze and legs moving so fast that they were simply a blur. As he was running past my driveway, I yelled out, "Freeway!" He stopped dead in his tracks and looked straight at me. I pointed in the direction of his house and sternly commanded, "You. Go. Home."

He turned his head, looked toward his home, then looked at me again, then took off running in the *opposite* direction. The line from the movie *Alice in Wonderland* ran though my head: "I'm late, I'm late, for a very important date. No time to say hello. Good-bye! I'm late, I'm late, I'm late." That was Freeway's modus operandi, and that's probably how he got lost in the first place.

Freeway eventually found his way home, thank goodness. I'll always remember him as a friendly little dog that was very strong willed. A dog who loved to run—*away*—on the road again!

A TALE OF A TAIL

The location of the battle scars reveal whether a cat is a lover or a fighter. Fighters usually have wounds around the head and neck as a result of head-on confrontations, while lovers invariably have "getaway" wounds on the hind end and tail. Miss Priss, a four-year-old silver-tipped Persian cat, was, as her name implied, definitely *not* a fighter.

I first met Miss Priss for a second opinion involving an ongoing chronic tail condition. Her owners, Al and Beth Dohr, told me that the problem started about two months earlier when the little lady stealthily slipped outside one day to "see what the real world was like." She found out very quickly that there are some very mean and scary street cats out there. Miss Priss didn't want any part of that action because she was a pampered girl, not a fighter. As she took off running for the safety of home, the neighborhood "bully" cat swatted her on the caboose, and his sharp claws sunk deep into her tail.

The Dohrs were understandably relieved when Miss Priss finally returned home. She appeared frightened, a bit disheveled, and there were a few drops of blood near the base of her tail. Over the next several days, Miss Priss's appetite tapered off. She became less active and seemed to sleep a lot more. That concerned Al and Beth, so they took her to their regular veterinarian to be checked over. He told them that Miss Priss had an elevated temperature of 103 degrees Fahrenheit, her tail was infected, and she needed to be placed on antibiotics. The infection, however, did not respond to the antibiotic therapy, and within days, a full-blown abscess developed. The veterinarian treated the abscess, but the tissue damage was very extensive, and the eventual outcome didn't look very promising. In time, the veterinarian elected to amputate Miss Priss's tail. The amputation site healed well, but Miss Priss licked the tail stump incessantly. There were times, according to her owners, when she'd be quietly sitting on a living room chair, then suddenly go at her tail, vigorously licking and chewing at it. Al and Beth knew something wasn't right, so they took Miss Priss back to their veterinarian and were told that she was merely adjusting to the tail being gone, and eventually she'd get better and stop licking, but she never did. That's when the Dohrs sought a second opinion and brought Miss Priss to me.

The Dohrs entered the exam room and placed a petite and shy little Persian cat on the exam table. As they were explaining Miss Priss's history and present condition, I simply observed the cat's mannerism and behavior. She was a gentle little girl, and she sat quietly where she was placed. Suddenly, as if shocked, she swung around and started frantically licking and chewing at her tail stump. Mrs. Dohr sternly said, "Miss Priss, stop that."

I took a closer look at the tail stump and noticed that there wasn't much of a tissue cushion between the remaining tail vertebrae and the skin. I told the owners that Miss Priss could be experiencing discomfort at the amputation site because of adhesions or a neuritis (nerve inflammation), causing a hyperesthesia (excessive sensitivity), and that would explain her sudden and spontaneous reactions, as if being shocked. I recommended that the tail be amputated at the next vertebra and a tissue cushion be reconstructed over the end of the remaining bone. Miss Priss would definitely look like a Manx cat then because she'd end up with almost no tail at all. I told Mr. and Mrs. Dohr that the surgery could likely solve the problem.

Mr. Dohr asked me, "When can you do the surgery, Doc? She's miserable most of the time, and we hate to see her go on this way." I told them, "We'll schedule her for surgery as soon as possible." Our receptionist checked the appointment book, and scheduled the surgery for the next morning.

Miss Priss was the first surgery of the day. She was placed under a general anesthetic, the surgical site was shaved and prepped, and the procedure began. The end vertebrae was removed, and I reconstructed a nice tissue cushion over the remaining vertebrae. She now had a protective layer between the bone and the skin, and hopefully she'd be more comfortable.

Miss Priss made an uneventful recovery, healed quickly, and never licked or chewed at her tail—or what was left back there— ever again. Miss Priss once had a beautiful, long, fluffy tail, but now she was much more comfortable with her new look, and so were Mr. and Mrs. Dohr.

AN OVERCOMER

All of us, mankind, as well as animals, often face life-altering health issues. We have a choice of how we respond to those challenges—either we give in to the problem or rise up and triumph over adversity. Sandy, an eight-year-old buff-colored Cocker Spaniel, was an inspiring example of courage and determination. She was a true overcomer.

Judy Granger had noticed that Sandy's eyes were looking a bit bloodshot and also observed that Sandy was rubbing her eyes with her paws and on the carpet a lot more than usual that hot, dry summer. Judy understandably assumed that allergies were causing Sandy's eyes to itch, and rubbing them was just a natural response to the irritation. Judy frequently washed Sandy's face with a damp washcloth and often scolded her to stop rubbing, hoping the problem would go away, but it never did. In fact, the eye rubbing seemed to be getting worse and had become an obsession. That's when Judy brought Sandy to the clinic for some help.

Sandy was a good patient. She sat quietly on the exam table, knowing that she'd get treats if she was a good girl. She was. And she did. As I began to examine Sandy's eyes, I noticed that her right eye was more involved than the left. The sclera (white portion) was reddened, and the eyeball itself appeared swollen and enlarged. The cornea looked slightly cloudy and steamy because of the edema that had resulted from the constant irritation of rubbing. The lens, however, was clear, so she didn't appear to have cataracts. I told Mrs. Granger that Sandy's problems didn't appear to be an allergy issue, and I needed to conduct several more tests in order to help clarify some of my concerns. I applied a topical anesthetic to her right eye, and used a chartreuse-colored stain to check for any corneal ulcers or abrasions. None were found. Next I used an instrument to check the intraocular (within the eyeball) pressure because the eyeball appeared to be bulging. The pressure was definitely elevated—not good news. Sandy had glaucoma, an eye condition where there is increased fluid pressure within the eyeball, and it could gradually lead to blindness, or even worse, loss of the eye itself.

Mrs. Granger understood the gravity of the diagnosis and asked if anything could be done for Sandy. I told her that Sandy needed to be placed on some medication to help regulate the intraocular pressure, but sometimes, if the condition had become too advanced, the medication wouldn't have any effect. If that were to happen, then the intraocular pressure would continue to build, there'd be much more discomfort, and it would then be necessary to remove the eye. Mrs. Granger was willing to try the medication and accepted the fact that Sandy could lose her eye.

Mrs. Granger faithfully gave Sandy her medication for several weeks, but there was no improvement. The eye, in fact, had actually become larger and much more painful for Sandy. Her appetite had drastically decreased, she'd become less active and sought seclusion. It was quite apparent that she could not go on this way. The eye had progressed to the point where it couldn't be saved. The decision was made to remove the eye as soon as possible, and the enucleation (removal of the eye) surgery was quickly scheduled for the very next day. Sandy was the first surgical case that morning. She was placed under a general anesthetic, the surgical site was shaved and prepped, and the painful blind eye was successfully removed. When Sandy awoke from the anesthetic, she acted relieved that the painful eye was gone. Sandy made a speedy recovery, and after all her hair had grown back, it was hard to tell that she only had one eye. There was no rubbing. She was happy, more active, and even played fetch with the ball. Her appetite was back to normal, and she was essentially her old self again, —- minus an eye. Everyone was pleased at how well she had adapted.

Several months had passed, and then the remaining eye started to swell. It became reddened and seemed painful to Sandy. My chief concern had become a reality. The remaining eye had also developed glaucoma, and it too did not respond to medical treatment. With each passing day, Sandy was experiencing more and more discomfort as the intraocular pressure continued to increase. She'd become virtually blind, was in constant agony from the pain, and I was faced with the distinct possibility of removing her only remaining eye. The big question was, "How would she adapt to being totally blind?" Her can-do attitude and easy-going personality gave me reason to be optimistic about the removal of her remaining eye. I knew that Sandy was an overcomer, and I was confident she'd find a positive way to deal with the absence of eyes, but it was, nonetheless, a big gamble.

The surgery went well, but now this sweet little dog didn't have any eyes at all. The gradual onset of glaucoma in Sandy's remaining eye had allowed her to adapt to her progressively diminishing eyesight. She had learned to rely more on her other senses to compensate for lack of vision. She'd turn and tilt her head, listen intently, and elevate her nose to sniff the air for any olfactory clues. If she'd bump into something, no problem, she'd back up, reassess, make adjustments, and try again—totally undaunted. She was still happy and enjoyed life, in spite of the "minor" inconvenience.

You couldn't help but marvel at the courage, true grit, and heart of this little dog with no eyes. Sandy was amazing! She was the perfect example of how an individual can adapt to a setback or physical challenge and triumphantly overcome. Sandy will always be a special friend and patient to me, one who really touched my heart and reaffirmed why I chose to become a veterinarian.

UNCONDITIONAL LOVE

Unconditional love is often defined as affection without limitations, to love someone as they are, completely, without reservation, and in all circumstances. That close, unselfish relationship can often exist between animals and their human companions, and in many cases, both have their lives enriched and prolonged by the experience.

" JULIETTE "

Strays tend to be independent creatures that are "on the lam." They've either run away from a bad situation, been abandoned, or have simply remained feral. Strays essentially are out there operating in survival mode, focusing on two basic needs—food and shelter. When they find a place where food is plentiful and the shelter is safe and secure, they seize the moment and often hang up their nomadic lifestyle and settle in. In many instances, if given a chance, these vagabonds can often become wonderful friends and faithful companions.

A four-year-old domestic shorthair cat of unknown ancestry was out there on her own—a stray. I don't exactly know how Kim

Olson crossed paths with the unkempt feline, but she felt sorry for the little waif. Kim thought the cat had probably been abandoned and decided to befriend the poor little thing and take her home. The cat quickly adjusted to her new surroundings, and Kim soon came to the realization that another cat had been added to the household. She figured that if the cat was going to stay, it needed a proper name, so Kim named the little ragamuffin Juliette. It wasn't long before a strong bond of love and trust was forged between the two of them, and it continued to mature through the years.

Juliette was about nine years old when she came to the clinic for her annual checkup and vaccinations. She appeared to be healthy and happy, but while examining her mouth, I noticed a small, hard bean-sized lump on the right side of her lower jaw, near her mandibular canine tooth. I asked Kim, "How long has Juliette had this lump on her jaw?"

Kim replied, "Not too long, I guess. I thought it might be an infected tooth or something, maybe a little abscess because she does get into some fisticuffs with the other cats once in a while."

As I continued to examine the lump, I found it to be very firm and immovable. It wasn't painful or warm to the touch, and the adjacent lymph nodes weren't enlarged—yet.

"What do you think is going on, Doc?" Kim asked, with some definite concern in her voice.

"It could be an infected tooth, an encapsulated abscess, a bone infection, or a bone tumor," I replied. "Most infections tend to be uncomfortable, and the animals usually have elevated temps, but Juliette's temp is normal, and the lump doesn't seem to be that painful to her when I press on it." I hesitated a few moments, then told her, "Kim, I seriously believe that we're looking at a tumor here, bone cancer, an osteosarcoma,—and that kind of tumor isn't very forgiving. They're usually malignant. An x-ray should tell us if that's what's going on here."

Tears began to well up in Kim's eyes as she said, "Oh, Juliette, why'd this have to happen to you?"

X-rays were taken and showed significant bone changes that were consistent with bone cancer, and the prognosis wasn't good.

When Kim asked how long Juliette had, I told her that Juliette had perhaps six to nine months or maybe a year to live. My heart felt heavy as I spoke those words. It was always difficult delivering bad news. Radiation treatments and chemotherapy were options and could possibly give Juliette some additional time, but there were no guarantees. Kim realized that and decided not to subject Juliette to all the treatments. She just wanted Juliette to be comfortable for as long as possible. Quality of life was Kim's primary concern. I completely understood and wholeheartedly agreed with her decision. I told Kim that I'd taken that approach with my own animals when they had cancers, and I'd be willing to treat Juliette as if she were my very own. Kim smiled wistfully and nodded her head in approval. She needed a hug, so I gave her a consoling embrace. I knew how she felt, I'd been there myself.

I placed Juliette on pain medication and anti-inflammatory drugs in an effort to make her more comfortable and slow the rate of tumor growth. I checked her frequently over the ensuing six months, and as the tumor grew, so did the degree of disfigurement of Juliette's face, but the love connection between Kim and Juliette never faltered. Their relationship was the perfect example of mutual unconditional love and devotion. It had been almost ten months since Juliette was first diagnosed with bone cancer, and the time had now come to help her gently cross over to the other side. Kim and Juliette had supported each other through some very tough times, yet their mutual affection never wavered. That committed resolve enabled them to endure till the end.

" ABIGAIL "

"Abigail" was a Siamese-cross cat whose better years were behind her. When she was twelve years old, her owner, Mary Mills, noticed that Abigail was getting thinner in spite of her voracious appetite. Abigail was still her happy, active self, but the progressive weight loss concerned Mary, so she made an appointment to have Abigail examined.

Mary entered the exam room, clutching a very thin cat in her arms. The cat seemed perfectly content as it periodically gazed up at Mary. My physical exam of Abigail revealed an active, older cat, that looked like a starvation case—basically skin and bones. Although her eyes were bright and lungs sounded clear, her heartbeat was quite loud and rapid. When I offered her a few cat treats, she devoured them without chewing and then frantically looked for more. I told Mary there were many factors that could contribute to a cat losing weight so rapidly. The most likely were malabsorption syndrome, parasites, diabetes, hyperthyroidism, and cancer. Several diagnostic tests needed to be performed in order to narrow the field of possibilities. The fecal analysis was negative, so internal parasites were not an issue. Abigail's lymph nodes were not enlarged, she didn't have any visible tumors, and most cancer cases weren't as active and animated as she was. Her blood analysis showed normal blood glucose levels, so she didn't appear to be diabetic, and she wasn't anemic or leukemic. However, the results of the T4 test, a blood test used to evaluate the thyroid activity, was extremely elevated! Abigail had a hyperthyroid condition; her metabolism was working at warp speed, burning up all her fat reserves. That's why she was losing weight, even though she was eating voraciously. Her body was running on high idle, which contributed to the rapid heart rate. The poor little cat may have appeared calm on the outside while resting in Mary's arms, but she had a raging metabolism on the inside. That's why she looked so thin, as if she was starving. She couldn't eat enough to maintain a normal body weight.

I told Mary that there were several treatment options for hyperthyroid conditions, surgical removal of the thyroid gland, radiation therapy to destroy the gland, or oral medication to slow down the thyroid gland's activity. Mary selected the oral medication. Abigail was a very good patient, and I checked her T4 values periodically to make medication dosage adjustments if necessary. Mary was totally committed to loving and caring for Abigail, no matter what the situation or circumstance. That display of unconditional love and devotion allowed little Abigail to live comfortably for nineteen years.

" SHELBY "

Barbara Wilson was one of the most compassionate, empathetic individuals that I'd ever met. Her snow-white hair, radiant smile, positive attitude about life, and genuine love for animals and their welfare definitely set her apart. It was always a joy to see her walk through that clinic door.

Barbara had recently adopted a dog from the local humane society, and it was scheduled for a courtesy health check and physical exam. I shouldn't have been surprised by her selection, but I was. You see, the dog wasn't exactly what most people would have chosen to rescue, but once again, Barbara wasn't like most people. The dog was a middle-aged spayed female Brittany spaniel–Shelty cross with a right ear that permanently stuck out to the side as if signaling to make a turn, and weak facial muscles on the right side of her head, which suggested some previous traumatic nerve injury or side effects from a stroke. Her hair coat wasn't that great either. It appeared dull and brittle, something often seen as a result of poor nutrition.

Curiosity got the best of me, so I asked Barbara, "Why'd you choose this dog?"

"I liked her, and she's a nice girl." Barbara glanced wistfully at the dog and responded, "Nobody seemed to want her, and I felt sorry for the poor little thing, so I thought I'd give her a chance. She deserved at least that much. Everybody deserves a chance, don't you think?"

I nodded my head in agreement, continued the exam, and proceeded to point out some of the dog's physical flaws. Barbara looked down at the dog, smiled, and reassuringly said, "I know." That was good enough for me, so I told Barbara, " I'll do all I can to help this little girl."

Barbara had named the dog "Shelby," but in my opinion, it should have been named "Blessed" because the dog was truly blessed when it was adopted by such a loving and caring person. The first order of business was to get Shelby on some quality food, and it didn't take long before her hair coat was shiny and supple. She still had flaccid facial muscles and a droopy upper eyelid on her right side, but she was happy and very devoted to Barbara. Those two sure loved each other.

Several years passed by, and on one of Shelby's routine annual exams, I noticed that the hair on her torso and hind legs was thinning. She also didn't seem as energetic and animated as before; in fact, she appeared quite lethargic. I told Barbara that I needed to draw some blood and test Shelby's thyroid activity. The test results revealed that her T4 value was definitely *below* normal. Shelby was hypothyroid. The thyroid gland was not functioning as it should, and that contributed to her hair loss and sluggishness. I immediately placed her on medication to specifically stimulate the thyroid gland. Barbara conscientiously gave Shelby the meds as directed, and Shelby's hair grew back nicely, she wasn't lethargic anymore, and she quickly returned to her normal, active self. Problem solved. But she needed to stay on the medication and have her thyroid values checked every few months for any dosage adjustments.

All went well for two more years, but then Shelby started showing different signs that raised some concerns. She was drinking more water and consequently urinating more. Her skin, especially on the abdomen, appeared thinner and more wrinkled than normal, and she had muscle weakness, especially in the hind legs. These findings raised a red flag for Cushing's disease, a disease that involves the adrenal gland. A routine blood chemistry screen showed that her serum alkaline phosphatase was elevated, as well as the serum cholesterol levels, and the leukogram (white blood cell analysis) revealed some signs of stress. I then ran a high-dose dexamethasone suppression test and a urine cortisol:creatine ratio test, and the results of both tests confirmed my suspicions. Shelby now had Cushing's disease along with her hypothyroid condition, and she needed to be placed on medication to shrink down the adrenal gland and slow its activity. There was, however, one major problem. The medication of choice made Shelby very sick. She vomited, had diarrhea, and refused to eat. Not good!

There were other methods of treatment available, including surgical removal of the adrenal gland and radiation therapy, but Barbara wasn't interested. My options were getting smaller pretty fast. I recalled reading an article in a recent veterinary journal about a new drug being used in England to treat Cushing's disease in dogs, and it was reported to be very safe and effective. Bingo! That would be just the ticket for Shelby. I had to get ahold of some of that stuff. Then came the fly in the ointment: the drug wasn't yet available in the United States for veterinary use. But I did manage to find out that there was a company in Boston that could import the medication through Canada. I phoned the company and ordered a bottle right then and there. Barbara was excited about the new find, and with her permission, Shelby was started on the new drug. It worked great! She had no side effects, and in short order, the little dog with the sticky-outy ear and weak facial muscles was enjoying life again.

Everyone has heard the saying, "Things happen in threes," and in Shelby's case, it unfortunately was true. The following year, during a routine physical exam, I detected a heart murmur and some lung congestion, which explained why she'd recently been coughing more than usual. X-rays showed that the poor little girl's heart was enlarged because the muscles had become stretched and weakened as a result of the tricuspid mitral valve not closing properly, which produced the murmur. The heart valve problem was not allowing the left side of the heart to efficiently pump the oxygenated blood from the lungs out throughout her body. As a result, there was back pressure into the lungs, and this caused fluid to accumulate in the lungs (pulmonary edema) and the reason for the cough. I placed Shelby on vasodilator medication for the heart and diuretics to remove fluid from the lungs. Her diet was also changed to a special cardiac diet, which was low in sodium, so as to decrease fluid retention. Shelby responded well to the treatment, the cough stopped, and the heart problem was managed successfully from that time forward.

Barbara Wilson and Shelby epitomized an unconditional love relationship, and it greatly enriched both of their lives. Barbara really loved that unusual-looking little dog. She gave it a chance just like she said it deserved, and faithfully cared for it through all its health challenges. Shelby and Barbara were a blessing to each other, and their close, unselfish relationship got them through the tough times and allowed them to have many wonderful years together.

CATCH OF THE DAY

Living and working in a small town surrounded by five very productive fishing lakes was absolutely wonderful! There were many times when I'd go fishing at five o'clock in the morning, catch my limit of rainbow trout, clean them, and be at the veterinary clinic at eight a.m. to see my first patient of the day. It was really a kick in the pants, and I wasn't the only one who enjoyed the fishing either. The lakes were like magnets, drawing people from miles around with their boats, dogs, fishing poles, and tackle boxes filled with fishing gear. Everyone seemed to be having a good time until something went wrong, and when trouble hit, it usually involved a fishhook. Those brightly colored, flashy fishing lures dangling on the end of a line or flying through the air were too tempting for most dogs. They'd instinctively leap and snap at the flying toy, and many, unfortunately, suffered the consequences. Some people got really creative and even put a smorgasbord of marshmallows, tasty red worms, and yellow stinky bait around the hook. That tantalizing morsel proved too much for some dogs, and down the hatch it went. Time to go to the vet!

Most of the time the barbed hooks got painfully embedded in the dog's lip, and the angled barb prevented the hook from being pulled out. The only solution was to sedate the dog and then painlessly push the tip of the hook completely through the lip. Once that was accomplished and the barb was exposed, a side-cutter tool was then used to cut off and remove the barbed end. Now, the remainder of the hook could be easily removed. It was a whole different story, however, when a dog swallowed the smorgasbord.

Everything had been going along quite routinely that day at the clinic until an unannounced emergency came through the front door. "My dog just swallowed a fishhook, and I think it's really down there," the owner said. His forty-pound Heinz 57 dog just stood there, flipping its tongue at the monofilament fishing line hanging out of its mouth. I quickly sedated the dog, whose name was Rufus, and took x-rays to identify the type of hook and pinpoint its location.

The x-rays revealed that the dog had swallowed a triple hook, and it was located at the bottom end of the esophagus, right next to the entry opening into the stomach. The owner was right; it was way down there! Now the big question, how to get it out! The triple hook couldn't simply be pulled out because all three hooks would then sink deeply into the esophageal tissue. Attempting to move and reposition the hook directly into the stomach and then retrieving it via abdominal surgery and a gastrotomy was a possible option, but much more complicated and time consuming. I didn't own a gastroscope to maneuver down the esophagus to grasp the hook, but a nearby veterinary specialist did; unfortunately their office was closed. As I was mulling over my options, I suddenly had an epiphany! I recalled a seldom-used instrument that I'd purchased several years earlier, and the thought occurred to me that it might be helpful in this particular case. The special instrument was a tubular scope about eighteen inches long and one-half inch in diameter, with a built-in light source. I muttered to myself, "This might actually work!"

I began the procedure by threading the monofilament fishing line through the tube. Thank goodness the owner didn't cut the line any shorter than he did. I then carefully moved the scope down the esophagus while maintaining light tension on the line until the shiny triple hook came into view. I gently dislodged the hook with the tip of the scope and managed to snag one of the hooks on the rim of the scope. Then, while maintaining light traction on the line, I carefully withdrew the scope along with the hook from the confines of the esophagus. Yahoo! It worked!

Rufus did great! He recovered quickly and didn't have any complications. I guess you could say that he was the "catch and release" patient of the day. Hopefully everyone, especially the dog, learned a lesson from the whole painful experience.

REFLECTIONS

We've all experienced special moments in our lives that have produced lasting memories—most of which were good, thank heavens. Some memories can fade over time, while others continue to endure. The following are a few amusing snippets from my memory bank.

" LOBO "

"Lobo" was a German Shepherd who honorably served in Vietnam as a guard dog. Upon completion of his tour of duty, he somehow managed to defy the odds and made it back to the United States. This was, in all honesty, a minor miracle, because most military dogs never left country. He eventually ended up living the remainder of his years on a small ranch located only a few miles from the clinic.

One might think that this dog's military training and wartime experiences would render him to be potentially dangerous and unacceptable for adoption, but that wasn't the case at all. The loud and threatening sounds of war were long gone. Lobo seemed to know that his military days were over, and it was now time for some well deserved R & R. He was a good boy, and his laid-back personality was not unlike that of Ferdinand the bull. Instead of sitting among the flowers in a pasture, Lobo spent much of his time lounging in the sun with his adoring horde of cats. It was a mutual love affair between that dog and his feline companions.

The image of Lobo that will be forever etched in my memory occurred when I went on a farm call to the ranch to work on one of the horses. When I got out of the truck, there was Lobo, sauntering across the farmyard, surrounded by eight cats with "happy tails" lifted high in the air. He looked like some sort of rock star with his groupies. Lobo was a great dog that lived life to the fullest and actually made it to the ripe old age of nineteen, a feat most German Shepherds aren't fortunate enough to attain.

" CY "

It was one of those beautiful spring Saturdays when everything was going right. The trees were leafed out, the lawn looked lush and green, and the flowers were beginning to bloom. Then suddenly, my moment in nirvana was interrupted by a stray cat jetting through the yard as if he were trying to evade the IRS. His low-profile running posture made it look like he was attempting to avoid a barrage of low-flying bullets. This guy was running scared.

It took some doing, but I managed to find the brown tabby cat hunkered down by the woodpile. He was young, about two to three years old, and I noticed there was something unusual about his appearance. Upon closer inspection, his eyes seemed to be positioned closer together than most cats. I squatted down and gently said to him, "Hey there, little buddy, I'm not going to hurt you. What's your name?" The cat shifted his eyes and blinked several times. Then out came a high-pitched *meow-ph*. I continued talking to the little guy while slowly getting closer to him. He started to relax a little, feeling less threatened, and that's when the lispy meowing really started in earnest. *Meow–ph, meow–ph, meow–ph.* I finally managed to get close enough to stroke his head, and that's when he actually started to purr. This frightened and homeless little cat was all alone in unfamiliar surroundings because he'd probably been dropped off and abandoned.

It didn't take long to gain his trust and confidence, and that enabled me to get close enough to pick him up and hold his trembling body in my reassuring arms. Now, the next hurdle— find this little cat with close set eyes and the lispy meow, a good home. I took the little fella to the clinic for a thorough physical exam. He was dewormed, vaccinated, treated for fleas, and blood tests for feline leukemia and feline AIDS were performed. He passed with flying colors, but he needed an identity, a name. Since his eyes were positioned so close together, I decided to name him "Cy", short for cyclops.

Cy quickly settled into his new digs. He was a real charmer and easily won over the hearts of the entire staff. Heidi, one of our veterinary technicians, was smitten with him, and needless to say, Cy couldn't have found a better home. He was one of my favorite rescue cases. Cy was definitely one of a kind, the cat with close set eyes and a lisp. *Meow–ph!*

" KINDLE "

A smiling dog is one thing that's sure to make almost anyone laugh. Those lighthearted canine expressions ranged from the wistful Mona Lisa–type smiles to the big toothy grins that looked very much like a threatening snarl. Sometimes those funny facial expressions were accompanied by gentle whines, squinted or winking eyes, and even gyrating hindquarters. It was really a hoot! Over the years I saw quite a few smiling dogs, but there was one special little Pomeranian named "Kindle", and she was one smiler that I'll never forget.

Harvey Kranek called the clinic and inquired about purchasing a dog shampoo that would treat dry skin and dandruff. He'd recently bought a dog in Montana, and it had been itching and scratching ever since he brought the dog home. He called the breeder and was told that the puppy just had dry, flaky skin, and that a little extra oil in the food and a good bath should solve the problem. The oil added to the food and a basic dog shampoo didn't seem to help, so Harvey was looking for a stronger shampoo. Our receptionist told Mr. Kranek that many things could contribute to a dog itching and highly recommended that the dog be examined. Mr. Kranek was at his wits' end and knew that something had to be done for the poor little dog, so he scheduled an appointment.

Several days later, Mr. Kranek walked into the exam room clutching the six-month-old tan-orange-colored Kindle. She was a cute little thing, and I could definitely see why the Kranek family chose her. When you'd say her name and gently pat her on the head, she'd squint her little eyes and slightly draw up the corners of her mouth. I commented to Mr. Kranek, "Have you noticed that she smiles when she's happy?"

Harvey responded, "Yeah. I know. Isn't that the funniest thing you've ever seen?" We both had a good chuckle. It actually seemed like the more we laughed, the more she smiled. It was crazy!

Now, enough of the levity, it's time to get down to business. Kindle could hardly stand still. She'd scratch almost nonstop at her back and sides with her hind paw. She was one very miserable little girl. I continued with the physical exam and didn't see any fleas or flea dirt (droppings consisting of dried blood), but there was flakey dandruff everywhere. I told Harvey that Kindle could have a mite infestation, and I needed to examine some of her hair, dandruff, and skin under the microscope. I took samples, placed them on a slide, focused in the microscope, and—bonanza!—we'd struck the mother lode! There, right before my eyes, were three chubby little Cheyletiella mites with their four sets of stubby legs moving in ultraslow motion. A few Cheyletiella eggs were lazily floating around on the slide too. I asked Harvey if he'd like to take a look. He was game.

"There's the culprit," I said. "That's why Kindle is itching and scratching so much and why she has all that dandruff." I told Harvey that Cheyletiella mite cases are often referred to as "walking dandruff" because the mites make the dandruff move ever so slightly. He thought that little fact was pretty neat, but I was sure that Kindle wasn't amused. She was too focused on scratching.

There were several treatment options available. Some were systemic (absorbed by the body), and some were non-systemic. Since Kindle was young and weighed only three and a half pounds, I felt the systemic treatments could possibly pose a safety risk. So I selected a non-systemic therapeutic shampoo, which contained pyrethrins, a safer insecticide compound. Harvey was instructed to bathe Kindle weekly for four weeks and wash all her bedding weekly as well. I was confident that treatment regimen would work, and it did! Kindle got relief with the very first therapeutic bath, but Harvey followed through and completed the course of bathing as directed, and when the treatment was finished, Kindle looked and acted like a new dog. Her hair coat was soft and shiny, the dandruff was totally gone, and best of all, she didn't itch anymore. One thing didn't change though, she still smiled. I fondly recall each time Kindle visited the clinic. I'd say, "Hey, Kindle, how's my girl?" She'd shyly dip her head slightly, squint those little brown eyes, and smile. Kindle was a delight and, without a doubt, one of my sweetest patients.

ASK, AND YOU SHALL RECEIVE

A farm call to the Neuland ranch was like taking a trip to Comedy Central—on the farm. The two hardworking ranch hands, Skip and Bill, found humor in just about everything, and it was always a blast working with those two guys. Actually, it was more like having Cheech and Chong as assistants.

The ranch's cattle herd was on a routine de-worming program, and periodic fecal exams were needed to evaluate the effectiveness of the medication. I'll never forget the time I called the ranch and asked Skip to drop off a small stool sample from the cows. Several days later, a personally addressed letter to "Doc Roloff" arrived in the mail. When I opened the envelope, I found a piece of facial tissue with a skid mark of cow manure on it. A small handwritten note was also enclosed. It read, "Doc, here's the small sample you wanted. Signed, Skip." I got a good laugh out of it, and so did everyone else in the clinic, but I needed a tad more manure in order to run the test. So I called Skip, and when he recognized that it was me on the phone, he about "split-a-gut" laughing. "Doc," he said, "you got the letter, huh? You said you wanted a little sample, so that's what we sent ya." Then there was more howling laughter on his end of the phone. He gave a tongue-in-cheek apology, in between snickers, and then told me that he'd drop off a "good" sample at the clinic in a few days. I fell for that one too.

Skip was true to his word. Two days later Skip and Bill walked through the clinic door, laughing and proudly carrying a Frisbee piled high with fresh cow manure. My mind instantly conjured up all kinds of images of how they got that much poop on the Frisbee, but the sample was sufficient. It was a weirdly comedic scene—two guffawing sunshine boys, dressed in coveralls, holding a Frisbee filled to overflowing with aromatic cow dung. As I took the Frisbee and its contents, I asked the guys if they wanted the Frisbee back.

They commented, "Nah. You can keep it."

Then more howling laughter broke out. They got me again. Oh, by the way, the stool specimen was negative for parasite eggs, and if any additional tests would have been needed, believe me, there was more than enough dung available.

HOUSE CALLS

House calls provided me the opportunity to witness firsthand the positive interaction between people and their pets—on their turf, instead of mine. It was always amazing to see how strong the human-animal bond could be and observe the close relationship that often exists between soul mates.

" LITTLE ORPHAN ANNIE "

As I walked into the clinic that morning, I couldn't help noticing a new patient in one of the recovery room cages. It was a noisy little tortoise shell–colored kitten, about sixteen weeks old, and she was very insistent about getting some attention. The cage card simply read, "Stray." I couldn't resist that cute little orphan so I opened the cage door, and she instantly jumped into my arms and started purring. I looked down at her contented little face and asked her in my Humphrey Bogart-like tone of voice, "Sweetheart, who the heck are you, and what's a nice girl like you doing in a place like this?" She didn't say much, but it was evident that she was overjoyed to get out of that cage and just be held.

It wasn't long before I got filled in on all the details. Melody, one of our veterinary assistants, had a neighbor suddenly move out of their rented home. They either knowingly or unknowingly left behind a very pregnant cat to fend for herself. The poor little mother-to-be was scared stiff and sought refuge under the vacated house. She went from having food constantly available to frantic scavenging for anything that was edible, but she was a true survivor. Melody set out food and water for the little abandoned waif, and that in itself was a lifesaver. Soon the cat delivered four beautiful kittens, and Melody spent many hours socializing the kittens with hopes of finding them good homes. In time, three of the kittens had been placed, and Melody brought the remaining kitten, who she'd named Annie, to the clinic for routine vaccinations, de-worming, and possible adoption.

When Melody mentioned adoption, one person instantly came to mind—Collin Sumpter. Collin was a bachelor who loved his cats, and he'd recently lost his beloved cat, "Callo". He was heartbroken and told me that since Callo had been such a huge part of his life, it would probably take a long time before he'd be able to have another cat. I completely understood because the grieving process can often take a while, but then Annie came on the scene two weeks later. I remembered what Mr. Sumpter had said, but I thought I'd give him a phone call anyway and try to convince him to at least take a look at Annie. When Mr. Sumpter answered the phone, there was profound sadness in his voice. He wasn't at all receptive to the idea of getting another cat so soon after Callo's passing. Perhaps he was patronizing me, but eventually he said, "I'll stop by sometime." Our conversation didn't leave me very optimistic, but it must have moved Mr. Sumpter because later that day he came to the clinic and asked to see the kitten. When I walked into the exam room with Annie in my arms, Mr. Sumpter's face lit up like a neon sign, and he smiled ear-to-ear as I handed him the kitten. Collin gently and lovingly stroked the kitten as he held it close to his chest. "What's its name?" he asked.

"Annie, Little Orphan Annie," I said. He was totally smitten with that little cat, who was now thoroughly engrossed with Mr. Sumpter and all the attention he was giving to her.

Then he said with a smile, "Little Orphan Annie, huh? I like that name. Would you like to come home with me?"

I'd become a mere bystander, witnessing two needy individuals finding a soul mate in each other. It couldn't have worked out any better. They really looked like a match made in heaven. Those two became devoted companions, and Mr. Sumpter provided Annie with the best of everything. Nothing was too good for his Annie. When it came time to go to the vet for her annual checkup and vaccinations, Collin requested that I make a house call because he thought that would be less stressful for Annie. I agreed and set up a time.

House calls were fun most of the time. Invariably, the cat would disappear the moment I stepped inside the door. The most common owner comment was, "Where'd she go? She was here just a minute ago." The usual hiding places were either under the bed, behind the big chair, or under the couch. It often turned into a hands and knees exercise, with the coffee table or dinette doubling as an exam table, but it all seemed to work out just fine! Annie, although a quiet protester, was still a very good patient. She had her favorite escape routes and "safe" places. Hiding under Collin's bed seemed to be the default location, and that was the first place we looked. It was quite the scene, three people on their hands and knees—butts in the air—looking under the bed, all the while trying to entice Annie from her safe haven with words of sweet nothings. Eventually the job got done, and we all had a good chuckle over what we put ourselves through for our feline friends.

ONE OF A KIND

Mr. Konig was a spry little gent in his eighties who had a soft spot in his heart for cats. He was our local Saint Francis of cats in the Lake and LeFevre Street region, befriending any sick and abandoned felines and bringing them to our veterinary clinic for care and treatment. Thank heavens for the generous donations to our compassion fund because those funds helped defray some of the medical costs incurred with treating all those strays.

As time passed, it was becoming increasingly more difficult for Mr. Konig to catch his own cats and bring them to the clinic for routine physical exams and vaccinations. He needed some help, so I offered him in-house veterinary care for his cats, and he gladly accepted. I always had a veterinary assistant accompany me on house calls. They helped find and catch the often reluctant patients and assisted with examinations, treatments, and any necessary paperwork. I really appreciated Megan and Heather's efforts. They were good!

House calls to Mr. Konig's residence were always an adventure, and just walking through the front door was a real experience. His two cats, Blackie and Whitey, took off with blazing speed and reckless disregard, as if someone had just yelled out, "Air raid!" Those two would knock over their food dishes, flip the water bowls, and send the throw rugs a-flyin' in their great escape. They were outta there! We had to clean up the mess before beginning the roundup. Blackie would usually ditch under the bed, and Whitey opted for safety behind the living room couch. I was thankful to have some young, fit, and flexible assistants because they were the ones who had to get Blackie out from under the bed in that very cramped bedroom. I'd swear, sometimes they had to get themselves into positions that resembled a contortionist doing yoga exercises, but they eventually retrieved the escapee. Now, Whitey had the whole routine pretty much figured out. Whichever end of the couch we'd approach, she'd jet out the opposite end and fly off to another room. This little rodeo went on for a while, but in time, we corralled the little buckaroo. Honestly, I think she thought we were playing a game of hide and seek because when we finally caught her, she started purring. Go figure!

House calls were also interesting in another way. We got to know the people on a personal level when they shared memorable photos, experiences, and cherished memories with us. Mr. Konig, for example, proudly showed us several framed photos of himself together with familiar showbiz celebrities. He was with comedian Jack Benny in one photo and with the famous ventriloquist Edgar Bergan in another. Mr. Konig nonchalantly reminisced about being on the same stage and billing with those entertainers and many others. He'd been a professional ventriloquist himself, performing on the East Coast for many years. Wow! Who would have known?

Mr. Konig was a very engaging individual. He always insisted upon giving the vet assistants a tip of $15 or $20 before we left. He'd say, "Here, I want you to have this. I appreciate you coming to my house. You're a nice young lady, and I know you can use the money."

At first they were reluctant to take the cash gratuity, but Mr. Konig was persistent, and eventually they graciously accepted the gift.

Without a doubt, Mr. Konig was definitely one of a kind.

PAW PRINTS ON THE HEART

Ask anyone about their most favorite pet, then sit back and watch what happens next. The person's eyes will light up as they recall and share cherished memories, often with vivid and exacting detail. You'd think that those events just recently happened, but in all reality, they'd taken place many years earlier. Those indelible memories prove how strong the human-animal bond can be and why animals are such an integral part of our lives.

Unfortunately, time stands still for no one, and it takes a heavy toll on all of us, including our pets. There will come a time when our faithful companion's health and quality of life has deteriorated to such an extent that we're faced with a difficult and agonizing question and decision: "Is it time to relieve the pain and suffering?" The final answer needs to be based upon the love and compassion we have for our devoted friend, but that still doesn't make it any easier.

Going on a final house call always weighed heavily on my heart. I knew it was an act kindness and compassion, yet I could empathize with the people because I'd been there many times myself. Invariably, the patient was lying on its favorite soft bed, surrounded by family members choking back tears. I'd kneel down and gently stroke the pet's head, telling them how good and courageous they'd been and that I'd come to help them go to a nice place where they wouldn't be sick or in pain anymore. A place where they could run, play, and chase butterflies all day long. The look in their eyes told me that they were ready to go. I then explained to those present that I'd first administer a sedative, and after a few minutes had passed, the final painless intravenous injection would be given.

Most families were at peace with what was necessary for their beloved companion. They'd wistfully reminisce about the good times and speak of how their four-footed family member had enriched their lives and taught them how to forgive and love unconditionally. As I administered the final injection, the family members would gently stroke their companion's head and tell them about a future reunion where they'd all be together again, and I truly believe they will be. The crossing over was always gentle, quick, and painless. Their faithful friend was now at peace. I often gave the family a lock of their friend's hair and made a keepsake paw print for them. Both served as a physical reminder that, although their companion wasn't here any longer, they'd never be forgotten. Then came the tears and the consoling hugs.

It was a bittersweet moment, an emotional roller coaster. For the family, it was a relief that the struggle was over, but a time of sadness in that their devoted companion was no longer with them. One thing was certain: there would forever be paw prints on their hearts.

A REAL DOWNER

Achilles was a Greek hero who fought in the Trojan War, and he was also the main character in Homer's *Iliad*. The legend tells us that when Achilles was an infant, his mother, Thetis, held him by his heel and dipped him into the river Styx in order to make him invulnerable, but his heel where he was being held remained dry and unprotected. The heel was Achilles's only vulnerable spot on his body, and he was later killed by an arrow wound to his heel. So the term "Achilles heel" was coined and used as a metaphor for a deadly weakness that, in spite of overall strength, could actually or potentially lead to a devastating downfall.

Not only do we as humans have our own particular areas of vulnerability, or Achilles heel, but so do our animal companions. The Achilles heel of the dachshund breed seems to be their back. A Dachshund, alias the "wiener dog," has a very interesting body type. It's long and low to the ground because they were originally bred to go down into badger holes and pull the critters out. The problem though, with such a long back, is that the midpoint of the back is particularly prone to intervertebral disk injuries, and when that happens, the consequences can often be devastating. Dachshunds tend to be very active little guys, and with all that gyrating and torquing of their long backs, they can often injure the pliable disks positioned between each vertebrae, causing them to either bulge or rupture, which then puts pressure on the nerves and spinal cord. It results in intense pain and is often accompanied by temporary or permanent hindquarter paralysis. Immediate medical attention is critical to having any chance of a favorable outcome for such a condition.

" FRITZ "

Terry and Chelsea Empler walked through the clinic door carrying their three-year-old Dachshund, "Fritz", who'd been "down in the hind end" for two weeks. When I heard Mr. Empler make that comment, my heart sunk because too much time had elapsed since the problem first appeared. Not a good situation for Fritz.

Little Fritz, bless his heart, did his best to support himself on the exam table. It was difficult to watch him struggle in an effort to make his hindquarters move, but it was all to no avail. He propped himself up with his front legs, held his head up high, and you could tell by the look in his bright little brown eyes that he really didn't understand what was going on. What really got to me was when I stroked his head, he actually licked my hand as if he were consoling me instead of visa versa.

My initial exam revealed that Fritz had a major posterior paralysis that involved both hind legs. Neither hind leg responded to the interdigital pinch reflex test. There was absolutely no feeling whatsoever. His tail was totally limp, and he didn't have any bladder control either. X-rays showed a profound narrowing of the intervertebral space between T13 and L1, suggesting that the intervertebral disk had been severely compressed, which caused it to bulge and rupture. That produced intense pressure on the spinal cord, which in turn resulted in the total restriction of nerve impulses to Fritz's hindquarters, causing the paralysis.

The treatment options for intervertebral disk syndrome cases included surgical decompression, anti-inflammatory medication plus muscle relaxants, strict inactivity, and acupuncture therapy. The success of the treatment regimens depended upon early initiation and the degree of severity of the injury. Unfortunately for Fritz, he'd been dealt a bad hand, and his paralysis, at this point, appeared to be untreatable and permanent. Mr. and Mrs. Empler were crestfallen when I explained to them the extent of Fritz's condition and the unfavorable prospects for his future. Then it hit me. "There is one other possibility," I said. "And that's a wheeled cart for paralyzed dogs. You know, kind of a wheelchair. I've got one here in the clinic, and I think it could be adjusted to fit little Fritz. Would you be willing to give it a try?"

"Oh yes, yes!" Mr. and Mrs. Empler said in unison as their tear-filled eyes lit up with hope. I told them that it often takes some dogs a little while to adjust to moving about in a wheeled cart, so I cautioned them to be patient with Fritz.

I retrieved the wheeled cart, made a few minor adjustments so it would fit Fritz's body, and then placed the little guy into his new wheels. He had a great attitude! He was excited and didn't appear intimidated whatsoever by the strange aluminum contraption. In fact, he looked quite confident as he stood there, supporting himself with his front legs while his hind legs were suspended in padded stirrups positioned over the wheels. We had a long central hallway in the clinic, and it was the perfect place for Fritz to make his "trial run."

Mr. Empler got down on his hands and knees at the far end of the hallway and called out, "Fritz, come!"

Fritz raised his head and perked his ears, then suddenly, off he went, full tilt, with ears flapping wildly and wheels a-turnin'. It was a sight to see! Fritz was having fun again! Then Mrs. Empler called him, and back down the hallway he went. Little Fritz was really getting the hang of it. Everyone was cheering him on, and the little guy gladly obliged, showing off his new motor skills.

Sometimes he'd get a bit carried away and turn too sharply. When that happened, the cart tipped over, but no big deal. Fritz just waited there patiently until someone put him back upright; then off he'd go full speed. He was one happy camper! He sort of reminded me of what Alfred E. Neuman of *Mad Magazine* would always say, "What? Me worry?"

Fritz's story is heartwarming and inspiring. He showed everyone what a positive attitude and sheer determination can accomplish. Fritz went on to enjoy a very good, free-wheeling life and demonstrated to all what it takes to overcome adversity.

ALTERNATIVE THERAPY

Intervertebral disk disease involving the cervical, lower thoracic and lumbar vertebrae, occurred primarily in long bodied dogs. This painful and potentially debilitating back problem ranged from mild to severe, and the treatment approaches varied accordingly. Most mild cases could be successfully managed with anti-inflammatory medications, muscle relaxants, and restricted activity, but a full-blown posterior paralysis was a whole different story. A hind quarter paralysis of any degree seemed to be the last straw for many doxies and their owners. Although the owners dearly loved their dogs, there were instances where the needed back surgery was financially impossible, and the people thought that humane euthanasia was their only recourse. I didn't want to go down that road, because there were other options available. For example, the Dachshund Rescue program. Those folks came to the aid of numerous downer doxies, hoping to provide some measure of relief and ultimately find new homes for those compromised little wiener dogs. Scenarios like these prompted me to find, offer, or suggest alternative forms of treatment, which could be effective and, most importantly, affordable.

My standard approach, other than surgery, was to use oral anti-inflammatory medication in combination with muscle relaxants and a special medicinal preparation that I'd formulate. It consisted of a penetrating reagent along with a potent steroid. I'd shave and clean an area along the dog's back that corresponded to the problem site, and then apply the liquid preparation topically with the aid of a dauber. The reagent carried the steroid deep into the tissue, reduced the swelling of the bulging disk, and took pressure off the spinal cord. The only problem—it smelled awful. But it worked, and the price was right! There were also occasions when I recommended acupuncture therapy, and the results were often amazingly successful at relieving a paralysis.

What was truly gratifying was the fact that the alternative procedures offered people hope for their beloved friend when initially all seemed lost. That hope was eventually realized in many cases, and as the word spread, I was called upon from far and wide to come to the aid of the little downers.

SUMMER TROUBLEMAKERS

Everyone enjoys the gentle warm breezes of summer, but those mild winds can sure dry things out. The green lawns become parched and turn brown, and so does just about everything else. When that happens, the weed and grass seeds also become dry and are easily scattered. Certain seeds can cause a myriad of problems, and the cheatgrass seed or awn, also referred to as a foxtail, seemed to be one of the worst culprits.

" BILLY BOB "

Norm Southwick had a three-year-old German shorthair dog named "Billy Bob", and that dog was one heck of a hunter. Billy Bob lived to hunt, and Norm put him through intense summer field training in preparation for the fall hunting season. Norm had noticed that Billy Bob was squinting his left eye and rubbing it for several days, so he made an appointment to have his dog's eye examined. Billy Bob came through the clinic door with his left eye completely closed, and tears were running down the left side of his face. He was definitely experiencing discomfort in that eye, so I immediately placed an anesthetic onto the eye in an attempt to relieve some of the pain. Once the eye didn't hurt anymore, he opened his eyelids, and that made the examination much easier.

It didn't take long to find the end of a cheatgrass awn or seed hiding under the eyeball. All Billy Bob's attempts to dislodge the awn hadn't worked because the tiny little barbs on the wispy tail of the awn were holding the offending seed in place, and the abundant flow of tears didn't seem to help dislodge it either. I delicately grasped the tail of the awn with a small forceps and gently removed it from its hiding place. Next, I examined the eyeball itself. The cornea, normally clear and transparent, appeared opaque and cloudy due to the swelling and edema that resulted from the irritation of the cheatgrass awn plus all the self-trauma from Billy Bob's rubbing. I applied a fluorescing stain to the surface of the cornea, and it revealed several abrasions plus a small corneal ulcer, both of which would heal with topical medication. Billy Bob's eye problems were solved, and he was now free of the pain and discomfort. He was good to go—hopefully not out into those weeds again.

" RUGER "

"Ruger" was a sturdy five-year-old Springer Spaniel who absolutely loved country life. He roamed freely and chased all kinds of birds to his heart's content, but his "no holds barred" lumbering technique didn't work in his favor. He really didn't care what he had to run through—brush, weeds, ponds—he was just having the time of his life, but that "C'est la vie" attitude is what got him into trouble.

Brad Welcher, Ruger's owner, had noticed Ruger licking his paws more than usual the last few days and thought that Ruger might have allergies or possibly had stepped into something sticky like pine pitch. When the licking and chewing didn't ease up, Brad decided to have Ruger looked at.

Ruger wasn't limping when he walked into the clinic, but I noticed the hair on all four paws appeared wet, stiff, and matted. Closer inspection revealed that all of his paws were swollen, reddened, and infected. The wet matted hair was not only from saliva, but also from the tacky, serous discharge that was coming from the numerous open sores between his toes. This guy had some major issues going on and needed medical attention ASAP.

I placed Ruger under a general anesthetic and proceeded to shave the serum-soaked hair off all four paws, exposing the full extent of his problems. There were multiple penetration openings in the web area between each toe on all four paws, and serum was visibly draining from each opening. Cheatgrass awns were everywhere—in the hair, some partially embedded into the skin, and others had totally perforated the skin and were now migrating deep into his tissue. There were also numerous festering, septic, fistulous tracts. It was a bad scene! Ruger's body was essentially attempting to reject the embedded offenders, but without much success. Some of the tails of the cheatgrass awns were visible in the openings, so I inserted a small forceps into each hole, grasped the awn, and gently removed it from its hiding place. That procedure was repeated over twenty times. Each tract was then flushed with antiseptics and antibiotics, the paws were bandaged, and for the time being, the ordeal was over.

When I showed Mr. Welcher the handful of cheatgrass awns that were removed from Ruger's paws, he said, "Holy cow! No wonder he was licking his paws so much. I guess I'd better check his feet more often." I definitely agreed and also recommended that the paws be kept shaved, especially during the warm months of summer.

Ruger was a good patient. He healed quickly, and it wasn't long before he was back out there running around like crazy. Brad Welcher had also learned a very valuable lesson. In the future, he kept the hair on Ruger's paws neatly trimmed and inspected the paws daily. The results—no more embedded cheatgrass awns, and that made everyone happy!

THE BODY INVADERS

It often seemed as if there wasn't a single place on the dog's body that was off limits to cheatgrass awns. Those pesky little varmints appeared to have a mind of their own, and just when you thought that you'd identified their favorite spots to invade, they'd throw you a curve and show up somewhere else.

A typical case often seen during the summer months involved a dog shaking its head, scratching and rubbing at one or both ears, and carrying its head cocked to one side. It sort of looked like someone trying to shake water out of his ears after going swimming. However, with the dog, all that head shaking was suggestive of two very plausible scenarios: (1) a serious ear infection or (2) a cheatgrass awn that had worked its way deep down inside the ear canal. In many cases it turned out to be the latter, and a quick look in the ear with an otoscope proved that to be true. The tiny barbs on the tail of the cheatgrass awn prevented it from being easily removed. So the only way to remove it safely was to sedate the dog and physically grasp the awn with a specialized forceps called an alligator forceps and pull the sucker out. Sometimes the pointed tip of the awn would contact and even puncture the eardrum, and needless to say, when that happened, it was very painful to the dog and serious damage to the eardrum and inner ear infections often resulted. Once the little invader was removed, the dog felt much better, as could be expected, and he was good to go. The odds, however, favored him to be a repeat offender somewhere down the road.

A twelve-week-old Brittany Spaniel puppy came into the clinic with a large soft domed swelling on the top of its head. A needle tap revealed it to be an abscess, and it was a bad one too. The little tyke was given a sedative, the abscess was lanced, drained, flushed, and then treated with antibiotics. Among the purulent drainage floated the culprit, a cheatgrass awn. The owner had been using some cheap bargain straw for bedding, and she confessed that she'd seen a lot of cheatgrass in the straw. One of the awns, along with some bacteria, had penetrated the puppy's skin on its head and caused the abscess.

The moral of the story: don't use dirty straw for bedding material! Oh yeah, the puppy recovered nicely, and the owner got rid of the straw and replaced it with a soft new bed. Problem solved!

· · · · · · · ·

Red was a beautiful Irish Setter, who was brought to the clinic with a grapefruit-sized lump on his left side. The hair over the lump appeared moist because the dog had been licking at the site for several days. Shaving off the wet, stiff hair revealed a very unusual-looking lesion. There were oodles of small penetrating holes, fistulous tracts, all over the surface of the lump, and tails of cheatgrass awns could be seen partially embedded in many of the holes. When I placed my hands around the lump and applied gentle pressure, multiple cheatgrass awns came popping out of the holes.

The owner happened to be standing right next to Red and witnessed the bizarre scene firsthand. She wrinkled up her nose and chimed out, "Eeeew! That's *really* gross! That's disgusting! How could that happen?"

I told her that Red probably laid down on a clump of cheatgrass, and the awns worked their way into and through the skin. Red's body was just trying to get rid of those pesky little foreign invaders. The owner responded, "Oh, I think I know how it happened. Red likes to go and lay on the hay bales in the barn, and that's probably where it all started." That sounded plausible to me.

I then sedated Red, removed scads of cheatgrass awns, cleaned and flushed the fistulous tracts, placed him on antibiotic medication, and sent him on his way, hoping that he'd stay out of the barn—or that the owners would buy better quality hay.

Over the years, I swear that I'd removed cheatgrass awns from just about every surface and orifice that a dog had—including the nose, mouth, and all the other very sensitive areas too, if you know what I mean. That benign-looking little plant, gently swaying in the warm summer breeze, appearing so innocent and totally incapable of causing any problems at all, —- but it does. It is undeniably one of the worst summertime troublemakers.

DOWN FOR THE COUNT

Who doesn't love animals? They're cute and cuddly when young and become devoted and loving companions as time goes by. We often form strong bonds with them, and they become an integral part of our life. That close connection frequently inspires people to learn more about their animal's health, behavior patterns, and basic principles of veterinary medicine. There were many occasions when interested individuals requested permission to observe procedures at the veterinary clinic. I was happy to oblige but soon discovered that some people were suited for it, and some definitely were not.

College students who were seriously considering the veterinary profession as a vocation were required to spend a specific number of hours with a veterinarian, observing examinations, treatment procedures, and surgeries. This was a requirement before ever applying to the college of veterinary medicine. It served as an opportunity for those individuals to test and evaluate their resolve and intestinal fortitude. Some students had never observed a surgical procedure before, and it proved to be a major eye-opener for them—in more ways than one.

I always set down ground rules prior to anyone observing surgeries. First and foremost, surgical masks had to be worn, and secondly, their hands had to be kept away from my surgical field—meaning, there should be no finger pointing or touching any of the structures. Thirdly, if they suddenly felt overly warm, sweaty, or dizzy, then they were to *please tell someone*! Most observers were interested, focused, and did just fine; however, there were others who didn't do as well. Comments like, "Boy, it's sure warm in here under those surgery lights" or "I feel a little dizzy" or "I don't feel so good" prompted me to immediately tell them to "sit down on the floor, lean your back up against the wall, and take some deep breaths."

Sandy, our office manager, was also a trained and licensed human nurse by profession, and when she heard my comments, she'd come rushing into the surgery room with smelling salts and cold packs in hand. She immediately went into action—broke open the smelling salts, placed the capsule under the victim's nose, and said with conviction, "Take a deep breath!" That first whiff was a doozie, —- a real eye opener! She then placed cold packs on their forehead and on the back of their neck, and it didn't take long before the person was back from their foggy experience. The students always felt embarrassed, but I reassured them that it wasn't a big deal and told them that they'd get used to it. And they did. In fact, many eventually became excellent veterinarians; however for some, they discovered that veterinary medicine wasn't their cup of tea.

I recall one particular case involving a large Bassett Hound that had been kicked in the muzzle by a horse. According to the owner, the dog's right upper canine tooth had been dislodged, and now all that remained was a big, empty, bloody socket. The dog was brought to the clinic and anesthetized, and preparations were made to close the opening.

I had a prospective veterinary student observing that day, and she was anxious to watch the procedure. As I began my preliminary exam of the empty socket, I noticed the very tip of the canine tooth, barely visible, way up inside the socket. The tooth hadn't been dislodged; it had been pushed back up deep within the facial bone. I nonchalantly said to the student, "Want to see me make his tooth reappear?" She looked at me with a puzzled expression on her face, and I then told her, "Watch this!" I delicately grasped the tip of the hidden tooth with a forceps and slowly pulled the huge, two-inch long canine tooth from its recesses. "See!" I proudly said as I held up my prize. I looked up just in the nick of time to see her eyelids flutter. She then slowly sank into the sunset — *out cold!* A call for help immediately went out for Sandy, and once again, she came to the rescue.

One thing was for certain. If we were going to allow clients and students to observe procedures, then we'd better keep the clinic well stocked with smelling salts and cold packs. Sandy had also become accustomed to the frantic call, "Help! We've got another one down for the count."

POINTS OF CONTENTION

Porcupines, also known as quill pigs, have a top-ground speed that's a little faster than a tortoise on steroids. Those gentle creatures with the wild hairdos walk around making mumbling, whiney, grunting sounds and prefer to be left alone. They don't attack anything, but when confronted, defend themselves very effectively with their barbed quills. The quills detach when touched and are not thrown, as many people believe. Once the quill penetrates the skin, the overlapping scales/barbs help move the quill inward, and many become deeply embedded. Quill cases were always considered an emergency because of the intense pain, discomfort, and disabling effects the quills had on the very unlucky dog. Some dogs had only a few quills in their paws or muzzle, while others had upward of a hundred or so of the barbed needles embedded all over their bodies. The treatment consisted of placing the dog under a general anesthetic and manually pulling out the quills individually—a one-at-a-time procedure. It often turned out to be a very long and arduous task.

The victimized dogs responded quite differently to their piercing ordeal. It all depended upon the number of quills and their locations. If the quills had found their mark in the dog's muzzle, mouth, or tongue, the dog usually pawed frantically at its face in an attempt to dislodge the mini-spears. Sometimes the dogs would stand almost motionless, because any movement on their part would cause the quills to slightly move, and that produced more pain and discomfort. Pain in itself can be, and often is, a very powerful motivator, one way or the other.

Trevor Masters brought his dog, Sparky, into the clinic with its head completely covered with porcupine quills. Sparky's face was almost unrecognizable, and it actually looked like a huge hedgehog was sitting atop of his neck. Sparky was an eighty-pound Lab-shepherd mix, and the evidence suggested that he'd gone in for the kill, but came out the loser. He'd definitely got his comeuppance.

Sparky was anesthetized, and three of us—myself and two veterinary assistants—began the challenging task of removing all those quills. Poor Sparky had quills everywhere throughout his mouth, lips, nose, cheeks, ears, and even some had impaled his tongue through and through. There were also a large number of porcupine quills in his front paws and chest. He looked like a totally defeated gladiator! It took the three of us well over an hour to remove all those quills, including multiple cut-downs where the embedded quills had to be surgically removed. One of the last places to check was the eyes. When I lifted the eyelid of Sparky's left eye, I saw the very end of a quill protruding from the conjunctival tissue, which is located next to and around the eyeball. I grasped the tip and began slowly pulling it out. That quill turned out to be two and a half inches long, and it had assumed a curved shape because when it became embedded, it conformed to the shape of the bony orbit of the eye socket. That was really weird!

Sparky recovered nicely, and as he walked out of the clinic, I said to Trevor, "I sure hope that he's learned his lesson."

Over the years I'd found that most dogs that had been impaled by porcupine quills didn't want to repeat that painful experience, so in the future, they avoided the quill pig like the plague. However, there were some, and unfortunately Sparky was one of them, that were repeat offenders. They were bound and determined to get even with the critter that caused them so much pain and discomfort. So I guess the saying applies to both man and beast, "Some learn. Some don't!"

MOMENTS IN TIME

Certain moments in time are like shooting stars in that they can leave us with some lasting impressions and specific mental images. The following are but a few of the interesting experiences that now reside in my memory bank.

CARRIERS

It was always amusing to see what people came up with for transporting their pets. It's been said that necessity is the mother of invention, and believe me, I saw some pretty interesting impromptu carriers.

There were the always handy and versatile laundry baskets. All sorts of things were used on top of the baskets to keep the pet inside, and the manner in which those things were attached was quite interesting too. Everything from duct tape to old shoe laces, bungee cords, leather belts, electrical cords, pieces of clothesline, and even old nylon stockings were used.

But the most unusual cat carrier that I'd ever seen was a birdcage. Shirley Kohler came waltzing into the clinic one day, toting a birdcage with her cat, Sam, sitting dispassionately inside.

Sam's hair coat and color patterns resembled the cartoon cat named Sylvester, so I laughingly asked him, "What'd you do with poor little Tweety Bird?" He just sat there and gave me a look of quiet resignation, appearing somewhat embarrassed with the whole situation.

Shirley quipped, "I was a little behind this morning. Couldn't find the dang carrier, so I grabbed whatever was handy. Pretty funny, huh?"

I couldn't have agreed more, but it worked! We both had a good chuckle; however, Sam didn't seem to be very impressed.

Other items used as quasi-carriers included pillowcases, storage totes, food and beverage coolers, old leather purses and satchels, and of course, the good ole reliable cardboard box with air holes punched in it all over the place. There was usually an eye staring out a peephole or a nose poking through a different hole, or a paw extended out of an opening and swiping aimlessly through the air. It really did look pretty comical. The unconventional carriers all seemed to do the trick though. A commercial carrier would have made the job a whole lot easier, but not quite as entertaining.

PICKPOCKET

Puppies and kittens are prime examples of pure energy and joy set into motion. Although playtime seems to be priority number one, they are, without a doubt, constantly learning from their litter mates, surroundings, and us. Those little guys are very impressionable and are quick learners, so we need to be mindful of how we interact with them, because bad habits can be inadvertently ingrained. I know. Been there. Done that.

Scout was a healthy, bright-eyed, fourteen-week-old German Shepherd pup, and he was a big one to boot. His calm, confident, self-assured demeanor definitely set him apart. Scout was a real charmer, and it wasn't long before the entire staff was drawn to him, oohing and aahing over how handsome, well behaved, and dignified he was. He just sat there, cool, calm, and collected, taking in all the accolades which he'd probably heard a hundred times before. His owner then proudly told me that Scout had come from an exclusive dog kennel in Germany that was known for breeding large, docile, German shepherds. That little bit of info explained a lot.

As I was in the process of examining Scout, his keen sense of smell honed in on a dog treat located in my uniform pocket. I'd completely forgotten about it being there. Scout unabashedly thrust his long snout deep down into the pocket, and in a flash, proudly withdrew the tasty morsel. We all got a laugh out of his little caper, but then he went back in the pocket for seconds. However, this time the cupboard was bare. Scout was determined to find another goodie in there, and I swear he checked out every thread in that pocket. When he withdrew his nose, he actually looked disappointed, and I couldn't have that, so I stealthily slipped another treat in there and one in the opposite pocket as well. Scout dove into my pockets with reckless abandon. Bonanza! He was in hog heaven. He was having a great time, and we were being entertained. It didn't dawn on me, at the moment, that I was actually training (conditioning) Scout to check out pockets for treats. Not just my pockets, but everyone else's too. Not good! Over the ensuing years, whenever Scout would visit the veterinary clinic, he eagerly trotted into the exam room, and the very first thing he'd do was to stick his big, long wet nose down into my uniform pockets, looking for the treats, and he always found some too. Only now, Scout's head and muzzle had become much, much larger, but the pocket size hadn't changed. No problem! He had to do a little extra maneuvering, but eventually he managed to get the tip of his long nose into the pocket, without tearing it off, and retrieved his prize.

Scout remained a big, lovable, happy-go-lucky German Shepherd, who just so happened to have a fetish for checking out people's pockets. I confess. I had taught him a very bad habit when he was a puppy. I'd unintentionally trained Scout to be a pickpocket.

ELEVATOR UP!

The profession of veterinary medicine, like many other professions, requires a specific number of continuing education hours periodically to maintain one's license to practice medicine. Veterinary conferences provide an excellent opportunity to attend relevant courses and learn new methods of diagnosis and treatment. These gatherings also offer an opportunity to check out all the current reference materials, new pharmaceuticals, and surgical instruments. In addition, it is an occasion to peruse all the new and interesting equipment. It's like going to a very big, expensive candy store!

As I wandered past all the vendors at one conference, something extremely interesting caught my eye—a hydraulic lift examination table! What a great idea! Now I wouldn't have to break my back attempting to lift a hundred-plus-pound dog onto a stationary exam table. I looked at the price tag. Believe me, it wasn't cheap. But it was a much better alternative to back surgery. So I took a long, deep breath and bit the bullet! My heart was pounding as I made the decision to buy that table, but I knew, without a doubt, that it was a necessary purchase.

The lift table was a wonderful addition to the practice. It truly was a back saver, and most dogs tolerated the table quite well. Oh sure, there were a few like "Bruce", a big seventy-five-pound, tricolor, rough-coat collie, who was petrified by the lift table. When he got on the table, he immediately laid down and tried to disappear. He started salivating, and then his teeth began to chatter nonstop until he got off the table. He was, what we referred to as a *quiet protester*, but his teeth weren't all that quiet. Usually one vet assistant consoled and reassured Bruce throughout the exam, but it didn't seem to help very much. When the ordeal was over and Bruce slithered off the table, he instantly returned to his usual confident self and pranced out through the waiting room with his head held high, acting as if the whole experience never happened. Ole Bruce—he was a real character, and you couldn't help but love him.

Then there was "Sebastian", a handsome black-and-silver ninety-pound Malamute with an energy level that would rival Mick Jagger. When that big boy entered the clinic, it was plain to see that he was a real handful for his owner, Tracy Heath. It took a major effort, on her part, to control all the twisting and dancing on the end of that hefty leash. Sebastian was one exuberant dude, and he let everybody in the entire county know it by his loud happy yips and long, low-pitched woo-woos. This guy really loved life! As I watched all the commotion, I thought to myself, *How in the world am I going to examine this noisy, powerful whirling dervish?* With Tracy's help, we eventually maneuvered Sebastian next to the lift table, and with the coordinated efforts of three people, we placed the loud, gyrating dog onto the platform.

At the precise moment Sebastian was placed on the lift table, an astounding transformation occurred,—he gently laid down and chilled out. Wow! What a change! As I was about to flip the switch to raise the table I told him, "Sebastian, hold on, the elevator's going up." The muffled whine of the hydraulics didn't faze him one iota. Sebastian remained cool, calm, and collected—thank goodness—throughout the entire physical examination, and then I lowered the table so he could easily step off. He hesitated initially, but with a little coaxing, we finally got him off the lift table, and immediately he started vocalizing and jumping around like a wild man again. I tapped the surface of the table with my hand to get his attention, then asked him, "Do you want to go for another ride?"

In the blink of an eye the big guy jumped back onto the lowered table, quietly laid down, and looked directly at me with an expression as if saying, "Whatcha waitin' for? Let's go again!"

So I flipped the toggle switch and said, "Elevator up, first floor, leashes and treats." He just lay there, quietly zoning, happy as a clam. I repeated the up and down elevator ride for him several times, and at that point, I was beginning to feel like a carnival ride operator.

The exam had been completed, and there were other patients waiting to be seen, but Sebastian was enjoying himself so much that he didn't want to leave. I told Tracy that Sebastian was welcome to come to the vet clinic anytime he wanted, and get his free ride, and he did—more than once. Sebastian was a great dog, and he sure loved to hear the words "Elevator up!"

STAND BY ME

It's always heartwarming to watch service dogs in action. They are dedicated canines who unselfishly provide assistance to the special needs of their human companions. These exceptional helpers aren't just limited to aiding people; sometimes they even help each other.

"Keto" and "Tonka" were litter-mates, but they sure didn't look like it. Tonka had the body type, color, and personality of an Australian Shepherd, while Keto resembled a small-framed Labrador Retriever. Keto also had one other major difference: she was totally blind from birth. She had a congenital anomaly called bilateral micro-opthalmia; meaning, both eyes were abnormally small, malformed, and nonfunctional. She'd never experienced the miracle of sight, so to her, she was normal. Keto instinctively compensated for her blindness by relying on her other senses of hearing, smell, and touch. That's where Tonka came to the rescue. She was Keto's point of contact and essentially become a seeing-eye dog —- to another dog. Keto would either lightly touch or be in close proximity to Tonka most of the time. Tonka seemed to be acutely aware of her sister's needs and avoided venturing into areas or situations that could potentially pose a serious threat or problem for either or both of them. Without question, it was Tonka's patience and gentle guidance that allowed Keto to enjoy a relatively normal life.

"Doodles" and "Petunia" were another interesting duo. Petunia, a Pomeranian-Boston Terrier combo, was the matriarch of the household, and Doodles, a black miniature Poodle, was her protégé. Those two got along well, but it was definitely obvious as to who was the teacher and who was the pupil. That was demonstrated each day as Petunia made her inspection trek around the premises. Petunia always took the lead while Doodles followed close behind, learning the routine from the master. As time passed and the dogs aged, Petunia's eyes gradually changed, and her vision had become quite dim. These changes went unnoticed by their owner until one day she saw that Doodles was leading the walkabout, and Petunia, now virtually blind, followed closely behind. What an astounding role reversal! Doodles had learned her lessons well, and now Petunia, with Doodles help and guidance, was able to enjoy life, in spite of her visual challenges.

I guess the singer/songwriter's lyrics said it all in the cases of Keto and Tonka and Petunia and Doodles: "I can get by with a little help from my friends."

A PROMISE KEPT

Carol Francis was an energetic, independent woman who had a sincere passion for animals and their welfare. She'd experienced more than her share of trials and personal tragedy during her life, but she'd always remained positive and strong through it all. Carol often said that it was the devoted companionship and unfailing love of her faithful animals that provided her the solace she needed to get through those very difficult times.

As Carol sashayed through the front door of the clinic and into the waiting room one day, it was plain to see that she'd mastered the art and technique of carrying two occupied cat carriers and her big purse all at the same time. She'd brought two of her cats, "Chrissy" and "Missy", to the vet clinic for routine physical exams, blood work, and vaccinations. Chrissy, a fifteen-year-old red-point Siamese cross, the matriarch of the household, was in relatively good health for her age, while Missy wasn't as lucky. Missy was a tortoise-shell-colored, portly little princess about three years younger than Chrissy. Unfortunately, she'd been battling chronic renal failure (CRF) for several years. The eventual outcome wasn't encouraging in spite of being fed a kidney friendly diet, receiving appropriate medications for associated conditions, and being given intravenous and subcutaneous fluids on a regular basis. We were all aware that as her kidney's filtering ability decreased, toxins would build up in her system and she'd be essentially poisoning herself, and regardless of all our heroic efforts, she wouldn't survive. Our goal was to help her feel as comfortable as possible, for as long as possible, and at the present time, we were ahead of the curve—she was stable, feeling good, and still enjoying life.

During the course of the physical exam, Carol asked, "Doc, if something were to happen to me, what would happen to Chrissy and Missy? Chrissy is old, and Missy has so many problems. Who would take them? I wouldn't want to have them put to sleep. Doc. What should I do?"

I thought for a moment, then said, "Carol, those are some pretty weighty questions you're asking. I'm sure we could find them homes, but finding the right person might be a challenge. Anyway, nothing's going to happen to you, so don't worry about that just now."

I could tell by Carol's facial expression that she was still very upset. Then she blurted out, "Doc, could you take them? I know you'd be able to find them good homes. Promise me, Doc. Please *promise* me that you'd take them and find them homes instead of putting them to sleep."

Carol was actually pleading. She sounded very desperate, almost panicky. So to calm her down I said, "Carol, okay! I promise to take them, but nothing's going to happen, all right? Nothing's going to happen."

That was exactly what she wanted to hear because as soon as I'd uttered those words, her face instantly lit up. She smiled and then said, "Thanks, Doc." Then she came around to my side of the exam table and gave me a big hug.

I told her, "Well, Carol, now that that's settled, can we finish the exam?"

She chuckled and appeared obviously relieved. "Okay. Sorry, Doc."

· · · · · · · ·

It was Friday morning, four days had passed since Carol's visit, and I was in the first exam room with a patient. The phone rang, there was a pause, and then I heard our receptionist Darlene say, "Oh, I'm so very sorry. Yes, I'll tell Doc." I surmised that Dar was talking to someone about an animal patient, so I finished up with my case, and then asked Dar, "What was that phone call all about?"

Dar looked me straight in the eyes and said, "That was Carol Francis's daughter on the phone. Carol went into a diabetic coma last night and never woke up. Doc, she died! Her daughter also wants to know what she should do with the cats."

I just stood there momentarily, dumbstruck by the shocking news. I had a flashback about Carol's recent office visit and the frantic request she'd made and what I'd told her. "Dar," I said, "call Carol's daughter, give her my condolences and tell her to bring the cats to the clinic. We'll find them good homes. They won't be put to sleep!" I paused briefly and attempted to process all that had just happened. Then the thought crossed my mind, *How did she know? Could she have had a premonition?*

The cats arrived at the clinic a few days later. Dar and her husband were totally smitten by Chrissy, Miss Personality. Chrissy couldn't have found a better home, and Carol would have been overjoyed. Missy, on the other hand, was liked by everyone, but was not adoptable. No one wanted to be saddled with that much responsibility and expense, especially with a cat having a terminal condition. So she became a clinic kitty, and a good one she was! Missy stayed at the vet clinic for a little over one year. She was placed on a strict, low-protein diet. She got her medications and fluid therapy on a regular schedule and had her blood chemistry values evaluated monthly. Missy appeared physically well, but the blood values for assessing kidney function were rising; meaning, the kidneys were wearing out, and the toxins were building up more in her little body. When that happens, a distinct ketone odor can be detected on the patient's breath, and it really smells bad. Poor Missy was now at the end stage phase of kidney disease. It was now time for basically hospice care, so Sandy and I decided that Missy could live out the rest of her days with us, at our home.

I transformed my fourteen-by-sixteen, two-story, heated, super-insulated Tuff Shed, often referred to as Doc's "man cave," into the premier, plush "cat house of Sherman Avenue." It had all kinds of feline amenities: multiple cushy cat beds, hammocks, toys, window seats, a television with a special "cat video" set on loop play, and a cat door to a secured outside exercise pen. Missy, the charmer, was definitely in her element. She was a real schmoozer, and it wasn't long before she maneuvered herself into the house and found an available lap. Her sweet countenance and non-confrontational attitude allowed her to be readily accepted by our other three male cats. Missy soon became part of our family. In the past, Missy had never been permitted outdoors, but we allowed her on occasion to roam free in our large, fenced, cat-friendly yard. She had a chance to be a "real" cat, if only for a short while. Missy relished laying on a freshly cut lawn, basking in the sun, chasing butterflies, and occasionally stalking birds. Outwardly, Missy looked and acted like any other portly princess, but on the inside, it was a whole different story.

Missy desperately needed her daily subcutaneous fluid therapy and oral medications in order to counter the awful effects of her failing kidneys. Through it all, she never complained; in fact, she actually purred throughout her treatment sessions. Missy really did live life to the fullest as long as she could. She'd enjoyed ten good months at our home, but then her condition rapidly deteriorated, and in spite of all our efforts, our sweet little Missy peacefully went home to be with Carol.

As I gently stroked Missy's little head for the very last time, I recalled Carol's requests, and I could honestly say, the promise was kept.

EPILOGUE

Looking back over the years, I can definitely say, without a doubt, that I had the greatest patients in the world. They were extremely honest, courageous, and quick to forgive. The animals were, in all honesty, some of my closest and dearest friends, and I really did love them, and I still do. It was a privilege to be entrusted with their care and an honor to devote my life to the mending of God's creatures. Would I do it all over again? Yup! In a heartbeat!